# Civil Judgment Recognition

*and the Integration of Multiple-State Associations:*
*Central America, the United States of America,*
*and the European Economic Community*

ROBERT C. CASAD

THE REGENTS PRESS OF KANSAS, *Lawrence*

Library of Congress Cataloging in Publication Data
Casad, Robert C.
    Civil judgment recognition and the integra-
tion of multiple-state associations.

    Bibliography: p.
    Includes index.
    1. Judgments, Foreign.   I. Title.
K7680.C37                    347'.077        81-11926
ISBN  0-7006-0218-6          342.777         AACR2

# Contents

*Civil Judgment Recognition and the Integration of Multiple-State Associations*

# *Preface*

Crowded onto a narrow volcanic isthmus between the Caribbean Sea and the Pacific Ocean, and linking North and South America, are six little countries with a combined population of over nineteen million (about two million more than Scandinavia without Finland) and a total area of about two hundred thousand square miles (roughly equal to Minnesota, Iowa, and Missouri).

The new Panama Canal treaty, the Nicaraguan civil war, and the political turmoil in El Salvador have combined to heighten within the United States the concern about the Central American region. The U.S. public, which traditionally has been largely ignorant of Central American affairs, is now being made aware of the strategic and economic importance of the area.

The significance of the relationship between the United States and Central America is even more obvious when viewed from the Central American perspective. The United States is, of course, the principal developed nation in the Western Hemisphere. As such, its influence—economic, political and cultural—is enormous throughout Latin America. The countries of Central America are among the least developed in the hemisphere; they are even more heavily influenced by the United States than are the rest of the Latin American countries.

U.S.–controlled firms have traditionally dominated one of the main export industries of Central America—the production of bananas—and many of the major utilities. The United States is the principal market for exports of Central American produce. In turn, Central America imports more products from the United States than from any other country (Secretariat Permanente del Tratado General de Integración Economica Centroamericana, *Integración de Cifras* [November 1977], *National Basic Intelligence Fact Book* [July 1977]). U.S. investment in Central American countries is generally encouraged by their governments. A stable, prosperous, peaceful Central America, thus, is of special importance to U.S. interests.

The goals of peace, prosperity, and stability in Central America will be difficult, if not impossible, to attain, however, if that group of tiny individual nations does not achieve some significant degree of regional integration. None of these countries is really capable of self-sufficiency in today's world—or yesterday's or tomorrow's. If they insist on maintaining total sovereignty within their respective territories—completely independent of each other—there is little hope for economic prosperity, and peace within the region will be ephemeral. Together, however, these countries might develop a regional economy that would be substantially stronger than the sum of its national parts. Social and political maturity might accompany economic development, and ultimately, democratic regimes that would be more sensitive to human rights might replace the military juntas that now control all of the countries except Costa Rica. It is probably unrealistic to expect such far-reaching changes to occur swiftly, but any significant step toward regional integration would seem to be desirable and should be encouraged by the United States.

The integration of several states into one politico-economic entity usually requires substantial modification in some existing national governmental institutions. The focus of this study is upon the judicial institutions of the six countries of the Central American isthmus. The objective is to see to what extent the acts of these sovereign agencies have effects throughout the region under present law. From this examination, we hope to identify problems that will require attention by the countries concerned if their judicial institutions are to be made optimally effective in fostering the process of integration. Our attention here will be focused upon questions involving the recognition and enforcement, throughout the region, of civil judgments rendered in the courts of one of the states. The existing regimes in Central America will be examined, and the regional composite will be compared to interstate judgment-recognition arrangements in more-developed multistate entities: the United States of America and the European Economic Community. The conclusion that we draw from this examination is that a system of intraregional judgment recognition comparable, in its significance for integration, to the more-developed schemes of the United States and the EEC would be possible in Central America without sweeping changes being made in existing institutions. This would require activating the Central American Court of Justice, already provided for in existing treaties, and it would probably require a special Central American judgment-recognition convention that would embody a more realistic balancing of the local, regional, and individual interests at stake in the judgment-recognition decision.

At this point it may seem futile to think about the integration of Central America. Relations among the states of the region are tense, and it is impossible at present to foresee the directions that Central America will take. This is not the first time in the history of Central America that has been marked by tension and turmoil, however. Previously, after the turmoil has abated, there has generally been a resurgence of the sense of their common interests among the states. It will take some time for the current atmosphere of distrust that exists between some of them to dissipate. Sooner or later, though, it will happen, at which time it is to be hoped that this study may make some contribution to the process of integration.

Apart from any practical value that it may or may not have for Central American integration, however, this study is offered for its possible usefulness to lawyers and legal scholars in North America, Latin America, and Europe who seek to know more about mutual judgment recognition among member states of multistate associations other than their own and about the relationship between judgment recognition and the integration process.

This study received some support from the Organization of American States and from the University of Kansas General Research Fund. I am deeply indebted to Professors Jerome Cohen, Kurt Nadelmann, and Donald Trautman of Harvard Law School for their counsel and guidance. Such flaws as the work contains are, of course, my own sole responsibility. In somewhat different form, portions of the work have been published in the *Hastings International and Comparative Law Review,* whose adviser, Professor Rudolf Schlessinger, gave me encouragement and stimulation. I also acknowledge gratefully the stimulation, counsel, and assistance that I have received in this and other projects from my distinguished friend and colleague Rogelio Sotela Montagné of San José, Costa Rica.

Finally, I note with gratitude the assistance of the Dana Fund for International and Comparative Legal Studies, which provided a subvention grant to permit the publication of this work.

# 1    *Central America: Integration and Reunification*

## THE LAND AND THE PEOPLE

North Americans who look at Central America find it hard to understand why those little countries never got together in a political federation as the thirteen American colonies did after gaining their independence from Great Britain. After all, they were united for nearly three hundred years during the Spanish colonial period under a single political authority as parts of the Captaincy General of Guatemala—a subdivision of the Vice-Royalty of New Spain (later Mexico).[1] They also share a common language. The Roman Catholic religion predominates in all of them. Why do they persist in being separate?

The problem is that despite the great similarities, there have been and still are significant differences between the Central American states that would make unification much more difficult than an outside observer might assume. Most important, probably, are the differences in racial compositions and in the social structures of the countries. Guatemala's population is said to be about 70 percent pure Indian; Costa Rica's, 80 percent white; El Salvador's, almost entirely mestizo; Nicaragua's and Honduras's are mixtures of white, Indian, and Negro.[2] Panama's racial mixture has a strong Negro component; Panama is more like the Caribbean countries than like other Central American countries in this respect.

The societies and cultures of the six countries are different too. A large proportion of Guatemala's Indians, almost untouched by the dominant *ladino* society, retain their tribal languages and resist assimilation. At the same time, this strong Indian element gives Guatemalan culture a unique character. El Salvador has the greatest population density in Hispanic America. It has no vacant land (unlike its sister states), and this profoundly affects its culture. Its people are deeply imbued with a work ethic, and their industriousness contrasts greatly with the conventional stereotype of tropical society. Culturally, Honduras is the least advanced of the group, and its overall state of development is among the most primitive in all of Latin America. The main themes of Nicaraguan society before the recent civil war are difficult to articulate. Its society (as distinct from its political institutions) had not been so much dominated by the capital city, as has been the case in the other five, and it still reflects to some extent the struggle of Liberal and Conservative elements (centered at León and Granada, respectively) that began in colonial days. It still bears some evidence of a literary tradition (exemplified most prominently by the famous poet Rubén Darío), along with the effects of an extended period of military despotism. Costa Rica is a country dominated by the middle class, with high literacy, strong democratic traditions, and a notable absence of the effects of militarism. It is the only one of the six that is not governed by a military regime. It does not even have an army. Panama is, naturally, more oriented toward the sea than is true of the other Central American countries. It is still struggling to establish its stature and identity as an independent nation, and this is a major feature of the Panamanian culture.

With such important differences, then, it is not surprising that Central America has not achieved complete political unification. What is surprising is that it has tried to achieve it so earnestly, and so often.

## THE HISTORICAL STRUGGLE FOR UNION

The truth is that five of these countries were once united into a federal republic. Central America became independent of Spanish rule in 1821 without the bloodshed that accompanied independence in other Spanish colonies. Almost immediately it was annexed to Mexico; but Mexican rule was overthrown in 1823, and the total independence of the United Provinces of Central America was declared. The constitution of the new country, adopted in 1824, changed the name to the Federation of Central America.[3] It also set up a republican government, modeled roughly after that of the United States in its principles of separation of powers and bicameralism.[4] One provision of the 1824 constitution that is particularly relevant to the theme of this study is Article 193: "Legal and juridical acts of one state will be recognized in all the others." From that early time the importance of a judgment-recognition regime has been appreciated, in theory at least.

The federal republic survived, in name, until 1838, but the federal government was never really able to consolidate its authority, not even by military force. Communications were difficult, and the state governments came to ignore the federal government.[5] Eventually the federal congress disbanded after passing a resolution that left the states free to establish any form of government they wished, so long as it was a "republican, popular, representative and divided-powers form of government."

Almost immediately, however, plans for a new union began to take form. The dominant theme of Central American history since 1838 has been the impulse toward reunification. Thomas Karnes has described it thus:

> A phenomenon was born in 1842 in the town of Chinandega, Nicaragua. It has lived a long life, made up of alternate years of lassitude and brisk activity, usually verbal, sometimes military. It is old and tired now, but it is not yet dead. This phenomenon is the peculiar motivation which causes Central American statesmen to drop whatever they are doing and get together for a new proposal to confederate their governments. It is made more strange by the fact that often the conferences are arranged in the midst of the ruins of the last great failure. Such was the case of the Chinandega agreements.[6]

The Chinandega agreements set up a new government, called the Central American Confederation. Only the three middle countries ratified the agreements, however, and so the confederation did not include all of Central America. Provision was made for Guatemala and Costa Rica to become members, but neither one ever did. The confederation lasted until 1845.

A new government was instituted in 1851, called the National Representation of Central America; but, again, it represented only the middle three countries. This government failed to get diplomatic recognition from the United States and Great Britain, so a new constitution for the union, now called the Republic of Central America, was proposed in 1852. This plan, too, failed.[7]

At about that time the strategic importance of Central America as a link between the Atlantic and Pacific oceans became apparent to the world. The discovery of gold in California stimulated travel, and one of the most convenient routes from Europe and the Eastern United States to California carried the forty-niners by ship to Nicaragua; by boat up the San Juan River and Lake Nicaragua; by road about fifteen miles to the Pacific coast; and thence by ship to California. The economic potentialities of controlling this route attracted an American sometime student of medicine and law, a journalist and soldier of fortune named William Walker. Walker took over the government of Nicaragua and made plans to unify Central America under his military control. Walker's scheme failed, however, when the natives of the five countries succeeded in acting cooperatively for a long enough time and with enough force to overthrow him in 1857.[8]

The next serious attempt at military reunification occurred in 1885. Inspired by the unification of Germany and Italy by military force, Justo Rufino Barrios, dictator of Guatemala, decided to do the same for Central America. His plan failed when he was killed in battle in that same year.[9]

Political attempts at reunion then began again. In 1886 the Guatemalan secretary of exterior relations sent a note to his counterparts in the other Central American states, urging the adoption of a treaty to facilitate reunion. Among the matters suggested for inclusion in the treaty were the unfettering of professional titles and the securing of the efficacy of all public documents granted in any of the countries "without requiring any requisites other than authentication." The note invited the establishment of a regime to "maintain the stability owed to the definitive resolutions of judicial tribunals."[10] In 1877 a treaty of friendship, peace, and commerce was signed by representatives of all five countries. Declaring that the five were "disintegrated members of a single political body," the treaty provided, among other things, that citizens of each would have the same rights as citizens in all of the five countries. It also provided for a commission to be appointed to bring about the unification of basic laws.[11] Most significantly for purposes of this study, it also contained a provision for the recognition and enforcement of civil judgments:

> Article 16. Judgments in civil and commercial matters arising from duly legalized personal actions and rendered by the courts of one of the parties shall have, at the request of those courts, in the territory of the other parties, equal force as those rendered by the local courts and shall be executed in the same way as them.
>
> So that these judgments may be executed, they must previously be declared final by the pertinent Higher Court of the Republic in which the execution will take place; and this court will not declare them to be such unless it has first ascertained in summary proceedings:
>
> 1. That the judgment has been rendered by a competent judicial authority and that the parties were legally summoned.
>
> 2. That the parties have been legally represented or declared legally in default.
>
> 3. That the judgment does not contain provisions contrary to the public order or the public law of the State.[12]

Every five years the representatives were to meet to discuss further reforms. This led to another treaty in 1890, which purported to recreate the Republic of Central America, although the states were to continue to be autonomous in internal affairs.[13]

In 1892 another attempt at confederation was made. A tentative government, this time called the Diet of Central America, was agreed upon by all but Costa Rica. As usual, it never really got off the ground,[14] but it may have given impetus to the adoption in one of the countries of a special law dealing with the enforcement and recognition of judgments of sister states of Central America: the Central American Procedural Convention of 1892.[15]

Another attempt at confederation was made in 1895. Again the three middle states were the initiators. The resulting entity was called the Greater Republic (*Republica mayor*) of Central America, although its name was to be changed to the Republic of Central America when (and if) Guatemala and Costa Rica should accede to it. The Cleveland administration in the United States recognized this new government initially, but the succeeding McKinley administration determined that the Greater Republic of Central America was not a federation but an association of separate states.

In 1898 the three constituent states decided to strengthen their union and therefore adopted a new constitution—with internal legislative, executive, and judicial organs—and a new name: The United States of Central America. The new union did not survive to see 1899.[16]

At this point it had become clear that reunification could not be achieved militarily or by the voluntary acceptance of a single sweeping political plan by all five countries. Union would have to come step by step, with the gradual improvement of each country's and the region's economic and cultural status. Accordingly, instead of new constitutions that would create a new federation or confederation, agreements that were aimed at reducing conflicts and promoting commerce and cultural integration began to be offered. This phase of the reunification story was accompanied by the clear-cut entrance of the United States into active involvement in the internal and regional affairs of Central America. Before 1903 the official United States posture toward Central America was one of nonintervention, and reunification was positively encouraged. The independence of Panama and the construction of the canal brought Central America to the consciousness of the North American people and government in a new way, and our historical Central American policy was altered.

A treaty was signed in 1902 at Corinto, Nicaragua, by all the states except Guatemala (which later expressed agreement in principle); it was aimed at relieving military tensions within the region. Among other provisions, it established the Central American Arbitration Tribunal to resolve difficulties that might lead to armed conflict. This institution did not, however, prevent the outbreak of war in 1906 between Guatemala, on one side, and El Salvador and Honduras on the other. The United States decided to intercede. President Theodore Roosevelt had been concerned about the unrest in Central America and about its potential effects on his plans to build a canal, and in 1904 he had issued a statement that came to be known as the Roosevelt Corollary to the Monroe Doctrine. In effect, the Roosevelt Corollary declared that while we would continue our policy of opposing European intrusion into the Western Hemisphere, we would ourselves intervene to restore order where chronic wrongdoing made that necessary. Acting under this doctrine, Roosevelt, with the concurrence of the government of Mexico, sent the cruiser *Marblehead* to the coast of El Salvador and induced the belligerents to meet on that ship. A new treaty resulted from this. The Arbitration Tribunal was reestablished, and two new international organizations were set up: the International Central American Bureau and the Central American Pedagogical Institute. Within a year, however, war had broken out again in Central America.[17]

The Washington Conference in 1907 was convened by Theodore Roosevelt to resolve these new military conflicts. The resulting treaties and conventions reaffirmed the International Central American Bureau and the Central American Pedagogical Institute, but they also contained two other provisions of particular importance. Article 15 of the General Treaty of Peace and Amity declared:

> The judicial authorities of the contracting Republics shall carry out the judicial commissions and warrants in civil, commercial or criminal matters, with regard to citations, interrogatories and other acts of procedure or judicial function.
>
> Other judicial acts, in civil or commercial matters, arising out of a personal suit, shall have in the territory of any one of the contracting Parties equal force with those of the local tribunals and shall be executed in the same manner, provided always that they shall first have been declared executory by the Supreme Tribunal of the Republic wherein they are to be executed, which shall be done if they meet the essential requirements of their respective legislation and they shall be carried out in accordance with the laws enacted in each country for the execution of judgments.[18]

This provision was amplified by a separate convention on extradition of persons who had been accused of crime, but no further amplification relating to the recognition or enforcement of civil and commercial judgments was promulgated. It is noteworthy that the provision specifically requires a decree of the supreme tribunal of the enforcing state before the judgment of a sister state is to be given effect. This requirement is reflected in the present laws of all but one of the Central American states, and it is a feature that will be discussed at greater length in subsequent chapters.

The other very important provision of the 1907 General Treaty was that of Article 1 relating to a new institution to replace the Arbitration Tribunal, which would be the key to a new peace plan: the Central American Court of Justice. A separate convention dealing with the court was signed at the same time.

The Central American Court of Justice was the first institution in the world to be set up with judicial power to adjudicate—not just to arbitrate or mediate—disputes between nations. All five Central American nations solemnly bound themselves to submit to its jurisdiction and to abide by its judgments. The court was to have its seat in Cartago, Costa Rica (it was later moved to San José). It was to have five judges— one from each country—and to have a life span of ten years, after which its existence might be continued or terminated, depending upon how successful its work had been. It was to be the representation of the "national conscience of Central America." The court had jurisdiction over:

> (a) all controversies or questions which might arise among [the Central American nations], of whatsoever nature and no matter what their origin might be, in case their respective Departments of Foreign Affairs had not been able to reach an understanding; (b) the questions which individuals of one Central American country might raise against any of the other contracting governments, because of the violation of treaties or conventions, and other cases of international character, no matter whether their own government supported their claim or not, provided, however, that the remedies which the laws of the respective country afforded for such a violation had been exhausted or that a denial of justice had been shown; (c) cases between two or more governments or between one government and one individual, when submitted by a common accord; and (d) international questions which any of the five governments and a foreign government might submit to it by a special agreement.[19]

In all, the court considered ten cases during the ten years of its existence, from the first in 1908 to the last in 1916. The last of these cases—the one that spelled the end of the court—involved the validity of the

Bryan-Chamorro Treaty, in which Nicaragua granted the United States the right to build a canal through Nicaragua, the right to build a naval base on the Gulf of Fonseca, and renewable leases for two Caribbean islands—the Corn Islands. Costa Rica claimed that the treaty violated longstanding agreements between it and Nicaragua which granted the former country free navigation rights in the San Juan River and the right of consultation on any plans for a canal. El Salvador and Honduras, which also have coasts on the Gulf of Fonseca, claimed that none of the three countries could cede control of any of the coast without the consent of the others. The court entertained the case, although it disclaimed having any jurisdiction over the United States and ruled that Nicaragua had violated earlier treaties with the plaintiff countries. When neither Nicaragua nor the United States would heed the decision, it became clear that one more helpful step toward reunification had failed. Central American historians are proud of the court and its accomplishments, and many have speculated that it could have been the key to solid reunification if the United States had accepted its judgment. But the United States did not, and the court was not renewed when its term expired.[20]

The International Central American Bureau survived somewhat longer. It had been set up to promote certain common interests, and its charges included the following: "(1) to contribute with all its efforts to the peaceful reorganization of the Central American Fatherland; (2) to impress upon popular education an essentially Central American character, in a uniform sense; (3) the development of Central American commerce in ways that would tend to make it more active and profitable and in its relations with other nations; (4) to promote agriculture and industries; (5) to foster uniformity of civil, commercial and penal laws, customs systems, monetary systems, weights and measures, general sanitation, etc."[21] The officials who initially staffed the bureau were dedicated and active, and that brought it into conflict with some entrenched interests. By 1910, its range of activity had been largely limited to promoting an annual Central American Conference and publishing a magazine called *Centro America*.[22]

In 1921, as the centennial of Central American independence approached, agitation for a new plan of federation mounted. A political party, called the Central American Unionist Party, formed in 1904, was now coming of age, and it played a major role, along with the International Central American Bureau, in promoting a conference to consider a new confederation plan. The meeting was held in 1920 in San José, Costa Rica, in the temple that Andrew Carnegie had built for the now defunct Central American Court of Justice. Nicaragua (at the urging of the United States, it was charged) refused to participate unless the other nations acquiesced in its obligation under the Bryan-Chamorro Treaty, which they in turn refused to do. The other four states, however, went ahead and produced a new plan for a new government, to be called the Federation of Central America, to take effect upon its ratification by three states, and to commence on 15 September 1921, the centenary of Central American independence. The three northern states ratified the plan, but Costa Rica rejected it. The new federation of the three lasted for less than six months. A coup toppled Guatemala's elected government, and the Harding administration, through Secretary of State Charles Evans Hughes, declared that the United States would not view lightly any interventionist steps taken by the Central American federal government to stabilize Guatemalan affairs. Thus another unification plan failed.[23]

In 1923 another Treaty of Peace and Amity was signed by the representatives of the five countries in Washington. In it the International Central American Tribunal was instituted to replace the Court of Justice. Its jurisdiction was much more limited, however, and it was an ad hoc, rather than a permanent, tribunal. It was not really a judicial body, and it had very little success in resolving international disputes.[24] The treaty did, however, reaffirm Article 15 of the 1907 treaty, dealing with intraregional judgment enforcement.

One more plan of union materialized in 1945, when Guatemala and El Salvador agreed to a full merger. Again, however, the signatory governments could not maintain themselves in power long enough to implement the plan.[25]

## THE ORGANIZATION OF CENTRAL AMERICAN STATES AND THE COMMON MARKET

In 1951 a new institution came into existence, and, with it, a new approach to reunification. Inspired by the United Nations—and the impetus to the formation of regional associations of nations that Article 52 of the United Nations Charter supplied—and more specifically by the 1948 Bogota Treaty promulgating the Charter of the Organization of American States, the five nations endorsed the Charter of the Organization of Central American States (ODECA). In so doing, they abandoned the idea of immediate refederation and adopted "regionalism" and a more gradual approach to integration as the basic policy. The preamble to the charter reflects this new orientation:

That the Central American Republics, disintegrated parts of a single nation, remain united by indestructible bonds that it is proper to utilize and consolidate for the collective good; That for the progressive development of their institutions and the common solution of their problems the organized fraternal cooperation of all is indispensable; That it is necessary to eliminate the artificial barriers that separate the Central American peoples and to achieve a common determination to resolve their problems and defend their interests through collective and systemized action; That in the course of the independent life of the Central American Republics the attempts at reinstating their ancient unity have been ineffective; and That modern International Law offers forms adequate to that end through the institution of regional organisms.[26]

The new organization was concerned about practical measures to reduce sources of conflict and to build, step by step, the "economic and social infrastructure" for a solid and permanent union.

At about the same time, the United Nations itself initiated some measures aimed at fomenting trade and industrialization on a regional basis in Latin America. Under United Nations auspices, the Economic Commission for Latin America (ECLA)[27] was formed to make studies and recommendations. The governing council of ODECA sought the assistance of ECLA in promoting the economic-integration phase of ODECA's objectives.

The Committee on Economic Cooperation was formed to work with ECLA in preparing the necessary economic studies and in formulating plans for integration. The processes for economic cooperation thus became somewhat separated from those aiming at political reunification.[28]

During the next four years, numerous lengthy studies of almost every phase of the economies of the region were conducted. Several bilateral treaties aimed at promoting free trade between individual countries were adopted.[29]

These steps led to the signing in 1958 of a multilateral treaty, which established free trade within the region on various items and provided for further liberalization of trade restrictions over the ensuing ten years, at the end of which time the goal of completely free trade within the region would be achieved. The parties also agreed to work toward the establishment of a regional customs union. In framing this accord, the Central American countries could draw on the experience of the European Economic Community for guidance.

In 1960 El Salvador, Guatemala, and Honduras, apparently acting independently of the Economic Cooperation Committee and ECLA and seeking to accelerate the integration process, adopted the Treaty of Economic Association, which called for further integrative measures that were not contained in the multilateral treaty.[30] The fear that this Treaty of Economic Association might splinter the movement and retard progress toward full regional integration led to an extraordinary meeting of the Economic Cooperation Committee. From that meeting there emerged in 1960 the General Treaty on Central American Economic Integration, which, when finally approved by Costa Rica in 1962, set the basic framework for the Central American Common Market. The institutions set up in the treaty were incorporated into the structure of the Organization of Central American States.[31] The treaty provided that "any Central American State not among the original signatories" could later adhere to it.[32] Presumably this referred to Panama as well as Costa Rica. Panama had been not only invited to join the Organization of Central American States in the ODECA charter but also encouraged to participate in plans for regional integration. So far, however, Panama has not joined either ODECA or the Central American Common Market.

Although the General Treaty plan drew extensively from the successful experience of the European Common Market, it is significant that the institutional structure of the Central American Common Market lacked any community judicial institutions comparable to the European Court of Justice. This is surprising in view of the relative success enjoyed by the earlier Central American Court of Justice. Judicial institutions have, by and large, functioned well in Central America. An outside observer might assume that the judicial process would be relied upon wherever possible. This was not done, however, in the Central American Common Market Treaty. The treaty was influenced more by economists and planners than by lawyers, and the importance of a court was perhaps not appreciated. The Secretariat of the Common Market Organization (SIECA) was charged with overseeing the "correct application" of the provisions of the treaty,[33] and the interpretation of the treaty has thus been handled by administrative rulings, for the most part. There is a provision for an arbitration tribunal, which is to be convened on an ad hoc basis when other measures do not resolve disagreements between signatory states,[34] but this provision has been criticized as being entirely inadequate and has not had much use.[35]

The ratification of the General Treaty by Costa Rica in 1962 set the Central American Common Market in motion. Also in 1962 another noteworthy development occurred. The Charter of the Organization of Central American States was significantly revised. The preamble of the new charter reflects a decline in emotionalism and an increase in pragmatism in its statements about reunification:

Whereas:
    It is necessary to provide the five States with a more effec-

tive instrument by establishing organs which assure their economic and social progress, eliminate the barriers which divide them, improve constantly the living conditions of their peoples, guarantee the stability and expansion of industry, and strengthen Central American solidarity,

Article 1: Costa Rica, Nicaragua, Honduras, El Salvador, and Guatemala are an economic-political community which aspires to the integration of Central America. For this purpose the Organization of Central American States (ODECA) has been established.[36]

The new structure of ODECA included a Central American Court of Justice,[37] but this is a pale imitation, similar in name only to the earlier one of 1908–18.[38] Again, it bears little similarity to the European Court of Justice. It has jurisdiction only over cases that are voluntarily submitted by disputing states. It has not really functioned, and has been called a "phantom entity" by one commentator.[39]

The Central American Common Market brought considerable economic progress to Central America. Intraregional trade, for example, had increased more than eightfold by 1970,[40] and the volume of external trade likewise increased substantially. Considerable advances in industrial development also were made, although this improvement was certainly not uniform throughout the region.[41]

Since 1970, however, the Central American Common Market has suffered some serious setbacks. Uneven economic development has contributed to the revival of traditional jealousies. Honduras, even before 1970, had complained vigorously of the lack of major industrial projects that could be located within its borders, which impaired its ability to be an equal participant in the benefits of the Central American Common Market. In 1970, Honduras in effect dropped out of the Common Market.[42] Costa Rica, the country with the greatest per capita consumption, has not been able to sell its products to its neighbors in sufficient volume to prevent serious trade deficits. It had, in fact, closed its borders to Nicaraguan goods—even before the onset of the civil war—and, in effect, had all but dropped out of the Common Market. The institutions of ODECA were not able to prevent the outbreak of open war between Honduras and El Salvador in 1969, and it required the resources of the larger Organization of American States to suspend the hostilities, which have been revived intermittently since then, most recently during the summer of 1976. The political situation in Guatemala has been far from stable. Riots rocked El Salvador in 1977 and Nicaragua in 1978, culminating in the overthrow of the Somoza government. It now seems unlikely that further progress toward full economic integration can be accomplished until there is further progress toward political stability within the region.

Nevertheless, this sketch of the history of the reunification struggle demonstrates how persistent the spirit is. The current constitutions of four of the countries reflect this officially in their basic charters:

> El Salvador, being a part of the Central American Nation, is obligated to promote the total or partial reconstruction of the Republic of Central America. The Executive Power, with the approval of the Legislative, will be capable of accomplishing that in a confederate, federal or unitary form, without the necessity of authorization or ratification by a Constituent Assembly [constitutional convention], so long as republican and democratic principles are respected in the new State, and the essential rights of individuals and associations are fully guaranteed. [El Salvador, Constitution of 1962, Article 10]

> Guatemala, as part of the Central American community, will maintain and cultivate fraternal relations of cooperation and solidarity with the other States that formed the Federation, and, faithful to the patriots' ideal that inspired it, will take all just and peaceful measures that will conduce to the total or partial realization of the union of Central America. [Guatemala, Constitution of 1965, Article 2]

> Honduras is a separated State of the Republic of Central America. Consequently, it recognizes as a primordial necessity the return to a union with one or more States of the former Federation. To this end, the Legislative Power is empowered to ratify treaties tending to bring that about, partially or totally, so long as they are proposed in a just and democratic manner. [Honduras, Constitution of 1965, Article 9]

> Sovereignty and territory are indivisible and inalienable. Nevertheless, treaties can be celebrated that tend to bring about a union with one or several republics of Central America. . . . [Nicaragua, Constitution of 1950, Article 6]

These solemn declarations may seem to be nothing more than pious hypocrisies. In practice, these countries, or at least their ruling juntas, have not been willing to sacrifice very much to bring about their union. It is paradoxical that the only one of the original five nations whose constitution lacks this kind of declaration is the one with the least tendency to resort to military aggression against a sister republic, at least during the twentieth century. Still, it seems likely that these declarations do reflect a spirit that is deeply felt by the people—or at least by those whose views are represented in constitutional conventions —even if they are not conscientiously followed by the juntas in power from time to time. It may well be that the absence of stable, effective democratic institutions in all the countries except Costa Rica is the most serious obstacle to reunion.

For purposes of this study, however, the constitutional provisions quoted above do have some significance. Their presence in the constitutions makes it constitutionally permissible for the governments of these countries to give legal force to some propositions that might otherwise appear to be beyond the scope of their constitutional powers. They can cede some of their sovereign legislative power, through treaty or otherwise, for the purpose of fostering reunification. Almost any step in that direction would be constitutional and could hardly be said to violate the public policy of that country.

The theme of this study is, of course, the recognition and enforcement of court judgments within the region. The thesis is that judgment recognition is an important, if simple, feature of any plan for multiple-state integration. Establishment of an effective and almost automatic regime of judgment recognition is certainly not enough to bring about the sort of full-scale integration to which the Central Americans aspire, but integration will be hard to achieve without it. It is a small step, but a necessary one.

The history of the reunification struggle shows that there have been a few successes along with the many failures. The Court of Justice worked well, indicating that Central Americans can use the judicial process effectively. Simple, concrete measures are more likely to be lasting and effective than sweeping reforms, judging from the course of reunification plans to date. The countries of Central America may not yet be ready to accept the exercise of sovereignty in all of its aspects on a region-wide basis, but the effects of the exercise of the sovereign *judicial* power could be extended to the whole region with almost no practical disruption of existing institutions and with beneficial consequences for the future of integration. The rest of this work will be addressed to that proposition.

# 2   *Recognition of Judgments*

## THEORIES AND POLICY GOALS

Civil controversies, of course, cannot always be finally and effectively resolved within the territory of a single sovereignty. The persons and property interests affected by the controversy may not all be within the reach of any one sovereignty's dispute-resolving processes. And persons and things that are within the range of territorial jurisdiction one day—even on a judgment day—may not be there the next. Conceptions of territorial sovereignty operate to prevent automatic extra-territorial recognition and enforcement of all judgments, and so the resolution of civil controversies may require the participation of two or more states or nations. If, in such cases, every affected jurisdiction were to deal with the controversy afresh—disregarding what may have already been done in another jurisdiction—waste, injustice, and disrespect for the ideal of the "rule of law" would be fostered. Accordingly, the laws of civilized nations generally provide that some measure of recognition should be given to at least some matters that have previously been adjudicated in other countries. Just *what* measure of recognition is to be accorded to *what matters,* and *why,* and *how,* are questions that have received widely variant answers.

Several different approaches to such questions have been used from time to time and from country to country. These approaches tend to parallel the theories underlying choice-of-law doctrines. Two or more nations can, of course, provide by treaty for the mutual recognition and enforcement of judgments. Through this approach the nations involved can consciously raise and weigh the competing policy considerations that should be faced in deciding what measure of recognition is to be accorded to what kinds of judgments. This approach was used to promulgate a judgment-recognition scheme for the nations of the European Common Market.[1] A judgment-recognition regime that would rest on a treaty has been proposed between the United States and the United Kingdom.[2] Two major judgment-recognition schemes are current in Latin America, their force resting on multilateral treaties: the Montevideo Treaty on International Civil Procedure, and the so-called Bustamante Code. The latter will be discussed at length in the next chapter. A new Inter-American Convention on Extraterritorial Validity of Foreign Judgments and Arbitral Awards has recently been proposed by the Inter-American Juridical Committee of the Organization of American States. That convention will be examined in chapter 11.

Even in the absence of a treaty or agreement, however, a nation may unilaterally adopt rules obligating its courts to recognize judgments of other nations under certain circumstances. Such rules may be explained as resting on the principle of "comity of nations": "the recognition which one nation allows within its territory to the legislative, executive or judicial acts of another nation, having due regard both to international duty and convenience, and to the rights of its own citizens or of other persons who are under the protection of its laws."[3] The conditions for extending or withholding comity are rarely examined. Even its nature is uncertain. Comity is said to be a matter neither of absolute obligation nor of mere courtesy and good will, but that does not help much in determining when one nation will or should give effect to matters adjudicated in another. The comity concept is simply too vague to serve a prescriptive function. It is more a conclusion than a premise. Moreover, reference to comity as though it were a meaningful normative principle tends to obscure the real interests that should be considered in deciding whether laws or judgments should be given extraterritorial effect.

Another theoretical foundation for judgment recognition, which is applicable more readily to the problem of enforcement of foreign money judgments than to more general problems of recognition, may be described as the "acquired rights" or "vested rights" theory. Rights, obligations, and other jural relations become fixed—or vested—in the winning and losing parties by virtue of the judgment of a competent court. These fixed relations are transitory: they adhere to the parties and are entitled to protection and enforcement anywhere in the civilized world without reexamination of the merits of the claim underlying the judgment. This view is said to be characteristic of the English approach to judgment enforcement.[4] Latin American theories of judgment recognition likewise rely heavily on this "vested rights" or "acquired rights" theory.[5] For a time it had considerable support in North America,[6] but not generally in continental Europe.[7] This approach rests on reasoning that is basically circular. The question of whether a fixed right, obligation, or immunity exists depends, in the final analysis, on whether it will be recognized and enforced outside of the country in which it was declared. This approach has been criticized as being even less helpful than the comity theory in providing guidance for the decision of actual cases.[8]

A better approach, and one that is more consonant with contemporary choice-of-law theories, starts with the obvious proposition that the question of whether one nation should give effect to the judgments of other nations chiefly depends on whether that nation's interests would be served or disserved thereby. If its interests would be significantly disserved, recognition of a foreign judgment is unlikely, of course. One nation will not normally sacrifice significant local interests merely to give effect within its borders to a sovereign act of another nation. However, insofar as the recognition of judgments that simply resolve disputes between private parties is concerned, the interests of the recognizing state may be involved only very indirectly, and these interests may not be very strong. The policy of all civilized states with respect to private disputes is to see that they are resolved in a just fashion. States may differ on the procedure for resolving them or on how the substantive merits should be resolved in the particular situation. But the laws that are provided by different states to regulate such matters often reflect merely administrative or convenience concerns, not deep national interests. Even when a citizen of country A may have been a party to litigation in country B, and even when a different result might have been reached if the case had been adjudicated in the courts of country A, it does not follow that any significant interests of country A would be disserved by giving effect to the foreign judgment. Every nation has an interest in seeing to it that justice is done between competing litigants, but that does not mean that every nation has an interest in trying in its own courts the merits of a case that has once been adjudicated elsewhere. Every nation also has an interest in economizing on judicial resources, an interest that should normally preclude the reconsideration of matters that have been fairly adjudicated anywhere. Clearly, relitigation should be precluded if there is no reason to believe that a different or better outcome would result if the matter were tried again. And even in cases where a different outcome might be likely, other concerns may nevertheless require that recognition and effect be given to the foreign judgment.

Trautman and von Mehren have identified five concerns that, arguably at least, are shared to some degree by all civilized states and that point toward the recognition and enforcement of foreign judgments:

[1] a desire to avoid the duplication of effort and consequent waste involved in reconsidering a matter that has already been litigated; [2] a related concern to protect the successful litigant, whether plaintiff or defendant, from harassing or evasive tactics on the part of his previously unsuccessful opponent; [3] a policy against making the availability of local enforcement the decisive element, as a practical matter, in the plaintiff's choice of forum; [4] an interest in fostering stability and unity in an international order in which many aspects of life are not confined to any single jurisdiction; and [5] in certain classes of cases, a belief that the rendering jurisdiction is a more appropriate forum than the recognizing jurisdiction, either because the former was more convenient or because as the predominantly concerned jurisdiction or for some other reason its views as to the merits should prevail.[9]

The relative strength of these interests can vary from country to country and from case to case, as can, of course, the nature and strength of local countervailing interests that might be impaired by giving effect to the foreign judgment without revision.

Local interests in the recognizing state that may oppose recognition of a foreign judgment include the interest in having its own substantive legal principles applied to the case (or, at least, in having the principles applied which its choice-of-law rules would identify) and the interest in seeing to it that minimal standards of procedural fairness were observed in any judgment that is to be given effect within its territory. A state may have a strong interest in seeing that its substantive rules or choice-of-law principles govern the merits of the case if one of the parties is a citizen or domiciliary of the state, or if events giving rise to the litigation had some significant impact in that state.

A sound regime of judgment recognition should produce results that would reflect a rational balance between the interests that favor and those that oppose recognition. Most existing regimes, however, do not call for a conscious weighing of the competing interests. Instead, they base the decision to extend recognition on the presence or absence of certain specific conditions, some but not all of which bear a relation to relevant policy principles.

One condition that is regarded as essential in all systems of judgment recognition is jurisdiction. The rendering court must have had jurisdiction to adjudicate the case. Anglo-American law analyzes jurisdiction in terms of jurisdiction over parties and over subject matter. The legal systems of continental Europe and Latin America employ the concept of "competence," or "competency," which is similar but not identical in content to our notions of jurisdiction, as may be seen in the discussion in the section titled "Basic Concepts," below. For this purpose, the standards of jurisdiction are not necessarily the same as those that either the rendering state or the recognizing state would apply to determine whether one of its courts could entertain the case, however. A distinction is generally made, in other words, between jurisdiction or competency in the domestic sense: that is, the conditions that must exist before a court can entertain an original action, and in the international sense. Jurisdiction in the international sense depends upon the factors that tend to connect the case and the defendant to the rendering state in a way that satisfies the recognizing state's conception of what is fair in "the handling of litigation involving significant foreign elements."[10] The bases for personal jurisdiction in Anglo-American law are factors that tend to connect the defending party to the forum state.[11] Competence standards in other systems, too, commonly require some enduring connection between some party and the forum state or else some significant connection between the subject of the action and the state.[12]

"Jurisdiction," as used in the Anglo-American world, also includes such matters as the form, content, and timing of the notice that is given to the defendant. In other systems the notice element is considered separately from competency. A foreign judgment will not be accorded recognition unless it satisfies the international standards, not only as to the bases for jurisdiction (or competency), but also as to notice. The jurisdictional requirement thus serves to prevent recognition of judgments that have been rendered under circumstances that indicate that the defending party lacked significant connections to the rendering state and those judgments in which minimal standards of procedural fairness were not satisfied. However, since the standards for competency and jurisdiction normally do not rest on a thoroughly rational analysis of the factors favoring and those opposing recognition in particular kinds of cases, the jurisdiction test may lead to the refusal of recognition in some situations in which no significant interest would be disserved.

In most systems, even if international standards of jurisdiction and notice are met, recognition will nevertheless be denied if the rendering court lacked jurisdiction under its own standards. If the rendering court lacked power to adjudicate the case under its own jurisdictional principles, the purported judgment should not have any validity at all—at home or abroad, so the theory goes. However, as von Mehren and Trautman have pointed out, some conditions that may be considered jurisdictional under the rendering state's law may reflect only local concerns that are not serious enough to warrant denial of recognition, in their absence, to a foreign judgment.[13]

In some countries a "choice of law" test is also applied to determine whether a foreign judgment is entitled to recognition.[14] That is, a foreign judgment will be entitled to recognition without reexamination of the substantive merits only if the rendering court applied legal principles that were consistent with those that the recognizing jurisdiction would apply. Although this test is not an established requirement in Anglo-American law, it does help to identify cases in which the local interests of the recognizing court may warrant denial of recognition.

> Such a test, like the jurisdictional test, tends to ensure that the defendant has been treated with at least minimal fairness by a jurisdiction which is not unduly parochial in its view of international transactions. Furthermore, when the requested jurisdiction has a legitimate interest in the parties or in the factual situation out of which the controversy arose, failure to apply the law which its courts would apply suggests that its interests may not have been properly protected. However, when choice-of-law practices are generally reasonable these arguments are not conclusive, and they may yield to considerations of convenience and simplicity.[15]

Some states that do not employ a choice-of-law test, as such, do give effect to local substantive policy concerns as well as basic notions of procedural fairness through a vague "public policy" doctrine. Even United States courts resort to this doctrine to avoid giving recognition to some judgments that have been rendered in foreign countries. The public-policy concept is difficult to define, and its application may be an unpredictable factor in the judgment-recognition scheme.

In some states a requirement of reciprocity is imposed. In those states, the recognition of a foreign judgment turns on whether or not the state in which the judgment was rendered would grant recognition to a judgment of the enforcing state under reciprocal circumstances. Presumably the justification for one state's adopting the reciprocity test is the pressure that it may exert on the other country to force the latter to grant recognition without revision to the judgments of the first state. This is a rather futile and ineffective form of pressure, however, since the foreign country's interests normally are not directly involved in the denial of recognition to a judgment affecting a private citizen. And it is the once-successful private litigant who must bear the burden of this means of exerting pressure on the other country. The reciprocity rule has been recognized in the United States in a limited way,[16] but it is generally assumed that this is not constitutionally required. Some states, at any rate, have refused to follow it at all.[17] The reciprocity rule is still widely followed in Latin America, however.[18]

In the discussions of the judgment-recognition regimes of Central America in subsequent chapters, attention will be given to the tests for recognition that are employed in connection with civil money judgments. An attempt will be made to see whether the results that have been reached under those tests tend to strike a rational balance between the interests that favor and those that oppose recognition. First, however, we must consider the significance that judgment-recognition regimes may have in fostering the integration of states into a larger entity.

## THE SIGNIFICANCE OF JUDGMENT RECOGNITION TO THE INTEGRATION OF MULTIPLE-STATE ENTITIES

### ASSOCIATION INTERESTS

Besides the relative strengths of particular policies and concerns that might be affected by the decision on recognition of a foreign judgment, the relationship between the jurisdiction where the judgment was rendered and the one in which it is sought to be enforced is also relevant. Of course, that relationship is an element of the enforcing state's own interests, but it is important enough to merit special attention.

When the two states are linked together in some sort of multiple-state association, the interests numbered 2, 3, and 4 in the von Mehren–Trautman model take on special relevance. These concerns are present to some degree, of course, in any case where recognition is sought in one state for judgments rendered in another, but their importance is intensified when the states are member states of a larger association that has been formed to promote mutual political or economic goals. Local concerns that might otherwise justify denying recognition to a judgment may be outweighed in that situation, for when states are thus linked together, additional interests, besides those of the rendering and enforcing states and the litigant parties must be considered: for example, the interests of the association and those of the other member states insofar as they relate to the goals of the association. The association interests will be shared by all of the member states, of course, but in particular cases the special interests of individual states may conflict with the association's interests. A sound scheme of judgment recognition should rest on an analysis that can identify and evaluate the association's interests that might be affected by a decision that would grant or refuse to grant recognition to the sister state's judgment.

The nature and strength of the association interests that might be affected by such a decision depends, of course, upon the character and purposes of the association. The interests of a loose regional association like the Organization of American States obviously are neither so extensive nor so intensive as are those of a federal union such as the United States of America. Somewhere in between the federal union and the OAS lies the situation of subregional organizations, such as the Organization of Central American States, and regional common-market organizations, such as the Central American Common Market.

In the Central American context, it is possible to identify several association interests that may be affected by a member state's rules relating to the recognition and enforcement of judgments rendered by other member states of the association. Probably most important is the interest in faithful and consistent application and interpretation of the provisions and policies of the association's basic charter and its implementing regulations. If the association is to be effective, this interest must be accorded great weight. Toward that end, multiple-state associations sometimes create special tribunals to review the decisions of constituent states involving such questions of interpretation. Probably the best example of this type of tribunal is the European Court of Justice.[19] Even that tribunal's jurisdiction is not broad enough to cover all situations in which the community's interests are affected by local tribunals, however. The General Treaty of the Central American Common Market provided for an Arbitration Tribunal to resolve disputes relating to the interpretations of provisions of the treaty that could not be otherwise resolved, but, as noted in the last chapter, it has had almost no use.[20] Likewise, the Charter of the Organization of Central American States (ODECA) provided for the Central American Court of Justice, but this tribunal, too, has been essentially nonfunctional.[21] The absence of an effective unifying tribunal makes it all the more important that the association's interests in faithful and consistent interpretation and application of the association's basic policies be accorded weighty consideration in decisions relating to recognition of sister-state judgments. The association's interest in uniformity and consistency would normally require one state to give conclusive effect to a judgment of another embodying such an interpretation, unless: (1) it was clearly wrong; (2) previous decisions of the enforcing state or of other states in the association had given the same point an interpretation different from the one embodied in the judgment; (3) some truly fundamental municipal interest of the enforcing state would be impaired by according the decision conclusive effect; or (4) some other important association interest (besides the interest in faithful and consistent interpretation of basic policy) would be impaired thereby. If the judicial decisions containing such interpretations are duly publicized and circulated among courts in the member states, inconsistent rulings should occur only rarely.[22] Incorrect and inconsistent interpretations, thus publicized, can be remedied legislatively by amending the basic documents so as to reflect the desired meaning. Recognition without revision of the interpretation, then, would normally be the best judicial response to a sister state's judgment interpreting the basic policy, even if the enforcing court disagrees with the interpretation.

Related to the association's interest in consistent interpretation of the basic charter and policies is the association's interest in the avoidance of conflict between local law and the association's policies. Presumably, member states will be conscious and careful of this interest in framing such legislative enactments or regulations as are promulgated after the adoption of the basic charter. Potential conflicts between the basic charter's policies and the preexisting corpus juris of the member states, however, are likely to go undetected until the issue is confronted by an actual controversy. It will normally be in the association's interest for such controversies to be resolved by according primacy to the association's policy over the local one, unless the local one is of such fundamental importance to the concerned member state that its further participation in the association would be jeopardized if its local policy had to yield. This interest would be relevant to the judgment-recognition decision even if no question of interpretation or application of the basic charter or policies of the association itself were directly involved in it. If the sister state's judgment embodied an application or interpretation of local law in a way that might conflict with association policy, the association's interest would be served by keeping the effects of that local law confined to the rendering state. The denial of extraterritorial recognition in such a case would serve to dramatize the potential conflict and bring it to the attention of both the lawmakers of the rendering state and of the association for appropriate consideration. In such a case, the enforcing state should weigh this interest against other interests tending to support extraterritorial recognition and enforcement of the judgment. Unless the conflict of the local rule with the association's policy is substantial and direct, it is doubtful that this interest would be weighty enough by itself to offset other concerns that would normally favor recognition; but it is a factor that should be considered, and it may require the enforcing state to look behind the face of the judgment in some cases if an issue is raised suggesting such a conflict.

Another association interest that merits consideration is the interest in the mobility of goods and persons between the member states. This, of course, may be one of the basic policies of the association, and so this interest could be subsumed in the broader ones that have previously been discussed. But since it is the very fact of international movement of goods and persons that makes international recognition and enforcement of judgments a significant problem, this interest merits special attention.

In the sense that is significant to the goals of an association such as the Central American Common Market, the association's interest in mobility of goods and persons argues for a general, association-wide policy of recognition and enforcement of judgments without revision of the merits. The main reason that mobility of goods and persons between the member states is important to such an association is that it facilitates responsiveness to opportunities for economic development within the region. Labor and capital, goods and services should be encouraged to flow from one place to another within the region in response to economic considerations. Artificial barriers and noneconomic concerns that tend to inhibit the free flow should be eliminated to the greatest possible extent if an integrated economy is to be realized. If havens from the claims of judgment creditors are eliminated from the region, then one potentially inhibiting consideration would be removed. The association's interest in mobility of goods and persons then argues for a rule, uniform throughout the region, calling for a virtually automatic recognition and enforcement of the judgments of each member state in all others.

Another association interest that deserves mention is the interest in fostering a climate of confidence and faith in the security of transactions. Ready enforceability and recognition of judgments throughout the region is obviously a factor that is conducive to such a climate.

## PROTECTION OF ASSOCIATION INTERESTS IN THE CONSTITUTION OF THE UNITED STATES

The importance of these interests was clearly seen by the draftsmen of the United States Constitution. Several provisions of that document are designed to serve such "association interests" as the ones referred to above. With respect to the interest in faithful and consistent application and interpretation of the provisions of the basic charter, our constitution not only provides for a special tribunal (the United States Supreme Court), but also authorizes the creation of a separate judiciary system (the lower federal courts) to deal with cases arising under our federal constitution, laws, and treaties.[23] The interest in ensuring the primacy of association policy over local policy is served by the Supremacy Clause,[24] by various express limitations on the scope of state power, and, again, by the institution of a supreme tribunal with power to enforce those constitutional provisions. The interest in mobility of goods and persons is served by the provision for federal control of interstate commerce, by the constitutional right of interstate mobility, and by the national policy of nearly automatic judgment recognition embodied in the Full Faith and Credit Clause.[25] That clause also contributes to the climate of faith in the security of transactions, as does the provision for federal-court jurisdiction of cases in which the parties are citizens of different states.[26]

Since principles of judgment recognition within the United States federal union are predicated mainly upon the Full Faith and Credit Clause, a brief sketch of the principles that have been developed in amplification of that clause is appropriate at this point.

The Full Faith and Credit Clause appears in Section 1 of Article 4 of the United States Constitution:

> Full faith and credit shall be given in each state to the public acts, records and judicial proceedings of every other state. And the Congress may by general laws prescribe the manner in which such acts, records and proceedings shall be proved, and the effect thereof.

Acting on the authority granted by this clause, the first Congress enacted a law clarifying only slightly the meaning of the phrase "full faith and credit."[27] This statute remains in basically the same form today:

> Title 28, U.S.C. § 1738. State and Territorial statutes and judicial proceedings; full faith and credit
>
> The Acts of legislature of any State, Territory, or Possession of the United States, or copies thereof, shall be authenticated by affixing the seal of such State, Territory or Possession thereto.
>
> The records and judicial proceedings of any court of any such State, Territory or Possession, or copies thereof, shall be proved or admitted in other courts within the United States and its Territories and Possessions by the attestation of the clerk and seal of the court annexed, if a seal exists, together with a certificate of a judge of the court that the said attestation is in proper form.
>
> Such Acts, records and judicial proceedings or copies thereof, so authenticated, shall have the same full faith and credit in every court within the United States and its Territories and Possessions as they have by law or usage in the courts of such State, Territory or Possession from which they are taken.

"Full faith and credit" was interpreted at an early time to mean that a valid and final money judgment of one state was to be given conclusive, not prima facie evidentiary, effect on the substantive merits in every other.[28] The words "same full faith and credit . . . as they have by law or usage in the courts of such state . . . from which they are taken" suggests that the money judgments of one state are directly enforceable without further formalities in every other state. This is not the way the phrase has been interpreted, however. A sister state can demand that a new judgment be obtained in its courts, based upon the debt created by the original judgment, before enforcing it by its own execution process.[29]

### REQUIREMENTS FOR RECOGNITION

*VALIDITY.* It is frequently declared that only "valid and final" judgments are entitled to full faith and credit in other states. Judgments, for this purpose, include determinations of administrative tribunals when acting judicially. Validity, for this purpose, means that the judgment must not be "void," that is, subject to collateral attack in the state of rendition.[30] It may be "valid" for purposes of full faith and credit even though errors were committed which make the judgment vulnerable to reversal on appeal.

A judgment will be subject to collateral attack and will therefore be invalid for purposes of full faith and credit if the rendering court lacked jurisdiction of the person of the defending parties or of the subject matter of the action. The rendering court must have had jurisdiction under its own law and under national standards. The national standards of jurisdiction under the Full Faith and Credit Clause are the same as those embodied in the due-process clause of the Fourteenth Amendment.[31] They must be met before a judgment can be valid either within the rendering state or outside of it.

*Jurisdictional Standards.* The due-process clause imposes limitations both with respect to the bases for personal jurisdiction and with respect to the process by which a court's jurisdiction is invoked. Traditionally, the authorized bases were said to be physical presence, consent, and domicile.[32] Under the traditional tests, a defendant could be constitutionally subjected to suit in a state only if he was domiciled there, if he was personally served with process while physically present there, or if he consented to suit there. This traditional approach was seriously deficient for a federal system such as the United States, however. Travel and commerce between the states is positively encouraged, and parties commonly engage in activities that are potentially productive of litigation in states other than the ones in which they make their homes. Under the traditional approach, however, a defendant could not be subjected to personal jurisdiction outside his domiciliary state against his will, unless by chance he could be found by a process server while he was physically present in that state. Corporations posed difficult problems for this jurisdictional system, since it rested on a personal, physical connection between the defendant and the forum state.[33] Eventually the Supreme Court, in the famous case of *International Shoe Co.* v. *State of Washington et al.*,[34] rejected the notion that personal process service on a nonconsenting nonresident defendant while he was physically present in the state was necessary for due process. All that was necessary in such a case (insofar as concerns the *basis* element of jurisdiction) is "certain minimum contacts with [the forum state] such that the maintenance of the suit does not offend 'traditional notions of fair play and substantial justice.' "[35]

The application of this very flexible test involves a weighing of the factors favoring the exercise of jurisdiction over that defendant for that case and the factors opposing such an exercise. It involves a consideration of "the quality and nature of the [defendant's] activity in relation to the fair and orderly administration of the laws which it was the purpose of the due process clause to insure."[36] Such questions as the expectations of the parties, regulatory concerns of the various states with which the case has an arguable connection, relative procedural convenience, and so forth, are relevant in determining whether enough contact exists between the parties and issues and the forum state to satisfy due process. A single liability-creating act or event with the state may be enough contact to satisfy the standard for an action arising out of that act, if the act or event was the result of the defendant's own conduct undertaken with awareness of its potential impact in that state.[37] A more substantial connection is required, however, to justify jurisdiction for a cause of action that is unrelated to the defendant's activity in the forum state.[38]

In 1945, then, physical presence in the state of a nonconsenting nonresident ceased to be a necessary condition for the exercise of personal jurisdiction by a state court. Until 1977, however, it continued to be widely assumed that physical presence was a sufficient condition. In that year, the Supreme Court, in the case of *Shaffer* v. *Heitner*,[39] declared that "all assertions of state-court jurisdiction must be evaluated according to the standards set forth in *International Shoe* and its progeny."[40] The full significance of this decision is not yet clear, but it may mean that physical presence of a nonconsenting nonresident is no longer sufficient for due process.[41]

Jurisdiction for purposes of full faith and credit and due process today, then, probably does turn on a weighing and balancing of factors that tend to make the rendering court a fair and convenient forum for the litigation of the case.

The "process" element of due process must also be satisfied, of course. This, basically, requires that a form of official notice reasonably calculated to afford the defendant actual notice be provided, and that the notice be provided in sufficient time to allow the defendant an adequate opportunity to prepare a defense.[42]

If local standards of the rendering state and these national standards for jurisdiction with respect to both basis and process are met, a judgment generally will be regarded as "valid" for purposes of full faith and credit. There is one notable exception to this proposition. If a judgment is subject to collateral attack or if equitable relief may be obtained against it on grounds of fraud in the rendering state, it need not be accorded full faith and credit in others, whether or not the local law of that state expressly treats the fraud as vitiating jurisdiction.[43] Normally only fraud that tends to deny the opposing party a fair day in court will provide grounds for collateral attack. Fraud in the form of false testimony does not have that effect.[44]

*Challenging Jurisdiction in the Requested Court.* The Full Faith and Credit Clause does not prevent the requested court from examining the rendering court's jurisdiction, at least if the party that opposed recognition made no appearance in the first action.[45] The recognizing court's ruling on the jurisdictional issue is subject to ultimate review in the Supreme Court of the United States. A denial of recognition to a jurisdictionally valid judgment, of course, would be a denial of the federal right to full faith and credit, while recognizing a judgment that is jurisdictionally invalid could be a denial of the federal right to due process.

If the defendant did appear and participate in the rendering court's proceeding, however, the right to challenge that court's jurisdiction in the enforcing state may be foreclosed. With respect to jurisdiction of the person, if the defendant makes a voluntary "general appearance," he will be deemed to have submitted to jurisdiction, thus curing any defect he otherwise might have raised.[46] Even if he appears solely for the purpose of challenging jurisdiction, without submitting to jurisdiction generally (as he is everywhere permitted to do today), he will be foreclosed from raising the same issue again if the rendering court determines, albeit erroneously, that it has jurisdiction to determine that question; and a judgment that is rendered subsequent to such a ruling will be entitled to full faith and credit in other states unless it is reversed on appeal in the rendering state.[47]

The issues of subject-matter jurisdiction, too, may be foreclosed from examination in the recognizing court under some circumstances, although the doctrine is not so clear as it is in the case of personal jurisdiction. In theory, the defendant's acquiescence or participation is irrelevant to the question of subject-matter jurisdiction. In fact, however, because of the principle that a court has jurisdiction to determine its own jurisdiction, the issue of subject-matter jurisdiction can, in some cases, be foreclosed from reexamination.[48] If the subject-matter jurisdiction of a superior court depends on a question of fact and if the parties actually litigated that question in the rendering court, the conclusion that jurisdiction exists will normally bind the parties and prevent relitigation of that issue anywhere.[49] In some kinds of cases the fact that the parties had an opportunity to litigate questions of subject-matter jurisdiction in the rendering court is enough to foreclose later litigation of that issue.[50]

*FINALITY.* Full faith and credit generally extends only to final judgments. Basically, this means that no interstate effect need be given to a judgment if further judicial action in the rendering state is necessary before the litigated matter is resolved.[51] Matters ruled upon in interlocutory orders need not be granted recognition in other states. The finality rule has also been invoked to deny enforcement in some cases where a complete adjudication has taken place. A judgment ordering the award of future payments in installments (for instance) need not be enforced in other states as to the unaccrued installments. Even accrued installments need not be enforced in other states if they are subject to retroactive modification in the state where the judgment was rendered.[52] This does not mean that a sister state is forbidden to enforce a judgment as to future or retroactively modifiable installments. The trend of modern cases, in fact, is to grant recognition and enforcement to such judgments or decrees,[53] and all states apparently will enforce such judgments when they fall within the scope of the Uniform Reciprocal Enforcement of Support Act.[54]

JUDGMENTS OTHER THAN MONEY JUDGMENTS

The application of the full-faith-and-credit requirement is not limited to money judgments. Other judgments are entitled to interstate recognition as conclusive adjudications of the matters litigated, even though they may not be enforceable in other states in the way that money judgments are. Defendant's judgments, divorce decrees, determinations of heirship, declaratory judgments, injunctions—all are entitled to such recognition. Whether any judgment that orders a defendant to do anything other than pay money is required by the Full Faith and Credit Clause to be enforced, however, is a question that has not been decided by the Supreme Court. Some states do accord enforcement to some kinds of decrees.[55] The Uniform Enforcement of Foreign Judgments Act apparently provides for the enforcement of such decrees, if they are of such a character as to be enforceable.[56]

The Supreme Court has held, however, that full faith and credit does not require enforcement of decrees ordering the conveyance of land or otherwise purporting to affect land title directly if the land lies outside the territory of the rendering court,[57] even though the defendant was clearly subject to personal jurisdiction there. Some courts have interpreted this as meaning that such decrees are void and are not even entitled to recognition for their res judicata effects,[58] but this seems to be inconsistent with the principles of recognition that are applicable in other cases. In any event, the majority of recent cases do afford recognition to sister-state decrees that purport to affect land outside the territory of the rendering court.[59]

GROUNDS FOR NONRECOGNITION

In the case of money judgments rendered by courts of foreign countries, United States courts may invoke several grounds for nonrecognition besides the absence of the requirements of jurisdictional validity and finality (unless a treaty provides otherwise). If the judgment was obtained in an action for taxes or for a penal fine, it need not be enforced.[60] This is also the case if the cause of action underlying foreign judgment is contrary to the "public policy" of the enforcing state.[61] Under some circumstances the lack of reciprocity may be invoked to resist recognition of a foreign country's judgment.[62]

If the judgment is one of a sister state in the United States, however, these defenses to enforcement are not available (with one possible exception). Lack of reciprocity is not a valid ground for nonrecognition of a valid and final money judgment. The Full Faith and Credit Clause virtually guarantees reciprocity. The famous case of *Fauntleroy* v. *Lum*[63] held that the public policy of the forum is not a valid defense to recognition and enforcement. A sister state's judgment for taxes is entitled to full faith and credit.[64] Whether judgments imposing a penal fine are entitled to full faith and credit is a question that is open to some doubt. Dicta in a late-nineteenth-century case[65] in the Supreme Court have sometimes been interpreted to mean that the Full Faith and Credit Clause does not require one state to enforce a penal judgment rendered in another.[66] The soundness of this interpretation is questionable, however, since it seems inconsistent with the rule that a court may not refuse enforcement to a money judgment of a sister state because the underlying claim is contrary to its public policy or because the judgment is for taxes. Accordingly, some courts have declared that full faith and credit cannot be denied to a money judgment merely because it rests on a penal claim.[67] If an exception exists in case of a penal judgment, however, it apparently is a narrow one. It applies only to penalties that are essentially aimed at punishing an offense against the public rather than providing a private remedy.[68] Judgments awarding multiple or exemplary damages to a private party are not penal judgments within the exception, according to most authorities.[69]

Although local "public policy" is not a legitimate ground for denying enforcement to a sister state's money judgment, the requested state can apply its own statute of limitations, rather than that of the rendering state, on judgement enforcement and can deny enforcement on that ground, even though the judgment is entirely valid and enforceable in the rendering state.[70] This proposition seems anomalous, since its effect is to ascribe more importance to the enforcing state's procedural interest in the prompt execution of judgments than to its important substantive policy concerns. The principle is well settled, however.

INCONSISTENT JUDGMENTS

Since the Full Faith and Credit Clause requires every other state to give basically the same effect to a judgment as it has in the state where it was rendered, instances of inconsistent judgments on the very same subject involving the same parties are relatively rare. They can happen, however. The parties may fail to call the attention of the court in the second action to the existence of the earlier judgment. Even if they do, the court in the second action may rule, erroneously, that the earlier judgment is invalid or that it is otherwise not entitled to full faith and credit. In such situations there may be two jurisdictionally valid but inconsistent final judgments. To which would a court in a third action owe full faith and credit?

The basic answer in the United States system is that it is the later (or latest) in time that must be given effect.[71] An erroneous refusal of full faith and credit to an earlier judgment does not make a later one void and subject to collateral attack. The error must be raised directly by appeal to the highest court in the second state, and ultimately review must be sought in the Supreme Court of the United States if the second judgment is to be denied conclusive effect. Thus, if a court of state B erroneously denies full faith and credit to a judgment of state A and determines the merits of the case differently than did the court of state A, and if review in the Supreme Court of the United States is not sought by the losing party, state A would owe full faith and credit to the state-B judgment rather than the earlier state-A judgment. If review in the Supreme Court of the United States was sought but was unavailable for some reason over which the losing party had no control, however, the result might be different.[72]

ENFORCEMENT PROCEDURE

The normal method of enforcing money judgments entails the bringing of an action in the enforcing state to collect the debt that the judgment declares to be owing. This mode of enforcement necessitates acquiring jurisdiction over the person of the defendant (or over the defendant's property) by proper service of process under the laws of the enforcing state. This procedure has been held to be consistent with the Full Faith and Credit Clause.[73] The enforcement action normally is brought in a general trial court. The cause of action may be proved by presenting a copy of the judgment, duly authenticated as prescribed by federal law.[74] The Full Faith and Credit Clause thus makes money judgments enforceable without reexamination of the merits of the underlying claim wherever the judgment debtor may have property. The only defenses that may be raised in the enforcement action are challenges to the jurisdiction of the rendering court (as prescribed above) or of the enforcement court. If there is no defect of jurisdiction or other invalidity that would warrant denial of full faith and credit, a judgment will be granted by the enforcing court, which can then be enforced by the same processes as are available for that court's domestic judgments.

An even more expeditious method is provided for the enforcement of a judgment of one U.S. District Court in others.[75] This procedure eliminates the need for initiating a separate action. The judgment, properly authenticated, can be registered with the clerk of the recognizing court, and the judgment thus becomes enforceable there.

The Uniform Enforcement of Foreign Judgments Act, which has been adopted in several states,[76] also permits enforcement of sister-state judgments by registration as an alternative to the conventional method.

RECOGNITION OF CONCLUSIVE (RES JUDICATA) EFFECTS

Besides making money judgments enforceable nationwide, the Full Faith and Credit Clause also serves to project the conclusive effects of judgments throughout the country. The policy of finality of litigation, embodied in the doctrine of res judicata, thus is given nationwide scope.

Res judicata, in modern jurisprudence, is analyzed as having two different aspects: claim preclusion and issue preclusion. The principle of claim preclusion serves to prevent a second suit from being brought on a claim or cause of action that has once been prosecuted to a valid and final personal judgment on the merits. The policy purpose behind the principle is to force a plaintiff to include in one lawsuit all he may ever want to assert in support of his claim. One cause of action, it is said, cannot be split into two or more lawsuits. Where applicable, the principle prevents a later suit on the same claim, even if matters that were not considered in the first action are presented in the second. The principle applies even if nothing was actually litigated in the first suit, so long as the first judgment was "on the merits." Thus, a default judgment or a judgment of dismissal "with prejudice" can preclude a later suit on the same claim. Some exceptions to the operation of the principle of claim preclusion have been recognized,[77] but the principle is applicable in most situations in which a money judgment is sought in the first action. The most difficult problem connected with claim preclusion is determining the dimensions, or scope, of the claim or cause of action that are precluded by the first judgment.

The principle of issue preclusion serves to prevent the relitigation of the same questions of fact (or sometimes of law) by the same parties, or persons represented by parties, in the earlier action.[78] Normally, it applies only to issues that have been actively and fairly litigated in the first action and that are necessary to the judgment rendered. The principle of issue preclusion rests on the premise that one trier of fact is as competent as another to determine factual matters; so that once parties have had a fair chance to prove their positions, justice normally would not be served by affording them a second chance. The principle may apply whether the later suit is on the same cause of action as was the first (in which case it may be referred to as the principle of "direct estoppel") or on a different cause of action (in which case it may be referred to as "collateral estoppel"). The principle does not normally apply to default judgments, but it may apply to judgments not on the merits, if matters actually were litigated which were necessary to the judgment rendered.[79]

Under basic U.S. doctrine, only parties—persons who were subject to the jurisdiction of the rendering court—or persons represented by parties, or persons in "privity" with parties are bound by judgments.[80] Persons who were not formal parties thus may be bound if their interests were represented in the action by one who was a party. A judgment against a guardian in his representative capacity will be binding on the ward; a judgment against a trustee, on the beneficiary; and a judgment against a properly represented class in a class action will bind all the members of that class. Persons in "privity" with parties may also be bound. Thus, matters relating to property ownership that have been adjudicated in an action to which a transferor was a party may bind one to whom he subsequently transferred his interest.

Limitations on who may be bound by the res judicata effects of a judgment are features of our conception of due process.[81] The federal constitution, then, restricts the states' power to enact laws that would make judgments binding on nonparties to the action. On the other hand, the states have been left free to prescribe different answers to the question of whether nonparties can claim the benefits of res judicata. Until the middle of the twentieth century, state courts generally looked to the principle of mutuality to answer that question.[82] Under the mutuality principle, only one who would have been bound by the prior judgment could claim the benefit of its issue-preclusion effects in a later action. Only parties and those represented by parties and those in "privity" with them, then, could claim the benefit of issue preclusion. Now, however, many states have rejected the mutuality principle and have adopted in its place a rule that would generally permit anyone to invoke issue preclusion (some states limit it to defensive use) against one who was a party to the earlier action, if the party to be bound had had a full, fair opportunity and incentive to litigate the issue in that prior lawsuit.[83]

The existence of different rules relating to the rights of third parties to invoke the issue-preclusion effects of a judgment poses the question of which state's rule should control when a judgment is asserted for its issue-preclusion effects in another state by a nonparty to the first suit. The full-faith-and-credit statute speaks of the "same" effects. This suggests that the recognizing court should permit the invocation of the judgment by a third party if the rendering state would do so, even if the recognizing state's own rule would not.[84] It is not clear whether the recognizing state should follow the rendering state's rule on this matter when the latter would *not* permit the third party to claim the benefit of the judgment but the former would.[85] The Full Faith and Credit Clause would not in itself prevent the recognizing state from giving more extensive conclusive effects to the judgment than it has in the rendering state, but the Due Process Clause might. If a party were held to more extensive conclusive effects of a judgment than he had any reason to foresee at the time of the original litigation, the principle of fundamental fairness that is embodied in our concept of due process might be violated. The Supreme Court has not yet ruled on this question, however.

This survey of the operation of the Full Faith and Credit Clause shows that through it, money judgments of one state can be enforced without reexamination (except for jurisdictional defects and sometimes not even for them) in any state in which the defendant owns property that can be used to satisfy a judgment. Moreover, the operation of the clause serves to project throughout the whole country the res judicata effect that the judgment has in the state where it was rendered. The clause thus serves a very important role in making our federation a single nation and a single economy.

Not all federal unions provide the same kinds of institutional arrangements to foster the association's interests as does the Constitution of the United States. However, a full-faith-and-credit clause is a common, if not universal, feature of federal constitutions.[86] Even the constitutions of the short-lived Federal Republic of Central America and the later, half-formed Central American Confederation contained specific provisions of that type.[87]

### JUDGMENT RECOGNITION IN THE EUROPEAN COMMON MARKET

The importance of strong judgment-enforcement provisions has not always been appreciated by the framers of plans for multiple-state associations that are not aimed directly at full political integration. Even the most sophisticated of economic-integration plans—the European Economic Community—initially contained no express arrangement for judgment recognition among the member states. The Treaty of Rome, which established the EEC in 1957, did refer to the problem but placed reliance on the member states to negotiate treaties with each other to provide for the "simplification of the formalities governing reciprocal recognition and enforcement of judgments."[88] It soon became apparent, however, that full realization of the goals of the EEC could not be achieved without the establishment in all the member states of uniform rules to ensure nearly automatic recognition and enforcement of civil and commercial judgments.

In October of 1959 the Commission of the European Economic Community sent a letter to the member states declaring that

> a true internal market between the six states will be achieved only if adequate legal protection can be guaranteed. The economic life of the Community will be liable to disturbances and difficulties unless it is possible, where necessary, by judicial means to ensure the recognition and enforcement of the individual rights which will arise from multiple legal relationships. As the power of the judiciary in both civil and commercial matters is derived from the sovereignty of Member States, and the effect of judicial instruments remains limited to national territory, legal protection, and consequently, legal security in the Common Market are essentially dependent on Member States adopting a satisfactory solution to the problem of recognition and enforcement of judgments.[89]

Accordingly, a negotiating committee was convened in 1960 to prepare a draft convention on Jurisdiction and Enforcement of Judgments in

Civil and Commercial Matters. The draft was completed in 1964, and after extensive debate was finally adopted and ratified by the six original community members. It became effective in February 1973.[90]

TYPES OF JUDGMENTS ENTITLED TO RECOGNITION UNDER THE CONVENTION

The convention covers all "civil and commercial matters whatever the nature of the jurisdiction" with certain specific exceptions.[91] This means that whether the convention applies or not depends upon the nature of the action, not upon the characteristics or title of the tribunal.[92] Thus, the judgment may be one of a civil, commercial, criminal, administrative, or labor court or tribunal, so long as the cause of action is characterized as civil or commercial.[93] The convention does not, however, define "civil and commercial," nor does it specify by what law that characterization is to be made. In 1976 the European Court of Justice ruled that the characterization was not governed by the law of any state, but by "the objectives and scheme of the convention" and "general principles which stem from the corpus of the national legal systems."[94] In view of the need for uniformity in the application of the convention, it has been suggested that all doubts as to whether a matter is "civil or commercial" should be resolved in favor of that characterization.[95] Thus, almost any action that has as its object an order requiring one private party to pay money or transfer property to another is covered by the convention if it does not fall within one of the exceptions. A suit between a private party and public authority, on the other hand, is not covered.[96]

The convention specifically excludes the application of it to certain common types of actions. Excepted are actions concerning the status or capacity of natural persons, marriage regimes, and wills or inheritances; bankruptcies, compositions, and similar proceedings; and social security.[97] The reason for excluding these matters from coverage was the difficulty of formulating rules regarding the conflict of laws and jurisdiction applicable to such cases that could be accepted by all contracting states.[98] These are matters in which local public policy is likely to be perceived as being very strong, and so, even if agreement could be reached on jurisdiction and choice-of-law rules, generally it was feared that refusals to recognize such judgments on public-policy grounds would be frequent.[99] Marta Weser, a member of the Committee of Experts who drafted the convention, urged that a different treaty be drawn up to deal with the excluded matters,[100] but this has not yet been done. It should be noted that a matter that is included among these exceptions is outside the scope of the convention only if it is the principal object of the action.[101]

Arbitration is another excluded subject.[102] The reason for having the convention's coverage exclude any matters resolved in arbitration was that other international arrangements were thought to be adequate to assure recognition and enforcement of arbitration awards.[103]

TYPES OF EFFECTS

*RECOGNITION.* When recognition of a covered judgment is sought in order to establish a point in a collateral proceeding, the convention provides that the judgment shall be recognized without the necessity for any formal procedure (other than proof).[104] Recognition means that the judgment must have the "authority and effectiveness" in every state that it has in the state where it was rendered.[105] This means that a judgment will be recognized throughout the Common Market region for its conclusive effects—what we would call res judicata effects. The civil-law countries of the European Economic Community do not attribute such extensive effects to judgments as does the United States, however. "In German law, for instance, which starts with very different propositions, only the ultimate dispositive holding (the *Urteilsformel*) has conclusive effects, and the underlying factual and legal conclusions (the *Sachverhalt* and the *Rechtsverhältnis*) can have such effects only to the extent that they are made a part of the holding; a cause of action (which may well be defined more restrictively than in American law) can be split; direct and collateral estoppel effects are not accorded."[106] The French doctrine is similar.[107] Where there are differences between the doctrine of the rendering state and of the recognizing state with regard to the scope of the conclusive effects of a judgment, those of the rendering state are apparently controlling. How effectively this principle works when the rendering country is England, where res judicata has much broader scope, is not yet clear.

Recognition is automatic when the judgment is proved in the collateral proceeding in accordance with Article 46.[108] If recognition of the judgment is the main object of the action, however, although no enforcement by execution is sought, the party who is seeking recognition of it must initiate a proceeding to have it declared valid. Such a proceeding is to follow essentially the same form as a proceeding of enforcement.[109]

*ENFORCEMENT.* A civil or commercial money judgment of one state that is enforceable there is entitled to enforcement in the other community states unless one of the specific grounds for nonrecognition applies.[110]

MECHANICS OF RECOGNITION AND ENFORCEMENT

No special proceeding is necessary to entitle a judgment covered by the convention to be recognized in a collateral action. It must be proved, however, to the court in which the collateral action is pending by producing a copy of the judgment, duly authenticated.[111] It is the law of the place where the judgment was rendered that determines the conditions for authentication.[112] If the judgment was rendered by default, a document establishing that the defaulting party was duly served with process must also be produced.[113]

If enforcement is sought (or if recognition is sought as the principal object of the action in the recognizing state), a special proceeding is required. The first phase of the proceeding is an ex parte application for enforcement, which is brought in the court that is identified in Article 32 of the convention as the competent one for each country. If the defendant is domiciled in the country where enforcement is sought, the court at the place of the defendant's domicile is the competent one. If the defendant is not domiciled in that country, then it is the court at the place where the enforcement is sought (i.e., where property can be levied upon) that is competent. No notice to the defending party is required at this stage.[114] The reason for the ex parte procedure is to give the party who is seeking enforcement some protection against the possibility that the defendant might remove property from the country before the execution could be levied.[115]

In the ex parte proceeding the applicant must submit the requisite proof to establish the validity of the judgment and its enforceability in the rendering state. No bond is required of the party who is seeking enforcement at this stage.[116] The court then examines the judgment to see if it qualifies for enforcement. The only grounds for refusing enforcement are those discussed below under "Defenses." The merits cannot be reexamined.[117] A prompt ruling on the application is to be made.

If the order of enforcement is granted, the other party must then be notified and be given an opportunity to appeal and present defenses against enforcement in a contested proceeding. He will have one month to appeal if he is domiciled in the enforcing state; two months if in another state of the community.[118]

The appeal is taken to the court specified for each country in Article 37. This appeal is a contentious evidentiary proceeding. The court may suspend execution if appeal is taken, and it can impose a bond requirement.[119] The possibility of further appeal on questions of law only is available.[120]

If the application for enforcement is refused at the ex parte hearing, the party who is seeking enforcement may appeal to the court specified for each country in Article 40. The opposing party must be notified and be given an opportunity to participate in the appeal. The ruling on this appeal may be further appealed on a question of law.[121]

DEFENSES

Recognition and enforcement can be denied under certain circumstances.

PUBLIC POLICY. The convention in terms seems to recognize the traditional public policy (*ordre public*) exception to judgment recognition. However, this exception is not so broad as the public-policy exception in the laws of individual states. The draftsmen of the convention, in fact, expressed the opinion that the clause ought to operate only rarely.[122] The public-policy exception does not permit a state to deny recognition merely because the law applied in the rendering court differs from that prescribed by the choice-of-law rules of the recognizing court.[123] It is not the foreign judgment itself but the recognition of it that must be contrary to the forum's public policy if recognition is to be denied.[124] The public-policy exception cannot be invoked to deny recognition to a judgment that has been rendered against a nondomiciliary of the EEC on the basis of one of the "exorbitant" jurisdictional bases.[125] Thus the public-policy exception is of limited scope.

LACK OF NOTICE TO THE DEFENDANT. If the judgment for which recognition or enforcement is sought was obtained by default, recognition will be denied unless it appears that the defendant was properly served with process sufficient to notify him of the proceeding against him and that the service was made at such a time as to permit the adequate preparation of a defense.[126]

INCONSISTENT JUDGMENTS. A judgment may be denied recognition if it is incompatible with a judgment between the same parties that has been rendered by a court of the state in which recognition was sought.[127] Presumably, instances of inconsistent judgments will be uncommon, since when actions are pending simultaneously in different states involving the same issues and parties, the court in which the later action was brought is required to declare itself incompetent to entertain the case.[128]

CHOICE-OF-LAW CONSIDERATIONS. If the judgment for which recognition is sought concerned the status or capacity of natural persons, marriage regimes, or wills or inheritances, and if the rendering court applied rules that were incompatible with those prescribed by the choice-of-law rules of the recognizing state, recognition can be denied for that reason.[129] This is an independent exception distinct from the general public-policy exception.

*JURISDICTIONAL DEFECTS.* Apart from the adequate-notice requirement discussed above, challenges to recognition that are based on jurisdictional infirmities in the original action can be made only in a very limited way. This is so because the convention adopts rules of competence that apply uniformly throughout the EEC in matters that are covered by the convention and imposes the obligation on the rendering court to ascertain whether the case falls within its competence or not.[130] The recognizing court is not permitted to review for itself the jurisdictional facts.

The jurisdictional standards prescribed by the convention are the following: Anyone domiciled in one of the contracting states is subject to jurisdiction in the courts of that state,[131] regardless of the nature of the claim (so long as it is "civil or commercial"). Persons domiciled in one contracting state may also be subjected to jurisdiction in the courts of another under some circumstances. In contract cases, for instance, a person can be sued in the place where the obligation is to be performed as well as in the country of his domicile.[132] In tort cases, he can be sued where the "harmful event occurred,"[133] or if the tort is one that may also be the subject of criminal prosecution, he can be sued in the court of prosecution, provided that court is empowered to entertain civil claims.[134] Suits for compulsory maintenance may be brought in the place of the claimant's domicile.[135] Suits concerning the way in which a firm's branch, agency, or other establishment conducts its business can be brought in the place where the branch, agency, or other establishment is situated.[136] If there is more than one defendant, all can be sued in the court of the domicile of one of them.[137] Special provision is made for claims arising from insurance contracts[138] and consumer contracts.[139] In a few kinds of cases, however, the convention provides that only one court may be competent.[140] Notable among these exclusive-jurisdiction provisions is the rule that limits actions involving rights in rem in real property to the courts of the situs of the property. Except in areas where the convention itself provides for exclusive jurisdiction and in certain situations involving insurance and credit sale-hire purchase contracts, the parties may by agreement specify a particular court as the one that is competent to entertain claims arising from their relationship.[141] Of course, if the defendant voluntarily appears, other than for purposes of challenging jurisdiction, the court will be competent to adjudicate his rights (except in those situations in which the convention expressly specifies that a certain court has exclusive jurisdiction).[142]

The convention expressly prohibits resort to certain "exorbitant" bases of jurisdiction in suits against defendants who are domiciled in one of the EEC countries.[143]

The most commonly cited of these rules of exorbitant jurisdiction are the following:[144] (1) In France and Luxembourg, jurisdiction can be predicated on the basis of the plaintiff's nationality.[145] Thus, a Frenchman, even if he is not domiciled in France, can obtain a judgment in a French court against a non-French defendant who is domiciled outside of the Common Market, even though the cause of action is unrelated to France.[146] (2) German courts can exercise jurisdiction on the basis of the presence of assets within Germany, and the judgment is not limited to the value of the assets themselves.[147] (3) A Netherlands court can entertain a suit against a nondomiciliary on the basis of the plaintiff's Netherlands domicile.[148] These "exorbitant" bases may be utilized in cases involving defendants who are not domiciled in one of the contracting states, and judgments obtained on such bases then become enforceable throughout the entire Common Market region.[149] This provision of the convention has provoked a great deal of criticism, particularly from the United States,[150] since it means that member states of the Common Market can adjudicate cases against noncommunity defendants on the so-called exorbitant jurisdictional bases recognized by some of the member states, and the judgments thus rendered are entitled to automatic recognition and enforcement throughout the community without reexamination of the jurisdiction of the rendering court. The fact that the convention framers have been willing to extend the principle of automatic enforcement to judgments resting on these "exorbitant" jurisdictional bases tends to emphasize how important the matter of judgment recognition is regarded.

The patent unfairness to noncommunity defendants that may result from the extension of the effects of these "exorbitant" jurisdictional bases to the whole Common Market region cannot be avoided even by having the enforcing court invoke the "public policy" exception.[151] Provision is made for the avoidance of the obligation to enforce such judgments, however, through bilateral or other treaty agreements between individual member states and nonmember countries.[152] Thus, for instance, in order to avoid the extraterritorial enforcement within the Common Market of judgments rendered against American domiciliaries based on "exorbitant" jurisdiction, the United States could either negotiate bilateral treaties with each of the member states or enter into a multilateral arrangement such as the proposed Hague Convention on Recognition and Enforcement of Foreign Judgments in Civil and Commercial Matters.[153]

A bilateral treaty, recently initialed, between the United States and the United Kingdom could become a model for treaties with other Common Market nations which would provide protection to U.S. defendants from judgments that had been obtained through resort to "exorbitant" jurisdictional bases.[154] The apparent abolition of one of our own "exorbitant" jurisdictional bases by the Supreme Court of the United States in *Shaffer* v. *Heitner*[155] may make it easier for our negotiators to arrange such conventions.

ROLE OF THE COURT OF JUSTICE

The Court of Justice of the European Economic Community serves the association's interest in faithful and uniform interpretation of the basic charter and legislation of the community. Article 177 of the EEC Treaty declares:

> The Court of Justice shall have jurisdiction to give preliminary rulings concerning:
> (a) the interpretation of this Treaty;
> (b) the validity and interpretation of acts of the institutions of the Community;
> (c) the interpretation of the statutes of bodies established by an act of the Council, where those statutes so provide.
>
> Where such a question is raised before any court or tribunal of a Member State, that court or tribunal may, if it considers that a decision on the question is necessary to enable it to give judgment, request the Court of Justice to give a ruling thereon.
>
> Where any such question is raised in a case pending before a court or tribunal of a Member State, against whose decisions there is no judicial remedy under national law, that court or tribunal shall bring the matter before the Court of Justice.

The role of the court, thus, is quite different from that of the Supreme Court of the United States in enforcing the Full Faith and Credit Clause. The European Court of Justice does not have appellate jurisdiction over national courts. It is empowered to act (in the kinds of cases referred to in Article 177) only when a matter is referred to it by a national court. Between thirty and fifty cases per year were referred to the court during the period 1972 through 1974.[156] Some of these cases concerned the interpretation of the Convention on Jurisdiction and Enforcement of Judgments in Civil and Commercial Matters,[157] thus providing unifying interpretations for some of the important provisions of the convention.

This survey of the judgment-recognition regime prescribed by the EEC convention suggests some interesting comparisons with the scheme that is embodied in the Full Faith and Credit Clause of the United States Constitution. These will be analyzed at length in chapter 10.

The convention serves to promote the goal of economic integration by providing within the region uniform, nondiscriminatory rules for the recognition of civil judgments, thus facilitating speed and certainty in the enforcement of obligations. Fairness to defendants is fostered by eliminating the "exorbitant" bases of jurisdiction in the case of defendants who are domiciled in one of the member states. "Exorbitant" jurisdiction is still available when the defendant is not a domiciliary of the community, and the effects of such exorbitant jurisdiction are now compounded by making judgments enforceable more or less automatically throughout the region. The unfairness of exorbitant jurisdiction can, however, be ameliorated by treaties with particular countries.

## JUDGMENT RECOGNITION IN CENTRAL AMERICA

In view of the long-standing commitment of Central American countries to political as well as to economic integration and in view of the early and continual reference to judgment recognition in bilateral and multilateral treaties, some of which were sketched in the first chapter, it might be assumed that the draftsmen of the agreements that led to the Central American Common Market would have been even more concerned than were those who formulated the European treaties about providing for expeditious judgment recognition within the area. In truth, however, the framers of the General Treaty of the Central American Common Market and the Charter of the Organization of Central American States, unlike the draftsmen of the Rome Treaty, made no reference at all to the matter of judgment recognition. Perhaps this omission is explainable as the product of a spirit of "antijuridicism" that seemed to dominate the formative meetings.[158] Perhaps the low volume of cases involving the recognition and enforcement of judgments from other states in the region contributed to the notion that no specific provision for judgment recognition was required. More probably, however, the main reason for the omission lies in the fact that all the signatory nations as well as the prospective additional member (Panama) were at that time parties to a multilateral treaty that covered, among other matters, judgment recognition and enforcement. That instrument is the Pan-American Code of Private International Law, more commonly referred to as the Bustamante Code (Código Bustamante).

## BASIC CONCEPTS

Before undertaking an examination of the Bustamante Code and the codes of the individual states of Central America, however, a brief comment on certain basic concepts is necessary. An understanding of what these concepts mean in the Central American civil-law systems is important to the subject that we are addressing. Because the words that are used to describe these concepts are similar to terms that are used to describe slightly different concepts in the common-law system, it is necessary to be aware of the differences.

One such concept is "jurisdiction." The term has many meanings in the common-law system, but in the context of judgment recognition it refers to the conditions that must be satisfied before a court can require a person to obey its orders. The court, we say, must have "jurisdiction of the subject matter" (sometimes referred to as "competency") and "jurisdiction of the person" (if the action is in personam). A court has jurisdiction of the subject matter of an action if the case in which the court is asked to issue binding orders is commenced in a procedurally proper manner and if the case is one of the class of cases that the sovereign has empowered that court to entertain. In the United States, there is in each state a court of general jurisdiction that is empowered to entertain any kind of case except those for which exclusive jurisdiction has been conferred upon some other court. Federal courts, on the other hand, are courts of limited jurisdiction and can entertain only certain kinds of cases—notably, controversies between citizens of different states and cases arising under federal law.

A court has jurisdiction of the person over a party if there is a valid "basis" for the exercise of jurisdiction over that person and if, in addition, the proper procedural steps are taken to connect the party to the court's authority ("service of process"). The "bases" for the exercise of jurisdiction in United States law were described in the section "Jurisdictional Standards" above.

"Jurisdiction," as the word is generally used in the civil-law system, does not bear the same meaning as that just described. The great Uruguayan jurist Eduardo Couture explains the term thus: "In the law of Latin American countries this word has at least four meanings: as a territorial range; as a synonym for competency; as the bundle of powers or authority of certain public bodies; and its precise and technical sense as the public function of doing justice."[159] It is in the last sense that the term "jurisdiction" is most commonly used in Latin America. The concept is broader than the idea that is generally associated with that term in common-law countries. It is the general power to resolve legal controversies.[160] In fact, even that definition may be too limited. To quote Couture again: "Jurisdiction, above all, is a function. Definitions that conceive of it as a power refer to only one of its aspects. It concerns not only a bundle of powers or faculties, but also of duties."[161]

Closer to our idea of jurisdiction is the concept of "competency." Here again, however, confusion is possible. The term "competency" is sometimes used in Anglo-American law to refer to what is more commonly today called "jurisdiction of the subject matter."[162] In Latin American law, however, "competency" is a mixture of concepts that we would describe as "basis for personal jurisdiction," "subject matter jurisdiction," and "venue." "Competency is a measure of jurisdiction. All judges have jurisdiction, but not all have competency to take cognizance of a given matter. Competency is the fragment of jurisdiction attributed to a given judge."[163] "Competency is the authority of the judge to exercise his or her jurisdiction in a given case."[164]

Before a given court can be said to have competency of a given action, two kinds of conditions generally must be satisfied. The first of these relates to characteristics of the action itself. Civil courts may not be competent to entertain commercial or labor suits, for instance. This kind of limitation on competency is referred to as competence *ratione materiae.* The second kind of condition relates to territorial factors. A civil suit for breach of contract may have to be brought in the territorial unit in which the defendant's domicile is located, for instance. This kind of competency standard is referred to as competence *ratione loci* or *ratione loci vel personae.*[165] Competency *ratione materiae* is said to be "absolute," meaning that nothing the parties themselves may do will enable a court that lacks such competency to hear the case. Competency *rationae loci,* on the other hand, is said to be "relative," meaning that the parties can, by agreement or by waiver, empower a court other than the one prescribed to hear the case.

The similarity of competency *ratione materiae* to "subject matter jurisdiction" is apparent, as is the similarity of competency *ratione loci* to our concept of venue. Competency *ratione loci,* however, differs significantly from venue in that a defect of such competency is not deemed to be waived if it is not positively asserted. Thus, lack of competency *ratione loci* may be a ground for collateral attack on a default judgment. In this respect it resembles our concept of "jurisdiction of the person" more than it does venue. Competency, however, is thought of as power, not over a person, but over the action.

Besides jurisdiction and competency, it is important to understand the difference between our conception of res judicata and the Latin American conception of *cosa juzgada.* The U.S. concept of res judicata was sketched above in the section "Recognition of Conclusive (Res Judicata) Effects." The Latin American counterpart is significantly different. The scope and effect of *cosa juzgada* vary from country to country, but certain generalizations can be made about it.

Couture defines *cosa juzgada* as "the authority and effect of a judgment when no means of impugning it exists by which it could be modified."[166] One usage of the term is to refer to judgments that have reached a certain stage of finality, since a judgment does not acquire the authority of *cosa juzgada* until all measures by which it could be reversed or modified have been exhausted or until the time for taking such measures has expired.

When a judgment has acquired that authority, it is said to be irreversible, immutable, and ultimately enforceable.[167] It has both negative and positive effects. The losing party cannot again relitigate the matter that has been decided, and a court in later actions must recognize the right of the winning party that was established by the earlier judgment.[168]

There are limits on the effectiveness of *cosa juzgada* in later litigation, however. It is generally said that the preclusive effects of *cosa juzgada* may be asserted only in a later suit that is identical with the former one in "object, cause, and parties."[169] Although there is much debate about the meaning of "object" and "cause" in this context, it is clear that the requirement of the three identities limits the preclusive effects of a judgment to a much narrower scope than is true of the Anglo-American res judicata.

Identity of parties may be met when the party to be bound in the second suit was a successor in interest to the thing that was the object of the former suit. Persons who would be "privies" in Anglo-American doctrine would normally be close enough to the original parties to satisfy the identity-of-parties test, as would be persons represented by parties.[170]

Although the analogy is not exact, the requirement of the dual identities of "object" and "cause" limits the conclusive effect of a judgment essentially to what Anglo-American law would describe as a later suit on the same cause of action. *Cosa juzgada* does not contemplate the effects that we would describe as collateral estoppel: that is, preclusion of relitigation of issues in a later suit on a different cause of action. Moreover, even in a later suit to which *cosa juzgada* does apply, the only conclusive part of the first judgment may be the ultimate result: the conclusion of ownership, or the existence of a contract, and so forth, as distinguished from the mediate findings from which the ultimate fact is inferred. Opinion is not uniform on this point, however.[171]

Although matters that have been adjudicated will normally not have conclusive effects in later actions in which one of the three identities is lacking, a prior judgment may sometimes be used as evidence of the facts on which it rests. In Anglo-American law, by contrast, a judgment normally cannot be used as mere evidence of the issues that it decided.

It may conclusively establish such issues through the doctrine of collateral estoppel, but if not, the prior judgment usually is inadmissible as evidence.

Execution of money judgments in Latin American law is generally accomplished by a procedure that is quite similar to that of the Anglo-American world: official seizure and sale of property. It is referred to by the Spanish cognate term of *ejecución*.[172] The execution procedure in Latin America is conceptually more distinct from the proceeding that led to the judgment on the merits than is true in Anglo-American law. Execution is seen as a separate action, and it may result in a separate judgment ordering the sale of the property that has been seized (*sentencia de remate*).

With these points in mind, we turn now to an examination of the judgment-recognition regime embodied in the Bustamante Code.

# 3   Execution of Foreign Judgments under the Bustamante Code

The Bustamante Code was named for its principal architect, Antonio Sanchez de Bustamante y Sirvén, Cuban jurist and scholar and former magistrate of the Permanent Court of International Justice. The code was promulgated as the Final Act of the Sixth International Conference of American States, 25 November 1928, in Havana. It codified principles of choice of law, jurisdiction, and judgment recognition.[1]

The Pan American Union, sponsor of the Conference of American States, did not see the Bustamante Code as a device to promote economic or political integration. It was adopted during a period when internationalism in general and Pan-Americanism in particular were flourishing. It was hoped that it would lead to a systematic and rational body of private international law that would be applicable uniformly throughout the hemisphere, supplanting the earlier Montevideo Treaty of 1889, which had been ratified by some South American countries. This hope could not be realized. One of the principal obstacles to wider acceptance of the Montevideo Treaty was a deeply rooted disagreement over the basis for determination of "personal law" of individuals—that is, the law relating to matters of civil status and capacity. That treaty endorsed the use of domicile rather than nationality as the connecting factor to identify the "personal" law applicable to such matters. Some of the most influential South American countries refused to ratify the treaty for that reason.[2]

The Bustamante Code was aimed at hemisphere-wide acceptance, and the participants in its drafting included North American, Mexican, and Central American representatives, as well as South American ones. To make the code more widely acceptable, it was expressly provided that signatory nations were free to apply as "personal law" either the law of the domicile or that of nationality.[3] Nations were also free to adopt the code with reservations.[4] This, of course, meant that uniformity could not be achieved under the Bustamante Code unless all nations voluntarily chose either domicile or nationality as the basis for "personal" law and accepted the code without reservation. This did not occur. Not all nations were willing to sign it at all, even with these concessions to local concerns,[5] and of those that did, several expressed significant reservations.

All of the nations of the Central American isthmus, however, ultimately ratified the Bustamante Code, although some of them expressed reservations. Nicaragua reserved the right to depart from the code in any situation in which its provisions conflicted with Nicaraguan law or with canon law as recognized in Nicaragua.[6] Nicaragua did not say that it would apply its own rules, but it reserved the right to decide whether to do so or not when the necessity should arise. Costa Rica joined Colombia in expressly reserving all matters in which the code conflicted with local law.[7] El Salvador expressly reserved, among other things, the right not to recognize foreign judgments in matters relating to inheritance and bankruptcy insofar as concerned Salvadoran immovable property,[8] thus rejecting Articles 327, 328, and 329 of the code, which appeared to make the court of the domicile of the decedent or debtor competent in such cases.

For all its inadequacies as a vehicle for hemispheric unification of private international law,[9] the Bustamante Code did, nevertheless, provide the framework for a general plan of judgment recognition, at least within the Central American region. It contained principles of competency[10] and general rules relating to enforcement of judgments that had been rendered in other "contracting states." It also contained some special rules relating to bankruptcy[11] and res judicata.[12]

The Bustamante Code reflects the theory of law espoused by Dr. Bustamante in earlier works.[13] The key to understanding his theory appears in the opening passages of the code: in the Preliminary Title, among the General Rules, the following appears:

> Art. 3. For the exercise of civil rights and the enjoyment of identical individual guarantees, the laws and regulations in force in each contracting State are deemed to be divided into the three following classes:
>
>   I. Those applying to persons by reason of their domicile or their nationality and following them even when they go to

another country, termed personal or of an internal public order.

II. Those binding alike upon all persons residing in the territory, whether or not they are nationals, termed territorial, local or of an international public order.

III. Those applying only through the expression, interpretation, or presumption of the will of the parties or of one of them, termed voluntary or of a private order.

Art. 4. Constitutional precepts are of an international public order.

Art. 5. All rules of individual and collective protection, established by political and administrative law, are also of an international public order, except in case of express provisions therein enacted to the contrary.

Art. 6. In all cases not provided for in this Code each one of the contracting States shall apply its own definition to the juridical institutions or relationships corresponding to the groups of laws mentioned in article 3.

Art. 7. Each contracting State shall apply as personal law that of the domicile or that of the nationality or that which its domestic legislation may have prescribed, or may hereafter prescribe.

Art. 8. The rights acquired under the rules of this Code shall have full extraterritorial force in the contracting States, except when any of their effects or consequences is in conflict with a rule of an international public order.

These passages introduce several important conceptions that the rest of the code is built upon. First, it will be noted that Article 8 seemingly places the code's theoretical basis on the "acquired rights" (or as we would call it, "vested rights") theory. This theory underlies both the choice-of-law and the judgment-recognition sections of the code. Second, Article 7 continues the Montevideo Treaty's emphasis on "personality" as contrasted with "territoriality" of law. Third, for purposes of the code, laws are divided by Article 3 into three classes:

1. Laws of an internal public order, or personal laws;
2. Laws of an international public order, or territorial (or "local") laws; and
3. Laws of a private order, or voluntary laws.

The terminology of this three-part classification is very confusing to one who is not schooled in Bustamante's theories. For one thing, the terms "internal" and "international" seem to be reversed, since laws of "internal" public order can apply outside the sovereign territory, whereas those of "international public order" apply only within.[14] For another, if "personal law" and "law of internal public order" mean the same thing, why are both terms used? And why both "voluntary law" and "law of a private order"? Professor Ernest Lorenzen, in an early commentary on the Bustamante Code,[15] ultimately despaired of ascertaining from the text of the code the meaning that was intended in various articles referring to "international public order" and "local" and "territorial" law. Even eliciting written explanations from Bustamante himself did not fully dispel Lorenzen's doubts. He noted that "the Code would have gained [in certainty of meaning], at least in the eyes of North American lawyers, if it had been more specific in its references whenever a provision is said to be 'local,' 'territorial' or one 'of international public order.' "[16]

Even Latin Americans have had trouble with this terminology. A Guatemalan lawyer made the following comment: "For someone beginning the study of Private International Law nothing is more confusing than the terms 'internal public order' and 'international public order,' each of which, by a strange paradox, expresses, grammatically and logically, the contrary of its true meaning."[17]

Perhaps the easiest discussion for a North American to follow concerning the "public order" concept and the division between "internal" and "international" that the Bustamante Code employs is that of the Mexican scholar Carlos Arellano García, which appears in his recent treatise.[18] He articulates the distinction, which is cloudy in the Bustamante Code, between "public order" (orden público) as a description of some kinds of laws, and the same term when it describes an exception to the application of otherwise appropriate foreign-law rules.[19] Since only the latter usage has any real functional role, Arellano objects to the emphasis placed on the distinction, which is featured so prominently in the Bustamante Code: "[the] distinction between internal and international public order, besides producing confusion in private international law, is unnecessary, because in reality it is enough to speak only of "public order" that impedes the application of the foreign rule."[20]

The confusion is compounded for a North American who is reading the Pan American Union's official English text of the Bustamante Code. By a subtle mistake, the translator inserted a superfluous and misleading "an" before "internal" and "international," and an "a" before "private." The meaning of the text would have been less difficult to comprehend if the translator had simply referred to "laws of internal public order" and "laws of international public order," without the unnecessary articles.

The choice-of-law provisions of the code contain many references to laws as being of "international public order" (and a few to laws of an "internal public order"). The meanings of these are quite confusing. Lorenzen provides the explanation (supplied by Bustamante himself) for some of them,[21] but certainly not for all. Generally, the Bustamante Code seems to use the "local"-"personal" terminology when it intends a statement about choice of law: that is, when the question to which the provision is addressed is "What law should the forum court apply?" The alternative terminology—"internal" and "international public order"— are mainly used when the question addressed is "Can the forum court apply its own rule?" By specifically declaring certain laws to be of "international public order," the code apparently was trying to harmonize local variations in the meaning of "public order," which could upset the choice-of-law scheme envisaged in the code. However, not all local variations in the concept were eliminated. Article 6 specifically allows each state to apply its own characterization scheme—that is, its own conception of what the forum's "public order" is—in all instances that are not specifically covered in the code. Article 4 expressly makes all constitutional precepts rules of "international public order," and Article 5 does the same for a very poorly defined group of rules of "political and administrative" law. In most countries, constitutional precepts supersede treaty provisions anyway. In general, then, individual states are left considerable latitude for invoking their own conceptions of "public order" so as to avoid application of the foreign-law rules prescribed by the code.

Fortunately, for purposes of this study, we do not need to deal at length with the formidable obscurities of the code's choice-of-law rules. Our concern is with the recognition and execution of judgments. The "public order" concept, however, cannot be escaped even there, as we shall see.

The judgment-recognition provisions of the code are mainly embodied in Articles 423 to 437.

Chapter I.—*Civil Matters*

Art. 423. Every civil or contentious administrative judgment rendered in one of the contracting States shall have force and may be executed in the others if it combines the following conditions:

1. That the judge or the court which has rendered it have competence to take cognizance of the matter and to pass judgment upon it, in accordance with the rules of this Code.
2. That the parties have been summoned for the trial either personally or through their legal representative.
3. That the judgment does not conflict with the public policy

or the public laws of the country in which its execution is sought.

4. That it is executory in the State in which it was rendered.
5. That it be authoritatively translated by an official functionary or interpreter of the State in which it is to be executed, if the language employed in the latter is different.
6. That the document in which it is contained fulfills the requirements necessary in order to be considered as authentic in the State from which it proceeds, and those which the legislation of the State in which the execution of the judgment is sought requires for authenticity.

Art. 424. The execution of the judgment should be requested from a competent judge or tribunal in order to carry it into effect, after complying with the formalities required by the internal legislation.

Art. 425. In the case referred to in the preceding article, every recourse against the judicial resolution granted by the laws of that State in respect to final judgments rendered in a declarative action of greater import shall be granted.

Art. 426. The judge or tribunal from whom the execution is requested shall, before decreeing or denying it, and for a term of twenty days, hear the party against whom it is directed as well as the prosecuting attorney.

Art. 427. The summons of the party who should be heard shall be made by means of letters requisitorial or letters rogatory, in accordance with the provisions of this Code if he has his domicile in a foreign country and lacks sufficient representation in the country, or in the form established by the local law if he has his domicile in the requested State.

Art. 428. After the term fixed for appearance by the judge or the court, the case shall be proceeded with whether or not the party summoned has appeared.

Art. 429. If the execution is denied, the judgment shall be returned to the party who presented it.

Art. 430. When the execution of judgment is granted, the former shall be subject to the procedure determined by the law of the judge or the court for its own judgments.

Art. 431. Final judgments rendered by a contracting State which by reason of their pronouncements are not to be executed shall have in the other States the effects of *res judicata* if they fulfill the conditions provided for that purpose by this Code, except those relating to their execution.

Art. 432. The procedure and effects regulated in the preceding articles shall be applied in the contracting States to awards made in any of them by arbitrators or friendly compositors, whenever the case to which they refer can be the subject of a compromise in accordance with the legislation of the country where the execution is requested.

Art. 433. The same procedure shall be also applied in respect to civil judgments rendered in any of the contracting States by an international tribunal when referring to private persons or interests.

Chapter II.—*Acts of Voluntary Jurisdiction*

Art. 434. The provisions made in acts of voluntary jurisdiction regarding commercial matters by judges or tribunals of a contracting State or by its consular agents shall be executed in the others in accordance with the procedure and the manner indicated in the preceding article.

Art. 435. The resolutions adopted in acts of voluntary jurisdiction in civil matters in a contracting State shall be accepted by the others if they fulfill the conditions required by this Code for the validity of documents executed in a foreign country and were rendered by a competent judge or tribunal, and they shall in consequence have extraterritorial validity.

Chapter III.—*Penal Matters*

Art. 436. No contracting State shall execute the judgments rendered in one of the others in penal matters in respect to the sanctions of that class which they impose.

Art. 437. They may, however, execute the said judgments in respect to civil liability and the effects thereof upon the property of the convicted person if they have been rendered by a competent judge or tribunal in accordance with this Code and upon a hearing of the interested party and if the other conditions of form and procedure established by the first chapter of this title have been complied with.

## KINDS OF JUDGMENTS ENTITLED TO RECOGNITION AND ENFORCEMENT

Article 423 provides that "[e]very civil or contentious administrative judgment rendered in one of the contracting States shall have force and may be executed" if it meets certain requirements. The article refers specifically to judgment enforcement—that is, the execution of a judgment for the plaintiff, as is clear from some of the requisites. Other articles (431 through 435) deal with other forms of judgment recognition.

Although commercial judgments are not expressly mentioned in Article 423, it seems clear that judgments of commercial tribunals or judgments that enforce obligations arising from the Commercial, as opposed to the Civil, Code are covered.[22]

The provision for execution of contentious-administrative judgments as well as civil judgments is curious, since the defendant in such cases is nearly always the foreign state or one of its agencies, and the situations in which the courts of one country could exercise jurisdiction over another country or its properties must be rare indeed.[23] The only extraterritorial effect that could be given to a contentious-administrative judgment, apparently, would be a nonconclusive, evidentiary effect.[24] The code makes no exception for tax judgments, so presumably such judgments in favor of one signatory state are fully enforceable in others, if they can be characterized as "civil" within the broad meaning of Article 423.

The code does refer to penal judgments,[25] and it specifically denies enforceability to judgments of another state that would impose penal sanctions. If the penal judgment would impose civil liability on the defendant, however, the judgment will be enforceable in other states to that extent.[26] In this respect the Bustamante Code's treatment of criminal judgments is essentially like that of the EEC Convention.[27]

## REQUIREMENTS FOR RECOGNITION AND ENFORCEMENT

### COMPETENCY

Article 423.1 expresses the universal requirement that the foreign judgment, to be entitled to enforcement, must have been rendered by a competent court. It also declares that the standards of "competency" to be used for this purpose are those prescribed in the code itself. Those provisions appear in Articles 314 through 343. The first four of those articles announce some general rules.

Art. 314. The law of each contracting State determines the competence of courts, as well as their organization, the forms of procedure and of execution of judgments, and the appeals from their decisions.

Art. 315. No contracting State shall organize or maintain in its territory special tribunals for members of the other contracting States.

Art. 316. Competence *ratione loci* is subordinated, in the order of international relations, to the law of the contracting State which establishes it.

Art. 317. Competence *ratione materiae* and *ratione personae*, in the order of international relations should not be based by the contracting States on the status as nationals or foreigners of the interested parties, to the prejudice of the latter.

Article 314 says that each state is free to prescribe the competency of its own courts and its own system of procedure. However, succeeding articles provide some limits. The limitation posed by Article 315 is clear, but the limitations of articles 316 and 317 are not. Again, the confusion arises both from the unfamiliarity of the concepts (*ratione loci, ratione materiae,* and *ratione personae*) to North Americans and from difficulties of translation.

An Anglo-American might be tempted to conclude that the three Latin terms in Articles 316 and 317 correspond to some jurisdictional concepts in our jurisprudence, to two of which we also give Latin names. *Ratione loci* suggests jurisdiction predicated upon the location of something, which suggests a "local" action, which in turn suggests what we have come to call jurisdiction in rem. The apparent implication of Article 316—that this is a matter in which forum law prevails over international standards—is consistent with our notions of in rem jurisdiction. Article 317 refers to a contrasting class: competence *ratione personae,* which is suggestive of what we have come to call jurisdiction in personam. Competence *ratione materiae* suggests what we call jurisdiction of the subject matter, a conception that is distinct from jurisdiction in rem and in personam.

As noted at the end of the last chapter, however, these suggestions are inaccurate. Competence *ratione loci* refers not just to jurisdiction that is predicated upon the location of things but to any rule in which the criterion for identifying the proper court is the location of something. The term applies to personal actions in which the proper court is the one at the domicile of one of the parties, for instance, as well as to real actions.[28] Moreover, rules of competence *ratione loci* do not correspond to what Anglo-American law calls limitations of the subject-matter jurisdiction. They are matters of "relative" as opposed to "absolute" competency, which simply means that the parties can, by agreement, submit the case to a different court.[29] They are not just like venue rules, however, in that they are not presumed to be waived if not positively asserted, and thus they can provide the basis for collateral attack on a default judgment.

Rules of competence *ratione materiae* and *ratione personae* are normally matters of "absolute" competence—that is, true provisions of subject-matter jurisdiction. *Ratione personae,* as used in the Bustamante Code, refers to any rule that bases the subject-matter jurisdiction of a court on characteristics of the litigant parties (other than alterable locational characteristics).[30] Only a certain court or courts, for instance, may be authorized to entertain suits against a corporation or against an autonomous institution (such as a public university commonly is). The parties cannot by agreement submit the suit to another court. Any rule that bases subject-matter jurisdiction on some characteristic of the claim (e.g., crime, amount in controversy, etc.) is a matter of competence *ratione materiae*. These rules cannot be circumvented by agreement of the parties. A court that is empowered to hear only labor cases, for instance, cannot entertain an ordinary civil suit. Article 317 declares that a state cannot use the fact that one or more of the parties is a foreigner as the basis for prescribing standards of subject-matter jurisdiction if the effect would be to prejudice the foreign party. What "prejudice" means here is not clear, but the apparent object of Article 317 is to complement Article 315 so as to establish the point that there should be no discrimination against foreigners with regard to access to courts.[31] Article 315, on the other hand, apparently permits the foreign domiciliary status of a party to be used as a criterion for the designation of competence *ratione loci*.[32]

Articles 318 and 332 (see Appendix) prescribe general rules for determining the "competence" of courts in civil and commercial cases. These rules are not stated in terms that are limited to use in determining whether a judgment is entitled to recognition and enforcement under Article 423.1. They are, like the competency provisions of the European convention, direct rules of competency and are to be applied to resolve "conflicts of jurisdiction" in the first instance as well. They do not apply, however, unless the jurisdictional conflict is between nations that are signatories of the Bustamante Code.[33]

The rules that are applicable to personal actions generally base competency on the location of persons, things, or events—rules *ratione loci*—and according to Article 316, each state may follow its own rules in the event of conflict in such cases. Thus, the code's competency provisions are not the exclusive rules of "international jurisdiction" that are applicable to ordinary civil or commercial money judgments.

Basically, the rules of competence[34] contained in Articles 318 and 332 are as follows:

A. For ordinary civil and commercial actions:
1. The court to which the litigants expressly or impliedly[35] submit themselves (if one of the parties is a national or domiciliary of the forum state) (Article 318); or, if none,
2. The court at the place where the obligation is to be performed (Article 323); or, if none,
3. The court at the domicile or nationality (or residence) of the defendants (Article 323).

B. For real actions respecting personal property:
1. The court at the situs; or, if unknown,

2. The court at the domicile (or, if none, residence) of the defendant (Article 324).
3. If the property is in two or more states, the courts of any of them (Article 326).
C. For real actions respecting real property:
1. The court at the situs (Article 325).
2. If the property is in two or more states, the court of any of them, unless the law of the situs prohibits resort to any other tribunal (Article 326).
D. For probate of decedent's estates: The court at the decedent's last domicile (Article 327).
E. For insolvency or bankruptcy proceedings:
1. Voluntary: The court at the debtor's domicile (Article 328).
2. Involuntary: Any court that would have cognizance of the claim giving rise to the bankruptcy, preference being given to the court at the debtor's domicile (if there is one) if he or the majority of the creditors demand it (Article 329).

There are some separate rules for matters of "voluntary jurisdiction" (Articles 330 and 331). The term "voluntary jurisdiction" is applicable to a variety of noncontentious judicial proceedings, such as adoptions, guardianships, declarations of death, and so forth. Just what kinds of proceedings are classified as matters of "voluntary jurisdiction" varies considerably from country to country.[36] There are also some special rules relating to jurisdiction of actions against foreign governments or their officials (Articles 333 through 339).

It should be noted that the standards of competency prescribed by the Bustamante Code include no "exorbitant" bases, such as those noted above in discussing the European Common Market Convention.[37] Such bases might be recognized by individual countries, but none of the countries covered in this study have adopted any such provisions.

NOTICE

Article 423.2 provides "that the parties have been summoned for the trial either personally or through their legal representative."

Again, the translation leaves quite a bit to be desired. The Spanish text says nothing about "trial."[38] A better translation would be: "That the parties have been served with process in the action, either personally or by representative."

This appears to exclude the recognition of judgments wherein the defendant was served by publication, but it does not necessarily require personal service (or service on the representative) within the territory of the rendering court. The summons can be served outside the country.[39] There is a procedure, generally recognized in Latin America, through which a court may appoint a representative ad litem for an "absent" party. Service on such a representative is usually adequate to give the ensuing judgment a binding effect on the defendant, even if no notice other than publication is given to the absent party, at least if the address of the absent party is unknown. It is not clear whether or not such service would be proper service on a "legal representative" that would be adequate to meet the requirements of the Bustamante Code. The code contains some provisions relating to the declaration of "absence," in Articles 78 through 83, but they do not deal with this particular question.[40]

Part of the difficulty in Article 423.2 is the fault of the original drafting, not the translation. It is not clear from the text of the code whether the requirement of 423.2 would be met in a case in which the defendant, although never summoned, "implicitly submitted" in accordance with Article 322. In terms, Article 322 relates to "competence" and, as such, is relevant to Article 423.1 rather than 423.2. It seems doubtful, however, that the "personal citation" requirement was intended to deprive a judgment in which the defendant had actively participated on the merits of its extraterritorial force. One must probably assume that Article 423.2 applies only to nonappearing defendant parties.[41]

FINALITY

Article 423.4 specifies that the judgment must be "executory" in the state in which it was rendered. The term "executory" was chosen by the official translator as the English equivalent of "ejecutorio." This may be a source of confusion to people who have been schooled in Anglo-American law. To us, "executory" usually carries an implication of incompleteness, whereas the term is used here as an indicator of finality. It means that the action has reached that stage of completeness at which execution could be obtained, if it is a judgment that is capable of execution. It also suggests that the court has formally indicated that the judgment is ready for execution, even though a special proceeding may be required to secure the order of execution against specific property. It means that the merits of the case have been finally determined and that the judgment is "definitive." The term describes, then, a condition that is very similar to a "final" judgment in Anglo-American terminology. One difference, however, is that, to us, a judgment may be "final" for full-faith-and-credit purposes when it still may be appealable. For a judgment to be "executory," on the other hand, as the term is used in the Bustamante Code, it normally means that the time for review after the order was rendered shall have expired. Some judgments are never "executable": they may be merely declaratory and require no coercive order to make them effective. A later provision, Article 431, covers the recognition of nonexecutable judgments.

The Bustamante Code also, under the sections dealing with judicial assistance (Articles 388 through 393),[42] provides for the execution of certain nonfinal orders that have been issued by foreign courts. These provisions cover such matters as serving notice and taking testimony in response to letters rogatory or requisitorial. The assistance that is rendered under such a request may also include the provisional attachment of properties, in the enforcement state, that belong to the defendant in the original action. In this last respect, the Bustamante Code prescribes a degree of extraterritorial effect for nonfinal orders that is greater than that required by the Full Faith and Credit Clause with respect to orders of courts of sister states in the United States.[43]

TRANSLATION AND AUTHENTICATION

Sections 5 and 6 of Article 423 merely require that the judgment be translated (if it is in a different language from that of the enforcing state) and that it be duly authenticated.

RECIPROCITY

The code makes no reference to reciprocity as a condition of recognition or enforcement. Of course, if both the rendering state and the requested state were signatories to the code without reservation, reciprocity would usually be guaranteed. Since several of the countries, including some in Central America, did not endorse the code without reservation, however, there is no complete assurance of reciprocity. Accordingly, some states, as we shall see, apply a reciprocity rule even in relation to judgments that have been rendered in other Bustamante Code countries.[44]

PUBLIC POLICY

Article 423.3 declares an exception to the recognition and enforcement of judgments that "conflict with the public policy or the public laws of the country in which its execution is sought."[45] In this passage, the official translator used the English term "public policy" instead of "public order" for the Spanish *orden público*. Probably the reason for this is that in Article 423.3 *orden público* appears without the modifiers "*interno*" or "*internacional*" that accompany it in other sections of the code. However, the meaning of "public policy" in this article is apparently the same as "international public order" in other provisions of the code. A foreign judgment that rests on substantive principles that are contrary to a law of "international public order" of the requested state need not be recognized or enforced. This, at least, was apparently Bustamante's intention. Among his three Rosenthal Lectures given at the Northwestern University School of Law in October of 1928 (after the code had been approved at the Havana Conference in February of the same year), Bustamante included "The Execution of Foreign Judgments." In that lecture he addressed himself, among other things, to the problem of executing foreign judgments based on laws that are significantly different from those of the enforcing state. After noting that a foreign judgment should not be denied effect merely because it is based on legal precepts that are different from those that would have been applied if the case had been first presented in the enforcing state, he made the following observation:

> The case is different when the judgment whose recognition is sought has applied principles relating to the conflict of laws that would differ from those accepted in the locality (of the forum) and would accordingly lead to the acceptance of a different national or local law. In this situation, and when the legal precept on which the judgment is founded, or the consequences of the same, would contravene the international public order of the country in which it has to be executed, for this last reason, and not solely for the first, its recognition would have to be denied. And this thesis is applicable in every identical situation, even apart from the conflict between the rules of Private International Law.[46]

The Bustamante Code's public-policy exception is much broader than that of the EEC Convention.[47] The public-order exception in the EEC Convention does not become applicable merely because the substantive issues involved in the foreign judgment were matters of great social importance to the requested state and were resolved in a way different from that which the requested state's law would prescribe. The Bustamante Code's provision, however, does contemplate the denial of enforcement to a judgment under such circumstances. Laws of international public order, according to Bustamante himself, are "the essential norms on which the Constitution of the State rests: those that indicate the conditions of life . . . and all the rest that establish moral, judicial, political, religious and economic principles which, because of their centrality in the spirit of the State's components, the legislator cannot dispense with."[48] Some nations regard all matters relating to rights in immovable property that is situated within their boundaries to be of such fundamental concern as to be of "public order." The Bustamante Code, in Article 144, adopted a principle of unity of successions, applying the personal law of the decedent to all matters of succession—testate or intestate—to property—movable or immovable. But it is also declared, confusingly, in Article 145 that the "precept by which the rights to the estate of a person are transmitted from the moment of his death is of an international public order." Apparently the latter provision means that instruments or other voluntary acts designed to transfer rights in a decedent's estate are subject to the law of the place where the act occurred or the instrument was executed. A will, invalid where executed, in other words, would be invalid everywhere by this rule. It did not mean, apparently, that a will that is valid where executed would be ineffective to devise immovable property in another country. The mere fact that the law of the situs prescribed some different formalities for an effective will would not automatically mean that the devise would be ineffective. However, the devise might be denied effect at the situs of the property by virtue of Article 423.3 if the attempted devise would contravene the "public order" of that place. Some of the signatories of the Bustamante Code expressly reserved the right to insist upon the *lex rei sitae* in connection with all matters of succession to immovables.[49] Others will deny effect to a foreign decree of succession to the extent that it would pass property in a way that is expressly forbidden by local law: for example, by directing that more than a certain percentage should pass to the church.

Another situation in which the "public order" exception has often been invoked concerns the recognition of foreign divorces on grounds that are not deemed proper under local law. The Bustamante Code makes a specific provision for this problem, however. In Article 53 the code concedes to the signatory countries the option to recognize or not to recognize foreign divorce judgments that have been granted on grounds that would not be sufficient under the personal law of the parties. Denial of recognition to such a judgment, then, would not have to be justified in terms of "public order."

## BASIC PROCEDURE FOR RECOGNITION AND ENFORCEMENT

Enforcement of a foreign judgment should be sought in the court of the enforcing state that is competent to issue and execute judgments of that type (Article 424). In most Latin American countries, however, a preliminary proceeding must occur before the judgment may even be presented to the designated court for execution. This proceeding, which is usually called exequatur and is usually brought in the highest court in the land, determines certain matters of enforceability. The Bustamante Code provides that a judgment or decree ordering the enforcement of a foreign judgment can be reviewed in the same way that an ordinary original declaratory judgment can be appealed (Article 425). However, in states that require a prior exequatur proceeding in the highest court in the land, that provision has no application.

The judgment debtor must be served with process in the enforcement action (or exequatur proceeding, if that is where the determination of enforceability is made). If he is not domiciled in the enforcing state and has no representative to receive service there, he can be served outside by means of letters requisitorial or rogatory (Article 427).[50] A period of twenty days is allowed to the defendant to appear in opposition to the enforcement (Article 426). A public representative of the enforcing state must also be notified and given the opportunity to appear in the enforcement suit according to the Bustamante Code (although only two of the signatory countries that we are concerned with in fact require this).[51] The public representative will normally be an attorney whose function is similar to that of our county or district attorney— usually called the *fiscal*.[52] After the twenty-day period has expired, the court can issue an order granting or denying execution, whether or not the defendant appears (Article 428). If execution is granted, it will be carried out as in the case of an original judgment of the enforcing state of like import (Article 430).

Judgments that do not require execution can be accorded recognition for their res judicata effects "if they fulfill the conditions provided for that purpose by this Code, except those relating to their execution" (Article 431). This provision is somewhat ambiguous. Does it mean that the judgment must meet the requirements in Article 423 and also be established by a decree of a court of the recognizing state, obtained through the same procedure that an executable judgment would have to satisfy (except the execution itself)? Or does it mean that no procedural steps in the recognizing state are necessary in order to entitle it to res judicata effects? Both interpretations have found acceptance. In any case, res judicata cannot be used as a defense unless the parties appeared generally in the original action (Article 396).

## RECOGNITION AND ENFORCEMENT OF SPECIAL KINDS OF JUDGMENTS

Awards of arbitrators or international tribunals (to the extent that they deal with private interests) are entitled to recognition and enforcement in accordance with "[t]he procedure and effects regulated in the preceding articles . . ." (Articles 432 and 433). Again we encounter ambiguity. Are the "preceding articles" those referring to other forms of nonexecutable judgments—that is, Article 431? Or do they include the procedures that point to execution which are provided in Articles 424 through 429? Presumably, in the case of the arbitration award, at least the full course of execution should be followed, even if the arbitration award is to be recognized merely for res judicata effects. Commonly in Latin American law, an arbitration award has no res judicata effect until it has been embodied in or approved by a judicial order of some sort.[53]

The civil judgments contemplated by the articles that have been discussed are judgments relating mainly to consensual transactions. Tort judgments for personal injuries are commonly products of penal proceedings. One country will not normally enforce the penal judgments of another. Under the code, however, such judgments can be executed insofar as concerns the civil liability of the defendant, if the judgment satisfies the competency, hearing, and procedural requirements specified in Articles 423 through 429 (Article 437).

Bankruptcy proceedings are dealt with in a separate title (Articles 414 through 422) (see Appendix). The code provides for recognition and enforcement, in all signatory states, of orders and decrees that are customarily entered in bankruptcy proceedings and of their effects: declaration of the bankrupt's incapacities; the decree of bankruptcy itself; retroactive annulment of transactions; discharge of the bankrupt, and so forth.

Special rules are also provided relating to recognition of various kinds of judicial orders that affect domestic relations. Notable is Article 53, which provides: "Each contracting State has the right to permit or recognize, or not, the divorce or new marriage of persons divorced abroad, in cases, with effects or for causes which are not admitted by their personal law."

From this survey, several observations can be made about the judgment-recognition scheme envisaged by the Bustamante Code and about its capacity to promote the various association interests identified in the preceding chapter.

First, its coverage includes every civil judgment (including judgments in commercial matters) and, at least theoretically, some effect even for contentious-administrative judgments. It covers the kinds of judgments that the EEC Convention excepted. In this respect its potential contribution to the association goals of integration would seem to be greater than that of the EEC Convention, and would seem to approach that of the full-faith-and-credit principle in the United States. There are, however, several features of the Bustamante Code's regime that prevent it from realizing that potential.

The most significant drawback is the fact that the signatory states are permitted to—and some in Central America do—reserve the right to apply different principles. Thus it does not have uniform application throughout the area, not even theoretically.

Secondly, in most kinds of civil actions in which money judgments are sought, signatory states are free to apply different standards of competence from those announced in the code. Thus, there is no single official standard of "international jurisdiction" as there is in the EEC Convention and in the full-faith-and-credit regime. The recognizing state is permitted to review the competence of the rendering court, contrary to the practice of the EEC Convention, but there is no single authoritative tribunal in which an erroneous denial of recognition can be reviewed, as there is in the United States. In this respect, too, then, the Bustamante Code lacks the institutional devices to assure uniform judgment recognition throughout the region that the EEC Convention and the full-faith-and-credit schemes provide.

Thirdly, the Bustamante Code permits a state to refuse recognition and enforcement on public-policy grounds, as does the EEC Convention (but as the full-faith-and-credit scheme does not). The permissible scope of its public-policy exception is much broader than that of the EEC Convention, however, and provides another source of uncertainty and nonuniformity in the judgment-recognition scheme of Central America.

Finally there is no tribunal that is empowered to render authoritative unifying interpretations of the Bustamante Code itself. The code contains several ambiguities that could lead different states to different decisions on questions of judgment enforceability in identical cases, even if the states both accepted the code without reservation.

In view of all these areas of uncertainty in the application of the Bustamante Code, the conclusion is inescapable: it is not really an effective mechanism for a judgment-recognition regime that aims at exerting optimum influence in the promotion of the goal of integration among the states of Central America. It was designed for adoption by states that lack the kind of association interests that the Central American countries supposedly share.

Even if the Bustamante Code alone is inadequate, however, it is possible that the individual states have independently adopted judgment-recognition regimes based on that code and other sources that may nevertheless work well enough in practice. We now turn our attention to the law and practice of the individual countries in order to shed further light on this point.

# 4 Costa Rica

## THE BASIC LAW

The basic law of Costa Rica relating to recognition and enforcement of judgments is contained in the Code of Civil Procedure, Articles 1020 through 1026. Costa Rica is a party to the Bustamante Code, but its delegates endorsed the code "with the express reservation as to everything which may be in contradiction with . . . Costa Rican legislation."[1] This reservation was repeated in the decree of the government of Costa Rica ratifying the code, with the additional commentary that "insofar as concerns our legislation, that reservation applies not only to that in force, but also to that which may be enacted in the future."[2] With these reservations, the Bustamante Code, "if not rendered practically nugatory at least is relegated to the position of a subsidiary source" in Costa Rica.[3] The provisions of the Bustamante Code, then, are effective in Costa Rica only to the extent that they are not contradictory to provisions in the internal legislation, and the Costa Rican Congress can avoid its provisions selectively by simply enacting contradictory rules.

Of course, apart from the express reservation, Costa Rica is permitted to apply its own rules that are of "public order," according to the Bustamante Code itself;[4] and some of the rules relating to judgment recognition and enforcement have been classified as being of "public order" by the Costa Rican Supreme Court.[5]

The relevant sections of the Code of Civil Procedure (my translation) are:

Article 1020. The execution of judgments [*sentencias*] pronounced by foreign tribunals shall be brought before the Sala de Casación.[6]

Article 1021. First, the order to be executed [*ejecutoria*] shall be translated, if it is not in Spanish. Then, after giving the opposite party an opportunity to be heard for a period of time that the court will fix, between 9 and 25 days according to the circumstances of the case, it will be determined whether or not compliance ought to be granted to said order, whether or not the defendant has answered. There shall be no further recourse against this resolution.

Article 1022. Exequatur shall not be granted to a judgment [*sentencia*] if from the allegations and proofs of the opposing party, or from the instrument itself, it appears:

1. That the document is not duly authenticated.
2. That it is not executory [*ejecutoria*][7] in the country of its origin.
3. That the litigation proceeded without the participation of the defendant except when he clearly has been declared in default for not having appeared after having been duly summoned.
4. That the judgment [*sentencia*] is contrary to public order.

Article 1023. If exequatur is sought for an order of embargo [attachment], it will not be necessary to provide the hearing referred to in Article 1021, and it will be granted if it appears that the party against whom it is levied was notified of the order directing the letter requisitorial [*exhorto,* request for the extraterritorial embargo] to be sent in sufficient time to have been able to have recourse here to protect his rights. If it appears from the letter requisitorial [*exhorto*] or if the interested party demonstrates that any of the conditions specified in the previous article exist, no effect shall be given to it. The execution of a judgment of sale [*sentencia de remate*], or its equivalent, will follow the rule for judgments generally.

Article 1024. Requests [*requisitorias*] from foreign courts relating to the service of process, interrogatories, the taking of evidence, or to other judicial proceedings will be carried out, after the Sala de Casación has granted exequatur, in the same way that they would have been if they had proceeded from a court in the Republic.

Article 1025. If compliance is denied, the order [*ejecutoria*] will be returned to the one who presented it. If compliance is granted, the order [*auto*] will be communicated, by certification to the court [superior court—*juzgado*] of the place in which the losing party is domiciled, and it will proceed to execute it in accordance with the dispositions of the prior chapter. If the debtor has no domicile in the Republic, the judge that the creditor chooses will be competent.

Article 1026. If the debtor has no domicile in the Republic, the creditor can seek from the judge he chooses an attachment [embargo provisional] of the debtor's goods, after giving the bond spoken of in Article 173, to assure the execution of the judgment [sentencia] once he obtains the exequatur.

## BASIC PROCEDURE FOR RECOGNITION AND ENFORCEMENT

Before a foreign judgment, order, or a request for judicial assistance can be given effect in Costa Rica, an order according it force within the country must be obtained from the Supreme Court, Sala de Casación.[8] That order is referred to as exequatur.[9] It is not a writ of execution. The exequatur procedure merely determines whether or not the foreign judgment or order satisfies the requirements for recognition and enforcement in Costa Rica. If it does not, the exequatur is denied, and no further steps toward enforcement can be taken. If it does, the exequatur is granted, and the matter is referred to a lower court to obtain compliance with the foreign judgment or order in accordance with the process used to obtain execution upon domestic judgments. Proceedings in two different courts, thus, are required in order to enforce a foreign money judgment.

The first step in the exequatur process is the filing of a petition, which must be accompanied by a duly authenticated copy of the order that is sought to be enforced (officially translated if it is not in Spanish). The authentication requirement is a real one. This requires not only the seal and signature of the clerk or other functionary of the court that is issuing the order but also the verification of the functionary's authority and the signature of the Costa Rican consul in that country and the verification of the consul's signature and authority by the Ministry of Foreign Relations. On several occasions the Supreme Court of Costa Rica has denied exequatur to foreign judgments because of defects in the proof of the signature or the authority of some official's act in the process of authentication.[10]

The next step is the notification of the opposite party. If the party is located in Costa Rica, process will be served as it is in other cases. If the party is outside of Costa Rica, the process will be sent through diplomatic channels to the country where the party can be found,[11] and service will be made there through a rogatory letter or other appropriate proceeding. The notification will tell the other party of the exequatur petition, and it will inform him of the opportunity to appear in opposition to the petition, if he so desires, during the nine-day to twenty-five-day period set by the court.

Where exequatur is sought in order to obtain execution of a foreign money judgment, the plaintiff can get a preliminary attachment of the defendant's property, if the defendant is not a Costa Rican domiciliary.[12]

If the opposing party avails himself of the opportunity to be "heard," he, or his lawyer, will submit a formal brief, stating his objections. The moving party can, of course, respond to the objections. The matter can be decided on the basis of the written presentations, but an oral audience may be granted on request. The issues that may be raised in opposition are those designated in Article 1022 of the Code of Civil Procedure as well as the question of the competence of the rendering court.

If the exequatur is denied for reasons relating to form or proof of the foreign judgment, another proceeding can be brought later when the errors have been corrected.[13] If the exequatur is denied for other reasons, however, no review is possible.[14] If the exequatur is granted, orders will be made directing a lower court or official to carry out the execution or other directive. No review of the judgment granting exequatur is possible.

The Civil Procedure Code does not specify whether or not the exequatur procedure that is prescribed for judgment enforcement is also required when only recognition is sought for the judgment. In some countries, exequatur is unnecessary in such a case. In Costa Rica, however, the court has apparently taken the position that exequatur must be obtained before a foreign judgment can be given any conclusive effect—be it recognition or enforcement.

Exequatur is uniformly required before foreign divorces are entitled to recognition in Costa Rica, even though the object of the proceeding is nothing but the enrollment of the new marital status in the Civil Registry. Exequatur probably is also required when a foreign judgment is used as a res judicata defense. In an important case the court considered this latter question along with a related question: namely, Is exequatur required before a foreign judgment can be offered, not as conclusive proof of what it declares, but as rebuttable evidence of the matter contained in that declaration?

The court identified three different situations that were commonly confused: "The first deals with the simple evidentiary value of the judgment document; the second with giving it execution in a positive sense; and the third with respecting what other judges have resolved with the authority of *cosa juzgada*." The Costa Rican Code of Civil Procedure, in terms, only requires exequatur for purposes of execution, the court noted. It then referred to the writings of two Argentine authorities, which express conflicting views as to the necessity of exequatur in situations other than those where execution was sought.[15] The court ultimately concluded:

> They adduce very persuasive reasons for concluding that exequatur is obligatory when a foreign judgment is invoked with the value of *cosa juzgada,* since fundamentally it is a problem analogous to that of execution. The courts of another country execute a foreign judgment or comply with it by respecting the authority derived from it. But if the judgment document is offered as evidence of certain facts without having any binding obligation on the local judge to follow the decision of the foreign judge, there would be no reason to require exequatur. In the absence of that binding obligation, which is the reason that justifies that requirement, the local judge retains full power to evaluate the efficacy of the document, just as he has in dealing with other elements of proof that the parties may have offered. . . . [T]he foreign judgment, insofar as it is offered as a simple evidentiary document, neither must nor can be submitted to the formality of exequatur. It can and must, by disposition of the law, if execution is sought for it, and that would also be the case if it was intended to be used as the basis for the exception (defense) of *cosa juzgada* if the laws dealing with the execution are considered applicable by analogy.[16]

The case clearly holds that exequatur is not necessary when a foreign judgment is offered as mere evidence which the local judge is not bound to accept as conclusive on the facts that it has been offered to prove. The court is not referring to what we would call direct or collateral estoppel effect of a judgment, of course, since that effect is conclusive.

The court hedges in its statement about the necessity of exequatur when a foreign judgment is offered as a defense to a pending action, however. In that case, the judgment would be conclusive. The tenor of the court's analysis indicates that the judgment should therefore be accredited by the Supreme Court through the exequatur procedure, just as a divorce judgment must be. This is the understanding that is generally attributed to the court's comments; it is also the view of the judge who wrote the court's opinion.[17] That requirement would be awkward, for a defendant who has a *cosa juzgada* (res judicata) defense would have to bring a separate proceeding for exequatur in the Supreme Court before he could assert that defense in the court of first instance. However, the Costa Rican court's view is that a judgment is a high act of sovereignty, and accordingly, a foreign judgment should be scrutinized carefully by the highest court in the land before it is given the force of law in Costa Rica, no matter how much cost, delay, or inconvenience this may pose to ongoing proceedings in lower courts.

## KINDS OF JUDGMENTS ENTITLED TO RECOGNITION AND ENFORCEMENT

Under the Costa Rican Code, Article 1022, a judgment that is executory "in the country of its origin" is entitled to recognition through exequatur in Costa Rica, with certain exceptions. This would include judgments for money and other judgments as well. Default judgments are enforceable if the defendant was duly summoned in the rendering court, but otherwise, judgments that were rendered without the defendant's participation are not entitled to recognition.

Although money judgments generally are enforceable without revision, there are some kinds of money awards that merit special comment.

### SETTLEMENT AGREEMENTS

A settlement agreement, even though it had been judicially approved, was held (one justice dissenting) not to be a "judgment" that would be entitled to recognition and enforcement through exequatur in Costa Rica.[18] This result is curious in view of Article 1385 of the Civil Code, which declares that settlement agreements have, "with respect to the parties, the same force and effect as res judicata (cosa juzgada)." The agreement can be enforced in Costa Rica through an original action on the agreement as a contract, but not through the exequatur procedure, apparently.

### ARBITRATION AWARDS

The Costa Rican Code of Civil Procedure (CCP) contains no reference to the recognition or enforcement of foreign arbitration awards. The Bustamante Code does, however,[19] and since Costa Rican law is merely silent on the point, not directly contrary, awards deriving from countries that are signatories of the Bustamante Code apparently may be given effect in Costa Rica through that code. No decisions in cases have held that, however. In any event, an arbitration award of a country with which Costa Rica has no relevant treaty ties presumably would not be entitled to recognition in Costa Rica.[20]

### JUDGMENTS OF SALE (SENTENCIAS DE REMATE)

The Costa Rican law recognizes the enforceability, under the exequatur procedure, of some foreign judgments that may not have been based upon contentious litigation. Enforcement of "judgments of sale" (sentencias de remate) is referred to in Article 1023. This is the order that is the end product of the execution procedure directing the sale of particular property. Such a judgment may be granted as a means of executing an unpaid money judgment. Property of the debtor is first seized (embargoed) and then ordered to be sold. Judgment of sale may be entered, however, in some situations in which it has not been preceded by an earlier contested judgment. This may be true, among other situations, when the obligation of the debtor is to pay a liquidated sum of money, and the debtor has contractually agreed to confess judgment—as in a cognovit note. In such cases an embargo that culminates in a judgment of sale may be obtained through the execution procedure simply on the basis of documents, duly authenticated, evidencing an obligation to pay the liquidated debt. A judgment ordering the sale of embargoed assets of the debtor may be entered in such an action, and the debtor is not allowed to contest the debt. If the debt was not in fact owing, however, the debtor can recover anything that he lost through the "judgment of sale" by instituting an independent action for restitution.[21] Foreign "judgments of sale," then, apparently are enforceable in Costa Rica, presumably after first honoring the foreign court's order embargoing property in Costa Rica.

## PENAL JUDGMENTS

It is not clear whether or not the common rule—namely, that foreign penal judgments will not be enforced—applies in Costa Rica. The Bustamante Code, Article 436, declares that such judgments will not be enforced insofar as concerns the penal sanctions that they impose, although, according to Article 437, they can be recognized for their effects in declaring civil responsibility or their effects on the goods of the defendant. The CCP is silent on the matter. There is one case that may suggest that a penal judgment that imposes a monetary fine might be enforceable in Costa Rica. In that case, the police court of Liege, Belgium, sought exequatur for a Belgian default penal judgment imposing a fine of 10,000 francs on a Costa Rican. The Supreme Court denied exequatur because no official Spanish translation of the judgment was submitted. The court did not mention the fact that it was a penal judgment.[22] In other cases where the court denied exequatur on a procedural ground, it pointed out that an alternative substantive ground for denial existed.[23] The failure of the court even to comment on the obvious fact that the judgment for which exequatur was sought was a penal judgment suggests that the court considered the point immaterial. Still, even if there is no rule against enforcing penal judgments per se, the court might find some such judgments to be unenforceable by virtue of the "public order" exception. An Ecuadorean decree confiscating a ship was denied recognition in Costa Rica on public-order grounds, among others.[24]

## REQUIREMENTS FOR RECOGNITION AND ENFORCEMENT

### Competency

The Costa Rican CCP does not expressly make "competency" of the rendering court a condition of exequatur. The Bustamante Code does make that a condition of recognition of foreign judicial orders, and the requirement would thus be applicable in Costa Rica when the rendering state is a signatory of the Bustamante Code. The Costa Rican court also imposes that requirement when the rendering state is not a signatory, however.[25]

The judgment must conform to the competency standards of the place of rendition. This is implicit on the requirement of Article 1022.2 that it be "in force" (*ejecutoria*) in the country of its origin. The Costa Rican Court will also examine the competency of the rendering court under Costa Rican standards—and if a Costa Rican court would have been exclusively competent for the original action, exequatur will be denied. In one case, exequatur was sought for a Spanish decree that declared null some mortgage certificates on Costa Rican land.[26] The certificates had been issued by a Costa Rican company. The court ruled, on the basis of Article 4 of the Civil Code,[27] that the competency of Costa Rican courts in matters relating to real rights in Costa Rican land is exclusive. Article 4 of the Civil Code is a choice-of-law rule. It says nothing, in terms, about competency. The court nevertheless read it as a competency limitation. Even if the Spanish court had validly applied Costa Rican law in ruling on these certificates, the judgment would not have been entitled to recognition in Costa Rica because of the rendering tribunal's lack of competency (under Costa Rican law). In another case the court refused to grant exequatur to a "notification" directing a Costa Rican domiciliary to appear and give testimony in a Nicaraguan court (what we would call a subpoena).[28] Even though both the Costa Rican Code of Civil Procedure[29] and the Bustamante Code authorize the serving of such notifications, the court refused to order it. Article 263 of the Code of Civil Procedure provides that the testimony of a witness in an action that is pending in a court other than the one whose territorial jurisdiction includes the area in which the witness resides shall be taken by interrogatories propounded by the court at his residence. This rule was interpreted as jurisdictional: *only* the court at his residence is competent to order him to give testimony. If another Costa Rican court would not be competent, *a fortiori* a Nicaraguan court would not be. Exequatur would be granted to a request by the Nicaraguan court to take the witness's testimony on interrogatories that would be administered in Costa Rica, but not to the subpoena directing the witness to go to Nicaragua.

The result seems curious. The Costa Rican court was not asked to *enforce* the subpoena, but merely to serve it—as a foreign summons would be served. Even if the provision of Article 263 is a rule of "competency," it is an example of that species of competency which is referred to as *ratione loci;* and as was noted in the previous chapter,[30] such rules are usually "relative," not "absolute" (i.e., the parties can waive them if they so choose). The Costa Rican court apparently treats this particular rule, then, as an "absolute" rule of competence *ratione loci,* even though the code provision that it is based upon does not, in terms, purport to be such.

Whether local rules of competency will have to be satisfied in connection with ordinary foreign money judgments cannot be determined with certainty, since there have not been any cases. One commentator has said, however, that Costa Rican rules generally must be observed and that a Costa Rican will not be precluded from collaterally attacking a foreign judgment on those grounds, even if he appeared in the foreign court and there challenged the court's competency on that basis.[31]

NOTICE

Article 1022.3 permits exequatur only when it appears either that the opposite party actually participated in the foreign proceeding or that he had been declared to be in default for nonappearance after due service. The provision does not specify whether "due service" is to be judged by the rendering court's standards or by Costa Rican standards, or by both. Professor Walter Antillón, commenting on this point, concluded that the requirement of Article 1022.3 is just a rather loose statement of one aspect of the general "public order" exception. It means, basically, that the foreign proceeding must have been accompanied by those minimal guarantees of fair notice and opportunity to defend that Costa Rican public policy considers to be essential.[32] Presumably, this means that both the foreign and the Costa Rican standards of what is "due" must be satisfied, since the order not only must be "enforceable" in the country of origin but also must satisfy the due-service requirement (if the opposing party did not participate).

If the judgment does not expressly recite that the opposing party appeared or defaulted after due notice, the petitioner will have to bear the burden of proving those facts by some means.[33]

If the judgment for which exequatur is sought does recite that the opposing party appeared (personally or by representative) or that he was duly cited but then defaulted, however, the court apparently will not allow extrinsic evidence to contradict that recital in the decree.[34] In one case, the court granted exequatur to a New York money judgment against a Costa Rican corporation. The judgment recited that the defendant had been "duly served," but it did not state the form or manner of the service. It also recited that the defendant appeared by its attorneys (although the judgment was a "default" judgment, which stated that the defendant failed to appear). The defendant resisted the exequatur, claiming that it was never served or notified, that it had not participated in the New York action, and that its first awareness of the action was when the exequatur proceeding was brought in Costa Rica. It denied that it had any connection with the attorneys who, the judgment said, had appeared for it (they did represent some other defendants in the New York suit, but the Costa Rican corporation denied that any agency relationship existed between it and the other defendants). The defendant also produced a certificate of the secretary of the Supreme Court of Costa Rica which declared that no rogatory request for service of the New York court's process in Costa Rica had even been received. In spite of this, the court refused to consider the defendant's contention in the face of the explicit recitation of service. Exequatur was granted.[35]

The court did consider extrinsic proof to show that the defendant in a Honduran divorce decree was not actually served personally in Honduras, as recited in the judgment, and it therefore denied exequatur on the basis of Article 1022.3.[36] Divorce judgments, however, according to Costa Rican decisions in other contexts,[37] implicate the "public order" in ways that ordinary money judgments do not.

One technique of invoking a court's jurisdiction over an absent defendant that is common in Central America is the device of appointing a local attorney to serve as the representative of the absent defendant. The appointed attorney then "appears" in the action and, in effect, confesses judgment (as in the cognovit procedure followed in some states of the United States). The record of a judgment that has been obtained under this procedure will recite that the defendant "appeared" through his representative, and so a foreign judgment based on such a procedure would seem to satisfy the requirement of Article 1022.3. However, the method of notifying the defendant in such cases may be no more than publication, and the absent defendant may never know about the action. Accordingly, to protect against abuse, this technique generally cannot be used unless the residence or whereabouts of the defendant are unknown. If the execution of a foreign judgment that has been obtained through this method of serving the defendant is sought in Costa Rica, can the defendant resist the petition for exequatur by showing that his whereabouts were not unknown? In two cases the Supreme Court of Costa Rica indicated that he could.

In one case, this method of service was used in a Panamanian action that sought a declaration awarding the custody of a minor to his father. The mother, who was a Costa Rican, did not receive actual notice in time to present her opposition in the Panamanian action. When exequatur was sought in Costa Rica for the Panamanian judgment (so that the change in custody could be duly recorded in the Costa Rican civil registry), the wife objected to the lack of notice. The court denied the exequatur. Even if Panamanian law permits service by publication, coupled with the naming of a representative ad litem in actions against persons located outside the country, Costa Rican law does not permit this without proof that their whereabouts are unknown. The Costa Rican rule is not merely a matter of procedure but an essential right— one of "public order." Here it was clear that the wife's domicile was known. She could have been personally served in Costa Rica with the assistance of Costa Rican courts. Under the circumstances, the judgment deprived her of fundamental rights recognized by Costa Rican law, so the Panamanian judgment was not entitled to recognition.[38] Whether the court would apply this rule if the defendant were not a Costa Rican national or domiciliary is not clear.[39]

The defendant can waive his right to resist exequatur on the ground of Article 1022.3,[40] or he may be estopped to assert it.[41] However, he will not be estopped merely because he raised the issue of inadequate or improper notice in the rendering court. A Costa Rican, at least, can resist exequatur even if the issue was unsuccessfully urged in the rendering court, according to Professor Gonzalo Ortiz Martin.[42] This opinion, however, is difficult to reconcile with the case of the New York judgment referred to above. The Costa Rican corporation in that case was not allowed to collaterally attack the New York money judgment on grounds of lack of notice where the judgment recited due service even though the corporation did *not* appear and make the challenge in the rendering court. If the defendant had appeared and had challenged the sufficiency of the service or notice, the judgment record would almost inevitably have recited that the defendant had been properly served and notified. It is hard to see why a defendant who did appear and contest the lack of notice should be able to attack the resulting judgment more easily than one who did not appear at all.

FINALITY

The exequatur procedure is prescribed for every situation in which effect is sought in Costa Rica for some directive emanating from a foreign court.[43] This means that not only those orders which are judgments, in the sense of final resolutions of litigation, but various interlocutory directives as well are dealt with by this procedure.

### FINAL JUDGMENTS

With respect to judgments, the text of Article 1022.2 of the CCP might suggest that only executable judgments for the plaintiff are entitled to recognition, since that section declares that exequatur cannot be granted if the judgment is not "executory" (*ejecutoria*) in the country of origin. In the last chapter we noted the ambiguity in the similar provision in the Bustamante Code,[44] but we saw there that the Bustamante Code contains another article that relates to judgments that are not "executable."[45] The Costa Rican CCP, however, does not contain such a separate provision. Nevertheless, judgments other than money judgments for the plaintiff clearly are enforceable by exequatur in Costa Rica. The word *"ejecutoria"* in Article 1022.2, then, is interpreted broadly to mean *"in force,"* not just *"executable."* An ordinary judgment generally must have achieved such finality and stature as to entitle it to res judicata effect,[46] but it may be a declaratory judgment, or a judgment to do or refrain from doing something, or a defendant's judgment. However, some judgments that are enforceable do not have res judicata effects. Notable are the "judgments of sale" which were discussed above.[47]

A decree for continuing support, calling for installment payments in the future, has also been given recognition and enforcement in Costa Rica, although execution could be obtained only for the accrued arrearages.[48]

### PROVISIONAL ORDERS

As noted previously, the exequatur procedure is a required step in the process by which letters rogatory and requisitorial and other requests for assistance that have been sent by foreign courts are carried out in Costa Rica. Assistance to foreign courts in connection with ongoing proceedings in the form of serving notices, taking testimony, and so forth, is provided in much the same way as in the United States, after the foreign court's request for assistance has been authenticated through the exequatur procedure. A summons informing a Costa Rican domiciliary that he is being sued in a foreign court can be served in Costa Rica through this means.

Some of the provisional orders of foreign courts that may be given effect and may actually be enforced in Costa Rica may have much more substantial consequences than mere notification or proof-taking procedures. Decrees awarding child custody[49] and support,[50] pending the resolution of a foreign divorce suit, have been enforced in Costa Rica.

What is most surprising to a North American observer is the willingness of the Costa Rican and other Central American courts to grant exequatur to provisional *embargo* (attachment) orders that have been issued by foreign courts against local properties. In our practice, courts of one state generally have been unwilling to attach properties of a person who is the defendant in an action that is pending in another state. Full faith and credit does not require this, and states have been unwilling to extend their provisional remedies to actions that are not pending in their own courts.[51] The Bustamante Code, however, has been interpreted as permitting this as a means of judicial assistance, and Costa Rican law authorizes this form of judicial assistance to all foreign courts,[52] provided certain prescribed conditions have been satisfied. The notice required by Article 1021 in the case of final judgments is not required in connection with the exequatur for a foreign *embargo*. However, the exequatur will not be granted unless it appears that the party whose goods are sought to be attached had sufficient notice of the request for the extraterritorial embargo order to have been able to present his defenses against it. Unless the letter rogatory seeking the embargo shows on its face that the defendant has been notified, exequatur will be denied.[53] It is not enough that the rogatory letter shows that the court ordered the defendant to be notified: it must appear that he was in fact notified.[54]

Another requirement that must be satisfied before exequatur will be granted to a provisional embargo is the requirement that is specified in Article 173 of the CCP—namely, the posting of a bond. That rule of the Costa Rican Code has been characterized as one of "international public order" and of "social order"—a fundamental guarantee of fairness. Accordingly, Costa Rica will not recognize or enforce a provisional embargo that has been requested by a foreign court without the bond that is required by Costa Rican law. This is true even if the law of the other country requires a guarantee.[55] It is curious that the court decided to enforce this requirement by making it a condition of exequatur rather than leaving it to the lower courts to impose the bond requirement, as they do in the case of domestic embargoes. Other local procedural rules relating to the remedy rather than to the validity of the order are imposed by the lower courts. The court apparently considers the bond to be of such fundamental importance as to be tantamount to a jurisdictional requirement, like the notice requirement. Notice, however, is required by the code itself. The imposition of the bond as a condition of exequatur is a judge-made rule.[56]

RECIPROCITY

In many countries it is necessary to show that the courts of the rendering state would give the requested effect to a judgment of the recognizing state as a condition of enforcing the foreign judgment. This is the so-called reciprocity requirement. Reciprocity is not a feature of the Costa Rican law relating to judgment recognition, however.

PUBLIC ORDER

The concept of "public order" as an exception to recognition of foreign judgments is somewhat confused in Costa Rica, as elsewhere. Only the term "public order" is expressed in Article 1022.4, but commentaries about the "public order" concept usually try to deal with it in terms of the Bustamante Code's distinction between "internal" and "international public order."[57]

"Public order" refers to principles that reflect the basic values of the society at any point in time, according to Professor Walter Antillón.[58] In the Costa Rican order, they are values of the Costa Rican society. He denies the utility of referring to principles that are basic to "civilized nations," because of the great variety of basic values among them.

Besides the principles relating to procedural fairness that have been discussed already,[59] two other situations commonly present instances of the "public order" exception to judgment enforcement: namely, foreign judgments relating to property in the enforcing state, and divorce judgments granted on grounds that are not recognized under the law of the enforcing state. Costa Rica uses the "public order" exception very extensively in cases of the second type, but less extensively in cases of the first type.

Article 5 of the Civil Code of Costa Rica declares that Costa Rican laws control all questions relating to immovable property in Costa Rica, including successions.[60] However, Costa Rica does recognize the principle of unity of succession for nondomiciliaries of Costa Rica, even with respect to immovable property. This may seem contradictory to Article 4 of the Civil Code, but Article 515 of the CCP specifically declares that judgments determining successions to properties of persons who are not domiciled in Costa Rica (whether foreigners or Costa Rican nationals) will be recognized and given effect with respect to properties in Costa Rica. The exequatur procedure must be followed, and in connection with that procedure, notice must be published for three months, so that persons who may have claims against the property will have a chance to assert them. If no claims are made (or, if made, the claims are rejected), the exequatur will be granted, and the property will be ordered to be distributed in accordance with the foreign judgment, subject to local taxes. Thus, Costa Rica will not invoke "public order" to deny effect to a foreign judgment of succession merely because it orders the property to be distributed in a different manner than Costa Rican law would. If, however, the foreign decree directs that Costa Rican property should pass in a way that is expressly forbidden by Costa Rican law— for instance, if it directs that more than ten percent of it should pass to the church—that part of the foreign decree will not be given effect in Costa Rica.[61]

The situation that has produced the largest number of cases involving the application of the "public order" exception in Costa Rica is the one involving foreign divorce decrees that have been granted on grounds that would not be regarded as valid under Costa Rican law. The matrimonial and familial relation is regarded as a matter of fundamental importance in Costa Rica, and the conditions under which marriages may be dissolved are matters of "public order." The Bustamante Code, it will be recalled, allows signatory states to refuse to grant recognition to otherwise valid foreign divorces if the grounds were not appropriate under the personal law of the parties.[62] Under the Bustamante Code, as we have seen, a country is free to use either domicile or nationality as the basis for identifying personal law, but Costa Rica has endorsed domicile for that purpose.[63] However, the Costa Rican Court has refused, in the name of "public order," to recognize foreign divorces that have been granted on grounds that are invalid under Costa Rican law, even when the parties were neither domiciliaries nor nationals of Costa Rica.

In a 1965 case, exequatur in Costa Rica was sought for an uncontested divorce that had been obtained in Honduras. The decree recited that both parties were domiciled in Honduras, although it did not mention their nationalities. The court characterized the uncontested divorce as one based on "mutual consent." It is a principle of "public order" in Costa Rica that people cannot get divorces by mutual consent. That principle, the court said, applies to divorce judgments that have been granted abroad and that were valid where they were granted, *even when the parties are foreigners.*[64] The marriage of the parties in the case had taken place in Costa Rica, but in the court's analysis, that fact was not regarded as being particularly important.

No reason is apparent to explain why a divorce, valid where granted, of persons who have neither a citizenship nor a domiciliary connection to Costa Rica should be denied recognition. No interests of the parties were served by such a rule, at least when the grounds were mutual consent. If the parties had formerly been Costa Rican citizens or domiciliaries who had changed their status in order to avoid Costa Rica's "public order," the matter might be different, but there was no indication of either possibility in the particular case. The very slight interest of Costa Rica, deriving from the fact that the parties had originally been married in Costa Rica, would not seem to be enough. The explanation for the decision apparently is a sort of "clean hands" rationale: the courts of Costa Rica will not give any aid to someone who has been a party to an arrangement that is immoral by Costa Rican standards. The interest seems flimsy, at best, in the light of the serious prejudice that the rule may expose the parties to. And when the parties are citizens and domiciliaries of a sister state of Central America, the rule has adverse implications for the association interest in the free mobility of persons. Nevertheless, in a case later in the same year, the court extended this rule in denying exequatur to a Panamanian divorce that was based on abandonment for less than the two years that Costa Rican law regards as sufficient.[65]

Fortunately, the court found a way to ameliorate the prejudicial effects of the rule to some extent. Exequatur was granted to a Nicaraguan divorce that had been granted on grounds of abandonment, even though the abandonment had not lasted more than the required two years at the time the Nicaraguan decree was granted. By the time exequatur was sought, the parties had been separated for more than two years, and that would have constituted valid grounds for divorce in Costa Rica. Thus, Costa Rican "public order" would not have been violated by giving effect to the Nicaraguan judgment.[66] This same device was used to justify exequatur to a Mexican divorce based on mutual consent, when the parties had remained separated for more than two years.[67]

The Costa Rican court has not applied this "clean hands" rule by way of the "public order" exception to ordinary money judgments that have been granted by foreign courts. However, the willingness to invoke it in divorce cases in which Costa Rica had no discernible legislative concern at the time the foreign decree was granted raises the fear that the "public order" concept might be invoked in some such cases to deny effects to judgments. The "public order" exception can be a serious impediment to a region-wide scheme of judgment recognition. If it is not eliminated (as it has been under the American full-faith-and-credit regime), it at least should be subject to some sort of limiting rules (similar to the limitations of the EEC Convention, perhaps).[68]

## RES JUDICATA (COSA JUZGADA)

Authority of *cosa juzgada* is an attribute of every contentious definitive judgment, according to the view generally prevailing in Latin America.[69] The exact meaning and scope of the effect of *cosa juzgada* is subject to considerable variation. It is not to be confused with "executability," which is an additional effect that some contentious definitive judgments have. As noted at the end of chapter 2, it is not identical in its scope to res judicata as understood in contemporary American jurisprudence, although it rests upon the same basic policy—namely, that a dispute, once it has finally been resolved by a court of competent jurisdiction, should not again be the subject of litigation by the same parties. Analytically, *cosa juzgada* has two basic functions: it establishes as an uncontestable fact the relation declared in the judgment, and it provides a defense (or "exception") that can be used to avoid a later suit.

Any form of judgment recognition other than enforcement (execution) involves the *cosa juzgada* effect. The Bustamante Code, Article 431,[70] provides for recognition of nonexecutable judgments for their *cosa juzgada* effects. The Costa Rican Code of Civil Procedure provisions that relate to foreign judgments, however, make no express reference to any form of recognition for final foreign judgments except execution. Nor does the Costa Rican legislation relating to *cosa juzgada* provide expressly that that effect can be attributed to foreign judgments. Nevertheless, foreign judgments are entitled to recognition for their *cosa juzgada* effects in Costa Rica.[71] Costa Rican standards prescribe the scope of those effects.

*Cosa juzgada* is dealt with in the Civil Code instead of in the Code of Civil Procedure in Costa Rica. It appears in a subsection of the title that deals with evidence or proof. The provisions in that code are typical of *cosa juzgada* doctrine throughout Latin America. The effects are limited to the dispositive part of the judgment; they do not extend to the grounds.[72] The three "identities" discussed above[73] are necessary before the *cosa juzgada* effect of a prior judgment will control a later one: identity of parties, identity of object, and identity of cause.[74] Determining when the requisite identities of "object" and "cause" exist is a problem that is very comparable in difficulty to determining the scope of the "cause of action" in Anglo-American res judicata doctrine.

The question of whether exequatur is required before a foreign judgment may be recognized for its *cosa juzgada* effects was discussed in the section "Basic Procedure for Recognition and Enforcement" above.

## INCONSISTENT JUDGMENTS

Costa Rican law makes no specific provision for the case in which exequatur is sought for a foreign judgment while an action is pending on the same claim in a Costa Rican court. Antillón's view is that the Costa Rican court would not entertain the defense of lis pendens to avoid exequatur in such a case, since there is no statute that specifically authorizes that defense.[75]

In the same vein, no specific provision is made for the case in which the claim that is embodied in the judgment for which exequatur is sought has already been adjudicated in Costa Rica or elsewhere. If there is an inconsistent Costa Rican judgment, exequatur will be denied to the foreign judgment, whether prior or not, on the ground of "public order."[76] Whether exequatur would be denied if the inconsistent judgment were rendered in another country, however, is an unsettled question. Couture declares that it is a matter of basic procedural logic that two contradictory judgments cannot coexist and that the later one in time cannot be valid.[77] In the full-faith-and-credit regime of the United States, however, as we have seen,[78] it is the later in time of two contradictory judgments that is entitled to recognition.

## EVALUATION OF THE COSTA RICAN REGIME

This examination of Costa Rican law and procedure relating to recognition and enforcement of foreign judgments indicates that judgments that have been obtained in ordinary actions seeking a money recovery in sister republics of Central America are generally recognized and readily enforced without examination of the merits. Even some kinds of foreign judicial orders that generally have not been regarded as enforceable among the states of the United States are given effect in Costa Rica—notably, provisional attachments (embargos) and some "judgments of sale." Penal judgments may be enforceable more readily than the Bustamante Code would require. Arbitration awards of signatories to the Bustamante Code are enforced, although settlement agreements—even if judicially approved—are not. There is no reciprocity requirement.

On the other hand, this survey of the Costa Rican law and practice has identified certain features of it that will, unless changed, make it difficult to achieve a judgment-recognition system in Central America that will serve both the association interests that were identified in chapter 2 and the overall goal of Central American reunification.

The principal problem is the Costa Rican application of local standards—substantive and procedural—in cases in which no strong national interests are jeopardized. This attitude is reflected in the country's broad reservation to the Bustamante Code. It is reflected in the cases that apply Costa Rican standards of competency to deny effect to foreign decrees, without regard to whether the foreign court in fact applied rules of decision that were inconsistent with those of Costa Rica.[79] It is reflected in the application of Costa Rica's "public order" doctrine to foreign divorce judgments involving nondomiciliaries and nonnationals of Costa Rica. The cases that apply these local principles in this fashion never discuss the costs to Costa Rica, to the litigant, and to the cause of regional integration that this parochialism entails.

Costa Rican doctrine sees judgment recognition as a high act of sovereignty, and thus the decision to grant or deny exequatur has political overtones that seem to make some sense in theory. That, no doubt, is one of the main reasons that underlie the lodging of exequatur jurisdiction in the Sala de Casación of the Supreme Court, rather than lodging it in some ordinary court of first instance, as is done in the United States, Guatemala, and some of the EEC nations. Whether these political concerns are worth the practical costs that they entail, however, seems questionable. When application must be made to the highest court in the land, rather than to an ordinary court, for the enforcement—or even for the passive recognition—of a sister nation's judgment, the effect cannot be to encourage mobility. The process of reviewing a foreign judgment to see if it is properly authenticated ordinarily does not require the attention of the highest court in the land. It is a rather rudimentary administrative exercise, in fact. The determination of whether the court that rendered the judgment was competent may require a judicial decision, but most rules of "competence" relating to money judgments can be waived by the parties in other contexts; and so, if the parties do not raise the issue, there should be no need to consider it. If the issue is contested, a judicial resolution will be required, but it does not follow that it should always be the Supreme Court that resolves the question. The parties may be satisfied with a lower court's ruling, which is likely to be correct in most cases.

The determination of whether the foreign judgment contravenes Costa Rican "public order" is a more serious matter, but whether it is serious enough to warrant the cost of requiring the Supreme Court to rule on all cases is doubtful. The "public order" exception should not be invoked unless some important local interest would be significantly impaired. It should be fairly obvious if such an issue is raised by a foreign judgment. A lower court judge would normally be able to identify and deal with the "public order" question, subject, of course, to ultimate review in the Supreme Court.

There is, however, one factor that may justify submitting some foreign judgments to review at some stage by the Supreme Court, at least when the judgment is one of a sister republic of Central America. The association interests identified in chapter 2 include the interest in faithful and consistent interpretation of the basic charter. This interest would normally require that automatic effect be given to a sister-state judgment implicating a charter interpretation except in a few situations.[80] One exceptional situation is that presented when the foreign judgment is inconsistent with another decision involving the same question. It was noted that inconsistency can usually be avoided if cases containing such rulings are regularly published and circulated. In Central America, however, cases, even of the highest courts, often are not published; so the interpretative rulings may not be readily accessible to courts generally. Nevertheless, exchange of opinions might be arranged between the highest courts in each country without great difficulty. It is more likely, under the present conditions, accordingly, that the Supreme Court would be able to identify a conflicting ruling than that a lower court could. Unless some such exchange arrangement were to be established, however, even this argument in favor of the prior Supreme Court exequatur requirement in cases that involve interpretation of the charter is rather weak.

A more pragmatic examination of just what interests of Costa Rica are implicated in the judgment-recognition decision, and in what way, might well lead to the abandonment of some of the tendency to localism that has been seen in some of the cases noted here. At present, though, it cannot be said that Costa Rica's judgment-recognition scheme would fit well into a region-wide recognition system aimed at optimal integration effects.

# 5 El Salvador

## THE BASIC LAW

Article 451 of the Code of Civil Procedure provides that "[j]udgments pronounced in foreign countries will have in El Salvador the force that the respective treaties establish."

Since El Salvador is a signatory of the Bustamante Code, that treaty establishes rules relating to enforcement of the judgments of other signatory states, which include, of course, all other countries of Central America. However, El Salvador, when it ratified the Bustamante Code, did express reservations, some of which are relevant to the judgment-recognition problem. El Salvador's delegation to the Havana conference expressly rejected the principle of articles 327, 328, and 329 of the Bustamante Code, which deal with competence of courts in matters relating to decedents' estates, creditors' compositions, and bankruptcy. The Bustamante Code makes the decedent's or debtor's domiciliary court competent. El Salvador's delegation rejected those provisions insofar as they would have application to immovable property in El Salvador. El Salvador's legislature not only repeated that reservation in the instrument of ratification but also added another restriction that had not been mentioned by the convention delegates. It reserved the right to enact future laws covering the matters that are dealt with in the Bustamante Code, and it declared that "[i]n case the juridical doctrines that the [Bustamante Code] contains oppose or restrict in any manner the laws of El Salvador, they shall not prevail over said laws."

These statements appear to place El Salvador in the same camp as Costa Rica: The code has effect only so long as and to the extent that it does not contradict the local law.

El Salvador's Code of Civil Procedure, then, is the basic law, augmented by the Bustamante Code in cases that involve judgments of other signatory states. The other relevant provisions of its Code of Civil Procedure are:

> Article 452. If there should be no special treaties with the nation in which [the judgment] was pronounced, it will have force in El Salvador if it meets the following circumstances:
> 1. That the order [*ejecutoria*] shall have been issued as a result of the exercise of a personal action;
> 2. That it shall not have been issued in default;
> 3. That the obligation with which the action sought compliance is lawful in El Salvador;
> 4. That the order [*ejecutoria*] meets the requirements necessary to be considered authentic in the nation in which it was pronounced, and those that Salvador's laws require for it to be given credence in El Salvador.
>
> Article 453. For the execution of judgments that have been pronounced in foreign nations, prior permission shall be obtained from the Supreme Court of Justice, which in order to grant or deny it, shall afford the opposing party an opportunity to be heard on three days' notice.
>
> Article 454. The judgment will be executed, if the case warrants it, in the manner prescribed in Article 450.

Article 450 deals with execution of money judgments. The Code of Civil Procedure does not refer directly to the enforcement or recognition of other foreign judgments, but such judgments are enforceable by the same methods that are prescribed in Articles 442 and 443 for the enforcement of nonpecuniary domestic judgments.[1] Articles 451 and 452 of El Salvador's Code of Civil Procedure are almost identical to provisions in the Spanish Civil Judgment law.[2] Three of the Central American countries have similarly drawn upon the Spanish law.[3]

## BASIC PROCEDURE FOR RECOGNITION AND ENFORCEMENT

El Salvador's recognition procedure is similar to that of Costa Rica in that it requires a determination by the Supreme Court before some kinds of foreign judgments may be enforced in El Salvador. All foreign judgments or orders must be duly authenticated and translated, if they are not in Spanish.[4]

The term "exequatur" is not used in the Salvadoran practice. The Supreme Court's permission, required by Article 453, granting recognition to the foreign judgment is called "*pareatis.*"

Article 453 prescribes only three days' notice to the opposite party in the *pareatis* proceeding. This contrasts to the twenty days that are specified in the Bustamante Code, Article 426. The body of Salvadoran *pareatis* cases is not so extensive as that available in Costa Rica,[5] and so it cannot be determined with assurance whether the notice provision of the CCP or that of the Bustamante Code applies to proceedings to enforce judgments of other signatory countries. It is not even clear that the two different notice provisions are contradictory. If Article 453 of the CCP is designed to ensure notification of the opposing party, the granting of the additional time to answer that the Bustamante Code allows does not appear to "oppose or restrict" the Salvadoran law. But if Article 453 is designed to limit the time, allowing the longer period would be contradictory.

The notice need not be given, of course, if the opposing party expressly waives its right to it.[6]

If the party who is seeking the *pareatis* was the losing party in the foreign action, no notice at all to the opposite party is required. The Supreme Court has declared that it would be "absurd to suppose . . . that the legislature wanted the victorious party to be heard . . . to argue against the same judgment that granted his petitions."[7] This situation can arise in connection with divorce judgments, where the losing party wants to register the changed civil status in El Salvador, but it could rarely occur in the case of a foreign money judgment.

If the *pareatis* is granted, the judgment is enforceable according to the procedure prescribed for domestic judgments.

## KINDS OF JUDGMENTS ENTITLED TO RECOGNITION AND ENFORCEMENT

### PERSONAL JUDGMENTS

Article 452.1 of the Code of Civil Procedure limits enforceability to judgments in personal actions. Personal actions are actions arising from personal rights.[8] Personal rights are all rights except real rights as defined in Article 567 of the Civil Code. Personal actions, then, are actions other than those to establish property rights of dominion; inheritance; usufruct, use, or occupation; active servitudes; pledge; and mortgage. Ordinary money judgments are usually personal actions.

The Bustamante Code does not limit recognition to personal actions as such. El Salvador's express reservation to the Bustamante Code,[9] however, would deny recognition to judgments of other signatory nations in cases of testate or intestate succession and in bankruptcy cases, insofar as those judgments might affect Salvadoran immovable property. If no immovable property in El Salvador would be affected, though, the rule appears to be that El Salvador will recognize judgments of other Central American countries even in nonpersonal actions. For example, a Nicaraguan nonpersonal judgment that designated a universal heir to the properties of a Nicaraguan decedent who left bank accounts in El Salvador was entitled to recognition in El Salvador.[10]

### DEFAULT JUDGMENTS

Article 452 of the Salvadoran CCP appears to deny recognition of all foreign default judgments. However, the court has interpreted this to apply only to countries with which El Salvador has no relevant treaties. The Bustamante Code is a "relevant treaty," and in spite of the Salvadoran reservations to it, that code provides the basic standards for recognition of judgments of other signatory countries. Default judgments of other Central American countries, then, may be enforced in El Salvador, in spite of Article 452.2, so long as the notice prescribed by Article 423.2 of the Bustamante Code was given before the default judgment was rendered.[11]

### ARBITRATION AWARDS

Foreign arbitration awards are enforceable if they concern subjects for which arbitration is permissible under Salvadoran law.[12] The same procedure applies as that which is provided for judgment enforcement.[13]

### PENAL JUDGMENTS

Presumably the provisions of the Bustamante Code, Articles 435 and 437, determine the enforceability in El Salvador of penal judgments of signatory countries.

### VOLUNTARY JUDGMENTS

Judgments that rest on voluntary jurisdiction are entitled to recognition in El Salvador, but the *pareatis* procedure is not required in order to give them effect.[14] Such judgments are essentially nonadversary ones, and so, ordinary money judgments would not come under this classification.

### DIVORCES BASED ON GROUNDS THAT ARE NOT VALID IN EL SALVADOR

A special provision relating to the effect in El Salvador of foreign divorces that have been granted on grounds that are not accepted by Salvadoran law deserves mention. Article 170 of the Civil Code declares: "The marriage dissolved in foreign territory in conformity with the laws of that country, but which would not have been dissolved according to Salvadoran law, will not enable either of the two parties to marry again in El Salvador as long as the other lives." This provision does not say that the divorce is not entitled to recognition as a judgment, but it does deprive the judgment of one of its most important effects; and in one case the court actually did say that *pareatis* could not be granted to a foreign divorce that rested on grounds that were unacceptable in El Salvador, citing Article 170 and also Article 15 of the Civil Code.[15] The Bustamante Code, Article 53, authorizes countries to recognize or not recognize divorces or remarriages of persons who had been divorced abroad on grounds that are not acceptable to the personal law of those persons. The Salvadoran provision in terms denies validity to the re-marriage in El Salvador without regard to what the "personal law" of the parties is or was. In terms it purports to apply to divorces of for-eigners who are not domiciled in El Salvador, as well as to those of nationals and domiciliaries. In terms it applies, no matter what the reason might be that the divorce would have had no effect in El Salvador. It has, however, been interpreted more narrowly. It has been inter-preted to apply only to divorces that have been obtained by or against Salvadorans and to apply only when the reason that the divorce could not have been obtained in El Salvador was that the grounds for the for-eign divorce would not have been valid grounds in El Salvador.[16] Fur-thermore, even a Salvadoran who was divorced abroad on grounds that are unacceptable to Salvadoran law, can validly marry again in another country, it has been said, since Article 170 of the Civil Code merely prevents a marriage "in El Salvador."[17]

## REQUIREMENTS FOR RECOGNITION AND ENFORCEMENT

### COMPETENCY

I was not able to find any cases that dealt with the "competent court" requirement, and so, I cannot draw any conclusions about how it works in practice with respect to such matters as burden of proof or the willingness of the court to consider evidence, outside the document itself, on jurisdictional issues.

El Salvador does apply its standard of "competence" to judgments affecting immovable property in the country. It expressly reserved this from its endorsement of the Bustamante Code.[18]

### NOTICE

The fact that the defendant was not notified of the action in time to defend in the rendering court will enable the defendant to avoid recognition of the judgment in El Salvador. Article 453.4 of the Code of Civil Procedure specifies that the judgment must have met all the requisites for validity in the nation where it was rendered, and such requisites would nearly always include notification of the defendant in some form. Whether the court will look behind express recitals of notification in the judgment itself is a question on which no answer can be given, owing to the lack of decisions on the point. In order to entitle the judgment to recognition in signatory countries, the Bustamante Code requires that the defendant or his representative must have been served personally,[19] and that provision applies with respect to judgments of other Central American countries, of course. However, the lack of formal service did not enable the defendant in a Guatemalan action to resist its recognition and enforcement in El Salvador when the defendant had actually participated in the action.[20] A "general appearance" doctrine, then, apparently operates to cure formal defects in notification or service.

El Salvador allows service on absent parties to be made by publication and appointment of a representative ad litem whenever the party is outside the republic, even if his residence or whereabouts is known.[21] This is not regarded as unconstitutional under the Salvadoran Constitution; and so, similar procedure practiced by another country would presumably be regarded as adequate service if it is allowed under the law of the rendering state and if it would not contravene Salvadoran "public order."

FINALITY

The Salvadoran Code contains no reference similar to the one used in the Costa Rican Code dealing with enforcement and recognition of provisional embargoes or other nonfinal orders emanating from foreign courts. This apparently does not mean that such orders are not entitled to recognition in El Salvador, at least if they come from countries that are signatory to the Bustamante Code.[22] However, if they are enforceable, the *pareatis* procedure is not required in order to give them effect.[23]

RECIPROCITY

The lack of reciprocity is not a defense to judgment recognition in El Salvador.

PUBLIC ORDER

The "public order" exception to judgment recognition clearly does apply in El Salvador. Article 452.3 of the CCP imposes, as a condition of enforceability, that the underlying obligation be "lawful" in El Salvador. This seems to suggest that enforcement may be denied on an even broader basis than the conventional "public order" exception, which applies only where the underlying obligation is contrary to some fundamental principles. I was not able to find any cases to amplify the meaning of Article 452.3, but this surely does not mean that enforcement of a judgment will be denied anytime that the underlying obligation is contrary to Salvadoran municipal law. An obligation may be lawful in El Salvador if Salvadoran choice-of-law rules regard it as being governed by the law of some other country, even though it would contravene Salvadoran internal law.

In the case of judgments of other Bustamante Code signatories, the "public order or public law" exception of Article 423.3 presumably applies. Whether this is in fact a different standard from the one embodied in Article 452.3 of the Code of Civil Procedure—and, if so, which standard should be applied—is a question that cannot be answered, owing to the paucity of judicial and scholarly commentary on the question.

Any attempt to articulate the real scope of the "public order" exception in El Salvador will have to deal with the fact that the Salvadoran Civil Code apparently endorses both the "domicile" and the "nationality" principle for identifying the personal law that is applicable in some cases. Article 14 declares that "the law is obligatory for all inhabitants of the Republic, including foreigners." Article 15, however, says that "Salvadoran citizens remain subject to the national laws, notwithstanding their residence or domicile in a foreign country: in matters relating to personal status and their capacity to perform certain acts which are to have effect in El Salvador; and in obligations that arise from family relations, but only in respect to Salvadoran spouses and relatives." These articles seem to make Salvadoran law the personal law of all domiciliaries and all Salvadoran nationals in the designated areas.[24] This could mean that the public-order exception is available on a somewhat broader basis in El Salvador than that contemplated by the Bustamante Code. I was not able to find any cases to clarify the point, however.

The absence of cases invoking the "public order" exception in El Salvador, in contrast to the situation noted in Costa Rica, is perhaps explainable in part by the fact that the kinds of cases in which the Costa Rican court found the exception applicable are dealt with much differently by Salvadoran law. The express reservation of matters relating to succession to immovable property, which El Salvador declared in ratifying the Bustamante Code, undoubtedly has deterred attempts to gain recognition for foreign judgments that purport to create such rights in Salvadoran land. The fact that El Salvador recognizes consensual divorces eliminates foreign judgments of that type as potential candidates for the "public order" exception. Finally, the Salvadoran conception of "due process" in relation to the form and manner of serving process on parties who are absent from the country is not so demanding as that which is observed in Costa Rica.[25]

## RES JUDICATA (COSA JUZGADA)

Salvadoran law (Article 451 of the Code of Civil Procedure) declares that foreign judgments will have such force in El Salvador as shall have been established by treaties. This would include the force of *cosa juzgada*. There is no other provision relating to *cosa juzgada* effects for foreign judgments, and so the provisions of the Bustamante Code are apparently determinative on this point, where judgments of other signatories are concerned. That code declares that judgments shall be recognized for their *cosa juzgada* effects,[26] and it limits the invocation of the *cosa juzgada* exception to cases in which the judgment was grounded on participation of the parties or their legal representatives and in which no question was raised about the foreign court's competence.[27] I was not able to find any cases or commentaries on the *cosa juzgada* effects of foreign judgments in El Salvador.

In a fairly recent case dealing with the *cosa juzgada* effect of a prior domestic judgment, the Supreme Court summarized the requirements that must be met before *cosa juzgada* would be available as a defense to a later action.[28] The court's statement of the doctrine describes *cosa juzgada* in traditional terms. It is available as a defense only where there is identity of person, object, and cause between the two actions. The first judgment must have been on the merits and must have been contested by the opposite party. Presumably, these standard requirements also apply when the first judgment was pronounced in another country.

A question may arise as to whether the fictitious "contest" that is authorized by the law of El Salvador and other Central American countries when a representative is appointed for an absent party is sufficient to warrant *cosa juzgada* effects. The Bustamante Code requires the appearance by a person or his legal representative. Conceivably, that requirement would be satisfied in cases where the "legal representative" is appointed by the court after publication notice to a nondomiciliary, noncitizen defendant. However, I was not able to find any cases to clarify the view that the Salvadoran court would take on this question.

In view of the fact that *pareatis* is not required in order to give effect in El Salvador to a foreign judgment based on voluntary jurisdiction,[29] it seems likely that the court would also rule that no *pareatis* is necessary in order to give a foreign judgment the defensive effect of *cosa juzgada*. The absense of decisions on the point makes this conclusion somewhat speculative, but that very absence suggests that foreign judgments offered as the basis of the *cosa juzgada* defense are normally presented directly to the lower courts of first instance rather than to the Supreme Court in a petition for *pareatis*.

## EVALUATION OF THE SALVADORAN REGIME

Although not so much information is available about Salvadoran practice as that of Costa Rica, there are a few features of it that are noteworthy.

The specific and general reservations from the Bustamante Code, along with the Costa Rican reservation, act to prevent that code from being the source of a uniform approach to judgment recognition throughout Central America. The Salvadoran attitude toward judgment recognition, however, seems to be much more liberal—less parochial—than that of Costa Rica.

The Salvadoran policy with respect to the "public order" exception does not seem to operate so actively to exclude foreign judgments as does that of Costa Rica (although generalization on this point is hazardous).

El Salvador, like Costa Rica, requires prior permission by the Supreme Court before foreign judgments may be enforced. Instances in which foreign judgments may be recognized without the *pareatis* are more numerous than they are in Costa Rica, however. El Salvador basically reserves the *pareatis* for cases in which some direct, positive effect must be given in El Salvador to a contested final judgment of the foreign court. Supreme Court involvement is not necessary in connection with interlocutory orders, rogatory letters, provisional embargos, and so forth, in contrast to the Costa Rican practice.

On the basis of available information, it appears that El Salvador's system of judgment recognition and enforcement would provide recognition without revision to most judgments that have been rendered in ordinary actions for money in its sister republics. A regime of automatic judgment enforcement within the region could be instituted with less displacement of established principles and practice than would be true of Costa Rica.

# 6 Guatemala

## THE BASIC LAW

Guatemala is one of the Bustamante Code signatories that endorsed that instrument without any reservation whatsoever.[1] Accordingly, the standards of that code are followed in all cases relating to the execution of judgments of other Central American countries. However, since the Bustamante Code leaves up to the local legislation the process by which effect is to be given to foreign judgments, it is necessary to consider the relevant provisions in the Code of Civil and Mercantile Procedure and in the Law of the Judicial Organism to get an understanding of the Guatemalan recognition process.

Chapter 2 of Title 4 of Book 3 of the Code of Civil and Mercantile Procedure (CCMP) deals with the execution of foreign judgments:

Article 334. Efficacy of the Foreign Judgment—In the absence of a treaty that expressly determines their efficacy, judgments of foreign courts will have in Guatemala the value that the legislation or the case decisions [*jurisprudencia*] of the country of origin attributes to judgments granted by Guatemalan courts.

Article 345. Conditions For Execution—Every foreign judgment will have force and can be executed in Guatemala if it satisfies the following conditions:

1. That it shall have been granted as a consequence of the exercise of a civil or mercantile personal action;

2. That it shall not have been granted by default nor against

a person reputed to be absent who is domiciled in Guatemala;

3. That the obligation for the performance of which the action shall have been brought is lawful in the Republic;

4. That it shall be executory [*ejecutoriada*] in accordance
   with the laws of the nation in which it shall have been
   granted; and

5. That it meets the requirements necessary to be considered
   authentic.

Article 346. Competent Judge and Requisites of the Title—
The judge that would be competent to entertain the action from
which it devolved is competent to execute a judgment granted
in another country.

After the order is presented to a competent court, translated
into Spanish, with signatures authenticated, the *pase legal*
granted, and execution requested, it will be proceeded upon as
though it were a judgment of the courts of the Republic.

*Pase legal* (or *pase de ley*, as it is more often called in the Guatemalan literature), which is referred to in the sentence last quoted, is
another name for the procedure called *exequatur* in Costa Rica and
*pareatis* in El Salvador. However, the present practice in Guatemala
does not require that there have been any prior Supreme Court ruling
before the judgment shall have effect in Guatemala. The promulgation
of the Law of the Judicial Organism (LJO) in 1968 abolished the *pase
de ley* procedure, and so the reference to that procedure in the CCMP
is obsolete.[2]

Guatemalan commentators have declared that "in no case does our
system submit the decision of a foreign jurisdiction to any revision
whatsoever."[3] This would seem to be inconsistent with the proposition
embodied in Article 345.3 of the CCMP, quoted above, to the effect
that the underlying obligation must be lawful in Guatemala. The reference to "lawful," however, is construed to mean "not contrary to public
order."[4] Accordingly, some partial revision—that contemplated by the
"public order" exception—is practiced in some cases.

## BASIC PROCEDURE FOR RECOGNITION AND ENFORCEMENT

The Guatemalan procedure dispenses with the necessity for a prior
Supreme Court ruling. In this respect it is closer to that of the United
States than are those of the other Central American countries. Once the
document containing the foreign judgment is duly authenticated and
"protocolized," it may be presented to the court or administrative agency
that is empowered to act upon it, as if it were a domestic judgment.
However, even if the only action that is being sought is enrollment of

the matter adjudged in the Civil Registry (in the case of divorce decrees) or in the Property Registry (in the case of succession decrees), it is still necessary to get a Guatemalan judgment recognizing the foreign judgment; at least this is the practice.

The procedures are contained in the LJO, Articles 190 through 195, which are applicable to any and all documents that originate in foreign countries, including judgments. The official authentication of the authority and signature of the court that issues the judgment is done by the Ministry of External Relations. Once the ministry has cleared it, it may be presented immediately to the court that is competent to act upon it, or it may first be presented to a notary to be "protocolized" before it is submitted to the court.[5] The advantage of protocolization is that the document will be readily available for other uses, if necessary. If it is not protocolized, it will remain in the file of the court and cannot be removed to be used for another purpose without a court order. All powers and all documents for which inscription in the Civil Registry or Property Registry is sought (which would include foreign divorce decrees or succession judgments, for example) *must* be protocolized, and the appropriate tax must be paid to the notary.[6] Within ten days after the protocolization, the notary must report the details of the instrument to the General Archives of Protocols, where an index of all such matters is kept.[7]

After this process has been completed, the instrument can be acted on as though it were a domestic judgment.

Because no Supreme Court action is required in the recognition process, cases involving recognition of foreign judgments are more difficult to find in Guatemala. The files are kept in the individual courts of first instance, and only a notation is recorded by the Archives of Protocols.

## KINDS OF JUDGMENTS ENTITLED TO RECOGNITION AND ENFORCEMENT

### PERSONAL JUDGMENTS

Article 435.1 of the Guatemalan CCMP limits enforceability to personal judgments in civil and mercantile actions. The Bustamante Code is not so restrictive.

It has been said that "it is absolutely clear that judgments and arbitral awards rendered as a consequence of a real action may not be executed in Guatemala. Only Guatemalan courts are competent to try such cases."[8] Nevertheless, foreign judgments declaring successions to Guatemalan property, real or personal, are entitled to recognition,[9] subject to certain formalities to provide notice to local claimants and to ensure the payment of local taxes. These are classed, not as "real actions," but as "universal actions." The Guatemalan "public order" exception will not be invoked, even if Guatemalan succession law would prescribe a different disposition of the property. If, however, the foreign judgment would transfer the Guatemalan property to someone who is positively forbidden to receive it under Guatemalan law (such as one who had murdered the decedent),[10] the Guatemalan "public order" would prevent recognition.[11]

## DEFAULT JUDGMENTS

Article 435.2 of the CCMP denies all effect to foreign default judgments, even to those that are not technically classified as default judgments, where a representative was appointed to represent an absent party, if the party was a Guatemala domiciliary. However, with respect to judgments of other Bustamante Code signatories, which includes all the Central American states, default judgments are entitled to recognition if the parties or their legal representatives were personally cited (not necessarily in the country in which the judgment was rendered).

The question has been raised previously whether service on a fictitiously appointed local representative would satisfy this requirement of the Bustamante Code. The view that has been taken in Guatemala is that it would not. Article 81 of the Bustamante Code declares that "local law" applies in determining when a declaration of absence is made and when it takes effect,[12] and that is interpreted as meaning that this question is to be resolved under Guatemalan law when the issue arises in Guatemalan courts and relates to a Guatemalan domiciliary. The Guatemalan definition of "absent" for this purpose is "a person who is found outside the Republic and who has or has had his domicile within it."[13] This is taken to mean that a declaration of absence issued by a foreign court (which would be necessary in order to permit the appointment of the local representative) with respect to a Guatemalan domiciliary would never be accepted in Guatemala, since such a person was not "found" outside the Republic. Accordingly, such a judgment would not be entitled to any recognition.[14] There is no resistance, on the other hand, to the recognition of foreign judgments that have been rendered under such a procedure against other than Guatemalan domiciliaries.

## ARBITRATION AWARDS

Arbitration awards are executable in the same way as judgments,[15] and this applies to foreign arbitration awards as well.[16] Certain subjects are not proper for arbitration, however, and as to such matters, neither foreign nor domestic awards are enforceable. Among the matters that cannot be the subject of arbitration (or of a settlement agreement in connection with judicial proceedings) are the validity of a marriage and the effectuation of a divorce.[17] Presumably, these exclusions would apply to such arbitration awards or settlement agreements if they had been rendered in Bustamante Code signatories. Money awards and settlement agreements, however, are enforced.

## REQUIREMENTS FOR RECOGNITION AND ENFORCEMENT

### COMPETENCY

The lack of competency on the part of the rendering court is a defense to recognition. Competency, in the case of judgments of Bustamante Code signatories, is judged by the standards of that code.[18] There is also a requirement that the judgment be "executory" in the state in which it was granted,[19] which means it must be valid (as well as final) under the rules of competency of the rendering country. The Guatemalan courts will not, however, review the question of the foreign court's competency under that court's internal rules. Muñoz, Camey, and Hall make that point forcefully: "Our courts must not engage in the ridiculous pretense of believing that they know, better than foreign judges, the internal norms to which they are subject concerning their competency. In any event, if the foreign judges were mistaken in this respect, the Guatemalan courts are not called upon to point out their errors."[20]

### NOTICE

Personal service on the defending party or its legal representative is a requirement of the Bustamante Code.[21] Whether the Guatemalan courts will look behind the recitals of due service in the judgment document itself is a question that cannot be answered with certainty, owing to the absence of decisions dealing with the point. It seems likely that they will do so, however, at least if the defending party is a Guatemalan domiciliary, although the problem would be approached, not as a question of jurisdiction, but as a matter of "public order."[22]

### FINALITY

#### FINAL JUDGMENTS

One of the requisites for recognition prescribed by the Bustamante Code, Article 423.4, is that the judgment be "executory" (*ejecutorio*) in the state in which it was granted. Article 345.4 of the Guatemalan CCMP contains the same requirement, although the Spanish word *ejecutoriado* is used. The difference is too subtle to be significant, and accordingly it is said that "no difference whatever exists between the two."[23] The term in the CCMP means simply that the judgment must not be subject to revocation or modification in the country of origin, which in turn means that there must be no possibility that it will be reviewed in the courts of that country.[24] The term is not limited to money judgments for the plaintiff. Defendants' judgments can be recognized for their *cosa juzgada* effects. Even judgments that order specific relief may be enforceable.[25]

PROVISIONAL ORDERS

The possibility exists in Guatemala, as it does in Costa Rica and El Salvador, for the enforcement of some provisional orders, including embargoes. That sort of recognition is considered judicial assistance, not judgment enforcement, and is given effect under the authority of Articles 388 through 393 of the Bustamante Code.[26]

RECIPROCITY

It will be noted that Article 344 adopts the principle of reciprocity as the basic condition for enforcement of foreign judgments, but this condition is not imposed on judgments stemming from countries that are signatories of the Bustamante Code.

PUBLIC ORDER

The "public order" exception is recognized by the Bustamante Code.[27]

Before 1968 the Fundamental Precepts contained in the Constituent Law of the Judiciary included the following:

> Article 17. The laws, documents and judgments of foreign countries, as well as any private agreements or provisions, will have no force or effect if they cause injury to national sovereignty, to public order, to our social institutions or to the provisions of Article 21 [which declares that only Guatemalan laws are applicable to properties located in Guatemala, whatever their nature, and even if the owners are foreigners].[28]

This precept meant that foreign judgments that applied other than Guatemalan law to properties—even personal properties—in Guatemala were not entitled to recognition. In 1968, however, the Constituent Law of the Judiciary was superseded by a new law (Law of the Judicial Organism). The new law retained, as Article 17, the provision that only Guatemalan law applies to properties in Guatemala (former Article 21), but it changed the limitation on the force or effect of foreign judgments to eliminate the reference to local properties. The law now reads: "Article 23. The laws, documents and judgments of foreign countries, like private agreements or transactions, will have no effect if they impair the national sovereignty of the Republic or the public order." With this change, the potential scope of the review to which a foreign judgment will be subjected under the "public order" exception has been considerably narrowed. I found only one case dealing with the "public order" concept in the context of judgment recognition. In that case,[29] a writ of *amparo* (an extraordinary proceeding to prevent or avoid some official act that allegedly infringes constitutional rights) was sought to set aside a decree effectuating a Costa Rican provisional embargo against Guatemalan bank accounts of a Guatemalan company. The embargo was issued in connection with an action that sought to impose civil liability on the company for negligent operation of a company truck by one of the company's employees while driving in Costa Rica. The company was named as a co-responsible party, but the correct company name was not used. No notice was served on the company in connection with the action. The Costa Rican court purported to act by virtue of the service on (and arrest of) the employee–truck driver. The company objected to the embargo, claiming not only that the Bustamante Code's requirements for execution of a judgment had not been complied with (owing to the lack of personal service) but also that, however viewed, to give effect in Guatemala to a foreign embargo over Guatemalan property of a Guatemalan company under the circumstances would violate the company's constitutional rights,[30] which were of "public order." Even if the Bustamante Code authorizes the enforcement in one country of provisional embargoes issued by another, it was argued, the Constitution takes precedence over it and must prevail.[31]

The Court of Appeals agreed with the company and granted the *amparo* to prevent the judge from carrying into effect the Costa Rican embargo. The Supreme Court reversed that ruling, however, on the ground that the company had delayed too long in seeking the *amparo*. The Supreme Court's decision did not touch upon the merits of the constitutional, "public order" ruling of the Court of Appeals. There is no reason to believe, however, that the decision of the Court of Appeals was not a correct application and interpretation of Guatemalan constitutional and "public order" standards. Thus it may be concluded, tentatively at least, that a foreign order affecting Guatemalan property of a Guatemalan will be denied recognition on "public order" grounds if the Guatemalan was not accorded the sort of notice that is considered to be essential under Guatemalan constitutional standards.

## RES JUDICATA (COSA JUZGADA)

Foreign judgments of other Central American states are entitled to recognition for their *cosa juzgada* effects. This, of course, is expressly provided by Article 431 of the Bustamante Code. The code, however, merely declares that the judgment will have the effects of *cosa juzgada*. The code does not define what those effects are, and it does not make clear whether the reference is to the effects that the judgment would have in the country of origin or the effects that a domestic judgment of the same type would have. I was not able to find any commentary on this issue, and so it apparently is not regarded as a significant problem in Latin America. It is probably assumed that the effects of *cosa juzgada* are the same throughout Latin America. This assumption is probably correct on the doctrinal level. Most discussions of *cosa juzgada* declare the necessity of the three identities: identity of persons, of things, and of cause.[32] But on the level of application there are differing views. Some countries endorse the view that only the juridical relation that is declared to exist has the *cosa juzgada* effect. Others take the position that any matter that is actively disputed may have *cosa juzgada* effect.[33] Views may differ on what may constitute the "identity of cause," since the term *causa* is as indefinite in Spanish as our English analog "cause of action." In view of the variations that exist from country to country in the application of the *cosa juzgada* concept, the question of which state's standards should apply deserves more attention than it has received.

In Guatemala the problem that is puzzling in other countries—whether exequatur is required when a foreign judgment is asserted as a defense or otherwise for its *cosa juzgada* effects—does not exist. Guatemala does not even require exequatur for the execution of a foreign money judgment. The *cosa juzgada* exception is a true defense in Guatemala. In some countries, a court may raise it on its own motion; but in Guatemala, it must be specifically asserted by a party, according to Guatemala's leading procedure scholar, Mario Aguirre Godoy.[34]

## EVALUATION OF THE GUATEMALAN REGIME

The Guatemalan approach to judgment recognition appears to be the most practical of those of all the Central American countries. Guatemalan commentators and legislators recently reexamined their rules and procedure to see what was really necessary and desirable in order to serve the interests affected. The requirement of prior Supreme Court review was found to have no sufficient justification and was therefore eliminated. The historical position denying efficacy to judgments affecting property in Guatemala has been relaxed and almost abandoned.

Guatemala does observe the discredited reciprocity principle with respect to judgments of non–Bustamante Code signatories, but that principle does not operate with regard to other Central American judgments.

Guatemala, in fact, follows the Bustamante Code without reservation. If the other states followed the Guatemalan example, a uniform scheme of judgment recognition would not be difficult to achieve.

Guatemala does, apparently, insist that standards of fairness which it considers to be fundamental must have been met by the foreign proceeding, at least if a Guatemalan domiciliary was a defending party; but this seems to be an entirely reasonable limitation. The states of the United States, bound by the Full Faith and Credit Clause, do review the judgments of sister states to ensure fundamental fairness. The interest in rendering individual justice is important enough to deserve primacy over interests in automatic recognition where fundamental fairness is involved.

# 7 *Honduras*

## THE BASIC LAW

Like Guatemala, Honduras signed and ratified the Bustamante Code without reservations.

The other Honduran legislation relating to recognition of foreign judgments is found in Articles 235 through 241 of the Code of Procedure:

Article 235. Judgments pronounced in a foreign country will have in Honduras the force accorded them by the relevant treaties; and for their execution the procedures established by Honduran law shall be followed insofar as that is not modified by the said treaties.

Article 236. If no treaties relative to this matter exist with the nation from which the judgments proceed, they will be given the same force that is given in that country to judgments pronounced in Honduras.

Article 237. If the resolution comes from a country in which compliance with judgments of Honduran courts is not granted, it will have no effect in Honduras.

Article 238. If the case should not be one of those spoken of in the three preceding articles, the orders will have force in Honduras if they meet the following conditions:

1. That the order shall have been issued as a result of the exercise of personal action.
2. That it shall not have been issued by default.
3. That the obligation with which the action sought compliance is lawful in Honduras.

4. That the document containing the order (*carta ejecu-toria*) meets the requirements necessary to be considered authentic in the nation in which it was issued, and those that Honduran laws require for it to be given credence in Honduras.

Article 239. The execution of judgments pronounced in foreign nations will be sought before the Supreme Court.

Article 240. Notice will be given to the party against whom the execution is sought, who will have a period of three days to make such presentation as he deems appropriate.

After the answer of that party or in his default, and after hearing from the Public Ministry, the Court will declare whether compliance with the resolution should be granted or not.

Article 241. If compliance is denied, the document will be returned to the one who presented it.

If it is granted, it will be promptly sent to the judge of the territory in which the party held liable in the judgment that is to be executed is domiciled, so that what was ordered in the judgment can be carried into effect, employing the measures of execution established in the preceding chapter [i.e., the same measures as for domestic judgments].

It will be noted that the statement (in Article 238) of the conditions that must be satisfied before a foreign judgment is entitled to recognition in Honduras is almost identical to the provisions of the Salvadoran code.[1] Both were copied from the Spanish Civil Judgment Law, Article 954.

## BASIC PROCEDURE FOR RECOGNITION AND ENFORCEMENT

A prior Supreme Court ruling is required before a foreign judgment will be given effect in Honduras. The term *pareatis* is used by the Supreme Court to apply to the proceeding, although litigants sometimes label their petitions "exequatur."

The provision of the jurisdictional statute (Law of Organization and Powers of Courts, Article 78.9) relating to this procedure does not in terms mention judgments as such. It confers power to "grant the permission [*pase*] to petitions and to declare the authenticity of judicial and notarial documents that come from abroad in order that they may have effect in the republic, and vice versa." The documents referred to would include rogatory letters and other requests for judicial assistance, as well as judgments. Notarial documents would include such matters as protocolized powers of attorney. The *pareatis* procedure is used to effectuate rogatory letters, for instance, seeking service in Honduras of process issued by a foreign court.[2] It is not required, however, to give effect to a power of attorney, according to a 1940 case.[3]

Article 238.4 refers to the requisites of authentication that are prescribed by Honduran law. These are found in Articles 325 and 326 of the Code of Procedure (CP), which contain the customary requirements of translation and verification of signatures by diplomatic or consular agents.

Although the Honduran law (Article 240, CP) only allows three days for the person who is opposing *pareatis* to respond, in contrast to the twenty days prescribed by the Bustamante Code (Article 426), the latter period is allowed in connection with judgments of Bustamante Code signatories.

It will be noted that Honduras requires notification of the Public Ministry (the *fiscal*, i.e., the attorney general) in connection with every *pareatis*. He may oppose recognition, or he may expressly acquiesce in recognition, or he may simply fail to respond (which is the equivalent of acquiescence). However, his presentation is merely advisory. The court can either grant *pareatis* over the *fiscal's* opposition or deny it in spite of his acquiescence.

Since Honduras requires *pareatis* to declare the authenticity of all judicial and notarial documents, presumably that procedure must be followed where the foreign judgment is sought to be established for its *cosa juzgada* effects. I was not able to find any case or commentary on the point, however.

## KINDS OF JUDGMENTS ENTITLED TO RECOGNITION

### PERSONAL JUDGMENTS

The requirement to Article 238.1—that the judgment be the result of a personal action—does not prevent recognition in Honduras of foreign decrees that declare the succession to the estates of decedents who left property—even real property—in Honduras. Such actions are characterized as "personal actions," at least if all potential heirs or devisees were parties.[4] Recognition may, however, be denied to such judgments on the ground that the court lacked "competence" (or on "public order" grounds) if the decedent was a Honduran domiciliary or national.[5] It may also be denied on reciprocity grounds.[6]

### DEFAULT JUDGMENTS

The condition of Article 238.2 of the CP—that the judgment not be a default judgment—does not apply to judgments of Bustamante Code signatories. It does not apply at all, in fact, if it is the defaulting defendant in the foreign action who seeks recognition for the judgment in Honduras.[7]

With respect to judgments of Bustamante Code countries, there is no prohibition against enforcing default judgments as such, but Article 423.2 of that code requires that the parties, or their legal representatives, have been personally cited. This condition will not be deemed to have been satisfied by the expedient of appointing a fictitious local representative with no actual notice to the absent party or to an actual representative if the absent party was a Honduran.[8]

### ARBITRATION AWARDS

Arbitration awards that have been granted in other Bustamante Code signatory countries are enforceable in Honduras by virtue of Article 432 of the Bustamante Code. That provision excepts matters that are not deemed to be proper subjects of "compromise agreements" (*compromisos*) in the country of execution. *Compromiso* is similar to arbitration, in that it involves the submission of a disputed issue to a third party for resolution. In some countries, no distinction is made between *compromiso* and arbitration. Honduras, however, deals separately with arbitration awards and *compromisos*. Arbitration is valid for any question that does not require the intervention of the Ministerio Fiscal—according to Article 847 of the Code of Procedure. This means that almost any private dispute can be submitted to arbitration. *Compromisos*, on the other hand, are regulated by Articles 2019 and 2020 of the Civil Code. Those articles, in turn, declare that the rules that regulate settlement agreements (*transacciónes*) also comply to *compromisos*. The provisions of the Civil Code that deal with settlement agreements contain several specific references to subjects that cannot be dealt with in that fashion, including matters of civil status and future-support obligations. Future-support agreements can be valid if judicially approved.[9] These limitations prescribed for *compromisos* will presumably be applied to foreign arbitration awards, as suggested by the wording of Article 432 of the Bustamante Code. If this is true, some foreign arbitration awards that would be valid and enforceable if they had been rendered in Honduras will nevertheless not be entitled to enforcement. I was not able to find any cases or commentaries dealing with this anomalous situation, however.

## REQUIREMENTS FOR RECOGNITION AND ENFORCEMENT

### COMPETENCY

Lack of competence of the rendering court is, of course, ground for denying recognition to a foreign judgment. Article 432.1 of the Bustamante Code declares that requirement. Presumably, the Honduran court will review the facts on which the foreign court's competency depends. Whether it will do so, however, in the face of a declaration of competency in the judgment and whether Honduran competency standards will have any relevance are questions that cannot be answered with certainty.

NOTICE

Notice requirements that are necessary in order to make the foreign judgment enforceable in the state of rendition must have been complied with if the judgment is to be recognized in Honduras. Even if the requirements of the rendering state have been satisfied, the Honduran court will not recognize a judgment that has been obtained by appointing a fictitious representative unless the party or its *real* representative received some form of actual notice.[10]

FINALITY

To be entitled to recognition, a judgment must have achieved the degree of finality that is necessary in order for it to be said to be "in force" (*ejecutoria*). Whether temporary, provisional, or interlocutory orders—such as the provisional embargoes that Costa Rica, El Salvador, and Guatemala do enforce—are so entitled is not clear. If these are enforceable in Honduras, it would surely be regarded (as it is in the other countries) as an instance of assistance to a foreign court rather than as a judgment enforcement. The *pareatis* procedure would nevertheless have to be followed, however, since it would involve giving effect to a foreign judicial document.

Modifiable decrees are enforceable. In one case the court granted effect in Honduras to a Florida divorce, which included an award for future child-support payments of $50 per month. The Honduran court reserved the right to modify the support in the future.[11]

RECIPROCITY

Articles 236 and 237 of the Code of Procedure endorse the principle of reciprocity as a condition to the recognition and enforcement of foreign judgments in Honduras. If there is a treaty, however, that calls for the recognition of judgments without regard to reciprocity, as the Bustamante Code does, it would seem, consistently with Articles 235 and 236 of the CP, that the reciprocity requirement would be dispensed with in connection with judgments from signatory nations. This conclusion is accurate, however, only with respect to judgments of countries that ratified the Bustamante Code without reservation. The reciprocity principle that is embodied in Article 237 of the CP apparently does apply to judgments of countries that endorsed the Bustamante Code with reservations, if the judgment is of a type that is affected by the reservation. It is apparently assumed that no treaty exists with respect to a matter that one of the other signatory countries refused to accede to. In this respect the Honduran practice appears to differ significantly from that of Guatemala, which likewise imposes a reciprocity requirement generally, but does not apply it to judgments of Bustamante Code signatories, even those that have expressed reservations from the code.

The reciprocity rule has been invoked frequently to deny recognition to Salvadoran succession judgments. El Salvador, it will be recalled, expressed a reservation with respect to Articles 327, 328, and 329 of the Bustamante Code, which recognized as competent the court at the decedent's or bankrupt's domicile in inheritance and bankruptcy matters, respectively.[12] The reservation was amplified by the Salvadoran delegation's declaration that El Salvador could not accept the jurisdiction of foreign courts over Salvadoran immovable property. The reservation, in practice, is not invoked by the Salvadoran court when a foreign court at the decedent's domicile grants a decree that affects *movable* property in El Salvador.[13] The Honduran Supreme Court, however, interprets the Salvadoran reservation *both* as refusing to recognize foreign inheritance judgments that affect Salvadoran immovable property and as refusing to recognize the court of the decedent's domicile as a competent court, even with respect to succession to movable property. Accordingly, the Honduran court refuses to give effect, not just to Salvadoran succession judgments that affect Honduran land, but to any Salvadoran inheritance decrees that relate to the estates of Salvadoran domiciliaries—even if the estate includes no Honduran land.[14] In one case the court persisted in the position in the face of the argument, vehemently urged by the petitioner, that the result left the matter in an absurd state. An original succession action could not be brought in Honduras, since the decedent was a Salvadoran domiciliary. The Salvadoran judgment, on the other hand, could not be enforced because of the reciprocity rule.

The Honduran court's interpretation of the scope of the Salvadoran reservation is clearly inaccurate, but in the absence of published and circulated judicial decisions within the region, such mistakes are probably inevitable. However, the retaliatory tenor of the opinions of the Honduran court probably reflect to some extent the continuing hostility that flares up into open warfare from time to time between the governments of Honduras and El Salvador. The court seems to be aware that these *pareatis* decisions do have some questionable implications. I sought leave, through a formal petition to the Supreme Court of Honduras, to photocopy at my expense one of the opinions in which the court had used this reciprocity argument to deny *pareatis* to a Salvadoran succession decree. The petition was denied without any explanation being given. In no other Central American country did the court or its functionaries indicate any reluctance whatever about allowing their decisions to be photocopied.

## PUBLIC ORDER

I was not able to find any cases dealing with the public-order exception. In the absence of some contrary indication, it is assumed that Honduras will invoke that doctrine in any situation in which the matter that has been adjudicated in the foreign action is a subject that is characterized as one of "international public order" by the Bustamante Code, and in which Honduran law would not permit recovery in such an action.

## RES JUDICATA (COSA JUZGADA)

Presumably the *cosa juzgada* effect of foreign judgments—at least those of other signatory countries—is controlled by Articles 431 and 396 of the Bustamante Code.[15] The same problem that was discussed in connection with other countries is apparent, however—namely, whether the scope of that effect is determined by Honduran law or by that of the rendering country.

Honduran legislation deals with the *cosa juzgada* problem in the following provisions of the Civil Code, in a section titled "Of Presumptions":

Article 1536. Against the presumption that the *cosa juzgada* is true, the only effective [rebuttal] is a judgment pronounced in an action of revision.

Article 1537. For the presumption of *cosa juzgada* to take effect in another action, it is necessary that the most perfect identity exists as to the things, the causes, the persons of the litigants and the capacity in which they were acting between the case resolved by the judgment and that in which it is invoked.

In matters relating to the civil status of persons and to the validity or nullity of testamentary dispositions, the presumption of *cosa juzgada* is effective against third parties, even though they were not litigated [by them].

It is understood that there is always identity of persons when the litigants of the second action are the assignees or successors of the contending parties in the earlier one, or are connected with them in a several liability relationship, or by the bonds that establish the indivisibility of performance among those that have the right to demand performance.

In those passages, borrowed almost verbatim from the Civil Code of Spain,[16] the Honduran code expressly declares the binding effect of *cosa juzgada* to extend to nonparties in some circumstances. The laws of the other Central American countries, except Nicaragua, do not, in terms at least, extend the effects so broadly. The question as to which state's *cosa juzgada* rules will apply to a foreign judgment is a real one, then, and one concerning which I was not able to find any case or commentary. Any plan for uniform rules dealing with the recognition and enforcement of judgments within the region should contain specific provisions to resolve this question.

## EVALUATION OF THE HONDURAN REGIME

Honduras's acceptance of the Bustamante Code without reservation and its willingness to apply its standards in preference to those that are prescribed by Honduran law suggest an attitude that would presumably be congenial to a region-wide system of judgment recognition and enforcement. However, other features of the Honduran system indicate that it is not really well suited for intraregional judgment recognition.

Like Costa Rica and El Salvador, Honduras requires that the highest court in the land participate in even the simplest kinds of cases. Moreover, unlike Costa Rica and El Salvador, the participation of the attorney general (*fiscal*) is solicited and expected in each case. This feature of the Honduran practice (which is borrowed from the Spanish) entails trouble and expense to the litigant and to the bureaucracy without having any apparent corresponding benefit. Although the Bustamante Code contains a similar provision for notification of the *fiscal*, it can hardly be assumed that it was intended to be mandatory on all signatories. This, with the requirement of Supreme Court participation, tends to foster a climate that is inhibiting to the free mobility of judgments by creating a sort of implicit presumption against recognition and enforcement.

Moreover, Honduras's insistence on applying its reciprocity standard to judgments of some other signatories of the code raises a problem that should be faced and expressly treated in any region-wide arrangement.

Finally, the scope of the *cosa juzgada* effects of judgments that are prescribed by the Honduran code differs from that which is recognized in other countries of the region. This fact emphasizes the need for a principle to determine whether the *cosa juzgada* standards of the rendering nation or the recognizing nation are to be applied to judgments by sister countries within the region.

# 8  *Nicaragua*

## THE BASIC LAW

In addition to the Bustamante Code, which Nicaragua's delegation signed with a curious reservation,[1] Nicaragua adopted a scheme of judgment recognition that is embodied in an instrument called the Central American Procedure Convention of 1892. The relevant provisions of that convention which are in force in Nicaragua as part of the Code of Civil Procedure are:

> Article 9. All persons have free access to the Courts in order to effectuate and defend their rights.
>
> Article 10. No bond or security will be required from Central Americans and juridical persons of other Central American states to assert their right, except in cases in which they would be required for Nicaraguans.
>
> Article 11. Actions and their incidents carried out in conformity with the laws of other Central American states will have effect in Nicaragua in the cases determined by the law.
>
> Article 12. Nicaragua recognizes that the laws of the Central American state in which a court has its seat determine the admission, weight and effects of evidence.
>
> Article 13. Testimony issued by a Notary Public under his signature and seal, duly authenticated and with the legal formalities, will have full credit in Nicaragua respecting the acts that have been performed before him.

Article 14. One who bases his right on foreign laws must prove their existence in authentic form.

Article 15. The courts of the State have the duty to carry out letters requisitorial [*exhortos*] and letters rogatory [*suplicatorios*] in authentic form addressed to them by the other Central American states, whether to receive declarations, serve notices, or perform any other proceedings, so long as the local laws are not thereby violated.

Article 16. The judgments, orders, or arbitration decisions of any of the states of Central America will have the same force in Nicaragua as in the state of their origin, if they meet the following requisites:

1. That they were issued by a competent court.
2. That they have the character of established decisions [*ejecutoriados*] in the place from which they proceed.
3. That the losing party was duly served and represented or was declared in default in accordance with the laws of the place of the action.
4. That they are not contrary to the public order or the laws of the State of Nicaragua.
5. That a prior declaration by the Supreme Court of the State of Nicaragua concerning the above points shall be issued.
6. That its authenticity and efficacy is clearly shown through a *Visto Bueno* or other sign of approval emanating from an ordinary superior court of the country where the decision has been issued.

Article 17. The documents that must accompany the judgment, order or decision in order for it to be executed are the following:

1. A complete copy of the resolution.
2. A copy of the passages necessary to show that the party has been heard or declared in default, as the case may be.
3. A copy of the order in which the executory character was declared and of the laws on which the resolution is based.

Article 18. The execution of the judgments issued in the other states of Central America, and the ensuing procedure, will be governed by the laws of Nicaragua.

Article 19. Acts of voluntary jurisdiction carried out in one state of Central America will have the same value in Nicaragua that they would have if they had been carried out in its own territory when they meet the requirements established in Articles 16, 17 and 18 insofar as they may be applicable.

Article 20. In Nicaragua resolutions issued by other states of Central America will be carried out, following the text of the request; but the judges and courts will decide the means appropriate for doing that, such as the designation of experts, appraisers, receivers or other analogous measures.

This convention, which only Nicaragua adopted, antedated the Bustamante Code. It appears to be based on the Montevideo Treaty on International Procedural Law of 1889. Nicaragua did not repeal it when the Bustamante Code was ratified in 1930, and so both sets of rules are applicable to the recognition of judgments of other Central American states. There is very little difference in the substantive standards of the two sets of rules, however; so the principal significance of the retention of earlier provisions relating to Central American judgments lies in the slightly different procedure that they prescribe.

The Nicaraguan Code of Civil Procedure contains the other principal body of legislation relating to judgment recognition, and the procedural rules are contained in its provisions.

Article 542. Firm judgments pronounced in foreign countries will have in Nicaragua the force accorded them by the relevant treaties; and for their execution the procedures established by Nicaraguan law shall be followed insofar as that is not modified by the said treaties.

If there be no special treaties with the nation in which they were pronounced, they will have the same force that is given in that country to judgments pronounced in Nicaragua.

Article 543. If the resolution comes from a nation in which by case decisions [jurisprudencia] compliance with judgments of Nicaraguan courts is not granted, it will have no effect in Nicaragua.

Article 544. If the case should not be one of those spoken of in the preceding two articles, the orders will have force in Nicaragua if they meet the following conditions:

1. That the order has been given as a result of a personal action;
2. That the obligation with which the action sought compliance is lawful in Nicaragua;
3. That the document containing the order [carta ejecutoria] meets the requirements necessary to be considered authentic in the nation in which it was issued, and those that Nicaraguan law requires in order that it may be credited in Nicaragua;
4. That the litigation proceeded with the participation of the defendant, unless it is clear that he has been declared in default for not having appeared after having been duly summoned;
5. That the judgment is not contrary to the public order;

6. That it is executory [*ejecutoria*] in the country of its origin.

These rules, and those of the preceding articles, are applicable to resolutions issued by arbitration judges. In this case their authenticity and efficacy shall be clearly shown by means of a *Visto Bueno* or other sign of approval issued by an ordinary superior court of the country where the award was granted.

Article 545. The execution of judgments pronounced in foreign nations will be sought before the Supreme Court of Justice.

An exception is made for the case in which, according to treaties, cognizance is granted to other courts.

Article 546. After the translation of the order, made in accordance with the law, and after giving the party against whom it is directed and the representative of the Public Ministry an opportunity to be heard for a period of three days, the Court will declare if compliance should or should not be granted to said order.

Article 547. In order to summon the party who should be heard according to the previous article, warrant will be sent to the judge in whose territory he is domiciled. The term set for appearance will be three days, plus one day for each thirty kilometers of distance. After that term, the Court will proceed with the case even though the one summoned shall not have appeared.

Article 548. In acts of voluntary jurisdiction, the Court will resolve the matter with only hearing the representative of the Public Ministry or in his absence, the *Sindico Municipal*.[2]

Article 549. If exequatur is sought for an order of embargo, it will not be necessary to provide the hearing referred to in Article 546, and it will be granted if it appears that the party against whom it is levied was notified of the order directing the *exhorto* [request for the embargo] to be sent in sufficient time to have been able to have recourse here to protect his rights. If it appears from the *exhorto* or if the interested party demonstrates that any of the conditions specified in Article 544 exist, no effect shall be given to it. The execution of a judgment of sale [*sentencia de remate*], or its equivalent, will follow the rule for judgments generally.

Article 550. Requests [*requisitorias*] from foreign courts relating to the service of process, interrogatories, the taking of evidence, or to other judicial proceedings, will be carried out, after the Supreme Court has granted exequatur, in the same way that they would have been if they had proceeded from a court in the Republic.

Article 551. If the debtor has no domicile in the Republic, the creditor can seek from the judge he chooses, an attachment [*embargo provisional*] of the debtor's goods, after giving a bond for costs, and damages, to assure the execution of the judgment [*sentencia*] once he obtains the exequatur.

Article 552. If compliance is denied, the order [*ejecutoria*] will be returned to the one who presented it. If compliance is granted, warrant will be sent to the judge of the place in which the losing party is domiciled, so that what is ordered in it can be given effect, employing the measures for execution established in the previous Title. If the debtor has no domicile in the Republic, the judge that the creditor chooses will be competent.

## BASIC PROCEDURE FOR RECOGNITION AND ENFORCEMENT

The code requires the issuance of an exequatur by the Supreme Court before foreign judgments may be executed.[3]

The procedure for execution is essentially the same as that used in Costa Rica. The time period for the opposing party's response that is prescribed in Articles 546 and 547 does not apply to judgments from Bustamante Code countries: The longer period prescribed by that code[4] is granted to the opposing party.

Unlike Costa Rica, however, Nicaragua does require participation of the *fiscal* in the exequatur process generally. This requirement is not applicable to judgments of other Central American countries, however.

The Nicaraguan Code expressly authorizes enforcement of provisional embargoes, following the same procedure as that discussed in connection with Costa Rica. Other matters of judicial assistance, such as serving foreign process, taking proof in a foreign action, and so forth, are also effectuated through the exequatur procedure.

Other orders that are not judgments, however—or even judgments that are based on voluntary rather than contentious jurisdiction—need not be presented through the exequatur procedure in order to be given effect in Nicaragua, in spite of the apparent requirement of Articles 19 and 548 of the CCP. Thus, no exequatur is required to give effect in Nicaragua to foreign orders naming an administrator of an estate,[5] or a guardian,[6] or declaring heirs,[7] or changing a party's name.[8] These are all classed as "voluntary actions" in Nicaragua. A provision of the Code of Civil Procedure declares that voluntary actions do not produce judgments that have *cosa juzgada* effects. This apparently does not mean that such judgments as those referred to above are entitled to *no* effect,[9] however.

An order declaring insolvency, on the other hand, even if it is not a final judgment, must be presented for exequatur before it will be recognized in Nicaragua.[10]

## KINDS OF JUDGMENTS ENTITLED TO RECOGNITION AND ENFORCEMENT

### PERSONAL ACTIONS

Article 544.1 of the Nicaraguan CCP limits enforcement to judgments and orders issued in personal actions. Neither the Central American Procedure Convention nor the Bustamante Code contains that restriction, however. Thus, various kinds of decrees that are not, strictly speaking, products of personal actions are given recognition when they emanate from other Central American countries. Declarations of heirship and declarations of insolvency are examples. Declarations of heirship are characterized as judgments based on "voluntary jurisdiction" and are expressly entitled to recognition, even though not all those persons who were potentially affected were participants in the foreign action.[11]

### JUDGMENTS OF SALE (SENTENCIAS DE REMATE)

Article 549 of the Nicaraguan Code permits execution of foreign "judgments of sale." The Costa Rican Code, contains a similar provision.[12] The basic features of the "judgment of sale" were sketched in chapter 4.

### DEFAULT JUDGMENTS

Default judgments are entitled to recognition on the same basis as other judgments if the defendant has been duly notified and given an opportunity to defend. Publication notice[13] is not due notice, however, nor is that provided by the procedure of appointing a fictitious local representative, except where the defendant's whereabouts are really unknown.[14] If the defaulting party who was not duly notified is the petitioner in the Nicaraguan exequatur proceeding,[15] however, or if he appears in the exequatur proceeding and accedes to its issuance,[16] the judgment will be accorded recognition.

### ARBITRATION AWARDS

Foreign arbitration awards are entitled to recognition under Articles 16 and 544 of the Nicaraguan CCP and under Article 432 of the Bustamante Code in those cases which, under Nicaraguan law, are suitable for arbitration.[17] It is arguable that arbitration awards of other Central American countries are entitled to recognition even if they do not concern matters that are appropriate for arbitration under Nicaraguan law. The provisions relating to the procedures and subjects of arbitration are found in Book 3 of the Code of Civil Procedure, Articles 958 through

990. One article in that section, however, Article 985, declares that the arbitration decisions of the other states of Central America are subject to the dispositions in Book 1. The only provision in Book 1 that is relevant is that quoted above (Article 16 of the CCP), which contains no restriction as to the subject matter of arbitration. It declares that the awards "will have the same force in Nicaragua as in the state of origin," which could mean that some matters that could not be arbitrated in Nicaragua may nevertheless be resolved in an arbitration award of another Central American country and be enforceable in Nicaragua. The Nicaraguan Court might invoke the "public order" exception (Article 16.4) to refuse enforcement in such a case, but otherwise the award would apparently be enforceable. I was not able to find any case or commentary to clarify this point.

## REQUIREMENTS FOR RECOGNITION AND ENFORCEMENT

### COMPETENCY

The competency of the rendering court is a requirement. If that factor is not shown, the proffered judgment will be denied recognition.[18]

In the case of judgments of other Bustamante Code countries, the jurisdictional standards of that code are used in order to determine the competence of the rendering court.[19] In the case of other countries, however, Nicaraguan standards will be employed—at least if the parties are Nicaraguans—and the court will make an independent determination of the jurisdictional facts.[20]

The competency requirement will not be a barrier to recognition, however, if the defending party is the one seeking exequatur in Nicaragua—at least if the question is one of competency *ratione loci*.[21]

### NOTICE

Notice, of course, is required by the Bustamante Code (Article 423.2), as well as by the Nicaraguan CCP (Article 544.4). On the other hand, the provision of Article 16.3, which specifically relates to judgments of other Central American countries, in terms seems to permit the enforcement of some judgments in which the defendant was not notified. It requires that the losing party must have been served or represented *or* "declared in default in accordance with the laws of the place of the action." If the laws of that place permit a default judgment on the basis of publication service, that would seem to satisfy Article 16.3.

The court has never knowingly given effect to a judgment that was entered without notice, however, except where the defendant who should have received the notice was the one who was seeking the exequatur.[22] The standards of the Bustamante Code are overlaid on the standards of Article 16, and the court will look *both* at the adequacy of service under the rendering court's procedure and at the personal notice or representation that is required by the Bustamante Code. Moreover, it will independently examine the facts relating to the process. When the judgment that is sought to be enforced against a Nicaraguan indicates that the defendant was "represented" in the action by a guardian ad litem who was appointed by the court because of the defendant's absence and unknown whereabouts, the court may deny exequatur if it appears that the plaintiff in fact knew where the defendant was and made no attempt to serve him through rogatory process.[23] In fact, unless the record shows clearly enough just what the procedure of notification was and that it was adequate to meet the applicable standards, exequatur will be denied.[24] Due notice is a matter of "public order" in Nicaragua,[25] and so, even if all the standards of the rendering court and of the Bustamante Code are satisfied, a judgment may still be denied recognition if basic Nicaraguan principles are not complied with.

FINALITY

Reference has been made in other connections to the Bustamante Code's requirement that the judgment be "executory."[26] That provision applies to judgments of other signatory countries in Nicaragua, of course. With respect to other foreign judgments, the Nicaraguan CCP appears, in Article 542, to grant enforcement only to "firm judgments" (*sentencias firmes*). This would seem to include only *judgments*, as opposed to interlocutory orders, and only those judgments that are firm in the sense that they are not subject to potential reversal on appeal.

The Nicaraguan CCP does, however, expressly authorize enforcement of some orders that would have to be characterized as something less than "firm." Article 549 permits the enforcement of embargoes. This does not expressly apply to *provisional* embargoes (i.e., attachments). Since Article 549 also makes reference to judgments of sale, conceivably it might apply only to those embargoes that are incident to the execution of a judgment. However, the order to which Article 549 refers is called an *exhorto,* a term that connotes an interlocutory order. The almost identical provision in the Costa Rican Code has been interpreted as covering provisional embargoes.[27] In any event, various other orders of a nonfirm nature are recognized, according to Article 550.

With respect to other Central American countries, Articles 15 and 20 of the Nicaraguan Code of Civil Procedure seem to authorize virtually every possible form of judicial assistance, and so all kinds of interlocutory orders and resolutions emanating from the courts of those countries will be entitled to recognition in Nicaragua.

RECIPROCITY

Reciprocity is not a requirement for judgment recognition or enforcement under the Bustamante Code, nor is it a feature of Nicaragua's special law relating to the judgments of other Central American states. Reciprocity is a requirement for recognition of the judgments of other countries, however, and Article 543 makes it clear that more than the text of a foreign code is relevant to this question. Reciprocity is to be judged by case decisions (*jurisprudencia*). This requirement is sensible in order to obviate the sort of misinterpretation of the foreign practice that is evidenced in Honduras with respect to Salvadoran succession judgments.[28] Earlier decisions treated the reciprocity principle as a matter of defense: that is, the one who opposed exequatur had the burden of proving the lack of reciprocity under the decisions of the courts of the rendering state.[29] The court has vacillated on this interpretation, however. In one case the court denied exequatur to a French money judgment because the petitioner failed to produce proof that the French courts would enforce a Nicaraguan judgment rendered under reciprocal circumstances.[30] The court changed its position on the burden-of-proof question, however, in a later case involving recognition of a California divorce and custody decree, noting that "*jurisprudencia* is not binding."[31]

PUBLIC ORDER

The "public order" exception is recognized in all three of the relevant bodies of rules.[32] The meaning of the reference is somewhat confused, however, by the other terms to which it is juxtaposed in each location. In the Bustamante Code, the exception covers matters of "public order or public law." In Article 16 of the CCP the exception extends to matters "contrary to the public order or the laws of the State of Nicaragua," which suggests a broader scope than that of the Bustamante Code provision. Article 544 of the CCP declares *both* that the underlying "obligation . . . is lawful in Nicaragua" (544.2) and that the judgment not be "contrary to the public order" (544.5).

The cases do not do much to resolve the uncertainties that these variant phrasings raise about the "public order" exception in Nicaragua.

The usage of the "public order" concept in the competency and notice settings has been discussed. The only case that I found which employs the concept in connection with the cause underlying the judgment, as opposed to the procedure by which it was obtained, dealt with causes for divorce, the allocation of child custody, and the obligation to pay for child support. These matters were said to be of "public order," and a California judgment that disposed of the questions in a fashion that was contrary to Nicaraguan law was held not to be entitled to exequatur.[33]

## RES JUDICATA (COSA JUZGADA)

Article 431 of the Bustamante Code declares that foreign judgments will produce *cosa juzgada* effects, without further defining what those effects are. Article 396 of that code recognizes *cosa juzgada* as an exception (defense) that can be invoked only if the parties or their representatives participated in the former action and if no question of competence was raised. *Cosa juzgada* may have other effects as well, but these are apparently left up to the local law either of the rendering or of the recognizing state, without specifying which.

If Nicaragua is one of the states, it is important to know which state's standards of *cosa juzgada* apply, because Nicaragua's Code of Civil Procedure contains some provisions relative to this matter that are unique in Central America.[34] The philosophy behind these provisions seems to be quite different from that of the traditional Latin American approach to *cosa juzgada*. Nowhere in them is there any mention of the "three identities" that other legislations and commentators insist are absolutely indispensable to *cosa juzgada*.[35] *Cosa juzgada* effects of criminal judgments may be asserted in civil actions in some cases, so the identity of cause and object requirements are not imposed. Moreover, some non-parties may claim the benefit of *cosa juzgada* for defensive purposes.[36] *Cosa juzgada* is said to be a ground for action as well as exception, although this apparently is nothing more than application of the term to the ordinary enforcement procedure that must be followed if a judgment is not complied with by the losing party. In allowing *cosa juzgada* effects of criminal judgments to be recognized in civil actions in certain circumstances, it appears to give conclusive effects to *facts*, not just to resolutions or cause of action.[37] In short, this Nicaraguan version of *cosa juzgada* seems to approximate much more closely than that of the other Central American countries the scope of res judicata in Anglo-American jurisprudence.

However, Articles 2358 through 2361 of the Civil Code contain provisions that are almost identical to those of the Costa Rican Civil Code,[38] declaring the traditional doctrine of *cosa juzgada*. This apparent contradiction leaves considerable doubt about the true effect of *cosa juzgada* in Nicaragua. The Supreme Court has tried to apply the standards of both codes. It has declared that the "three identities" (parties, cause, and object) really are requisites of *cosa juzgada*. The provisions of the Code of Civil Procedure that do not seem to be consistent with those requirements are viewed as modifiers or interpretations of those hallowed concepts,[39] rather than as independent principles that supersede the traditional ones where they conflict.

Nothing definite could be found that would help resolve the question of whether Nicaragua will apply its own rules or those of the rendering state to determine the *cosa juzgada* effects of a foreign judgment.

With respect to judgments of other Central American countries, Article 16 of the CCP says that they will have the same force in Nicaragua as in the state of origin. This would seem to apply to *cosa juzgada* effects as well as to effects relating to enforcement, but I was not able to find any cases that would affirm this conclusion.

It is not even clear that exequatur is required if a foreign judgment is to be recognized for its *cosa juzgada* effects. The court has dispensed with exequatur for judgments resulting from voluntary actions,[40] but those have no *cosa juzgada* effect anyway under Nicaraguan law.[41]

Exequatur probably would not be demanded before a judgment could be introduced as rebuttable evidence, however, if the analogy of the voluntary jurisdiction cases is sound.

## EVALUATION OF THE NICARAGUAN REGIME

Nicaragua's implementation of the 1892 Central American Procedural Convention is an important precedent. It demonstrates that at least one country appreciated the significance of a judgment-recognition plan that focused especially on the Central American region. Moreover, it was apparently adopted as an expression of Nicaragua's *own* policy interests, although, of course, the framers of the convention hoped that it would be adopted throughout Central America. The requisites for recognition that were prescribed by the convention are about the same as those of the Bustamante Code. Participation of the Supreme Court is necessary, but participation by the *fiscal* or other public minister is not required in the case of exequatur proceedings that relate to judgments of Central American countries.

The convention does specify that the "force" that a judgment of a sister Central American state is to have in Nicaragua is the same that it has in the state of origin. This is a potentially significant provision. If the regime of judgment recognition in Central America is to be modified to approximate more closely that of Full Faith and Credit in the United States or that of the European Common Market Convention, this point should be a feature of the plan.

The elimination of the reciprocity principle from the process of recognition of judgments from other Central American countries is a beneficial feature of the Nicaraguan scheme.

To anyone who has been schooled in the Anglo-American res judicata doctrine, the *cosa juzgada* provisions of the Nicaraguan Code of Civil Procedure seem to be much more sensible than the traditional ones that are embodied in the Civil Code. Since the provisions of the Civil Code are more like those of most of the other Central American countries, however, elimination of them probably would disserve the interest of uniformity within the region unless a new uniform approach were to be adopted. The provisions of the Nicaraguan Code of Civil Procedure could serve as a model for such a uniform region-wide approach.

Finally, the publication of all rulings that relate to foreign judgment recognition is a beneficial feature of Nicaragua's practice that should probably be included in any region-wide scheme of judgment recognition.

# 9 _Panama_

Central Americans have not considered Panama to be part of Central America. It was not one of the original United Provinces of Central America, and it has not been a participant in the many reunification schemes. Indeed, it was part of Colombia until 1904. The Charter of the Organization of Central American States (ODECA), however, expressly provides that Panama may join the organization whenever it chooses to do so and that it may join any of the organization's subsidiary agencies even if it does not join the ODECA itself.[1] Presumably, this would permit Panama to join, for instance, the Central American Court of Justice, if it saw fit to do so, even if it was not a regular member of ODECA.[2] Any study of the process of Central American unification, then, should include Panama.

## THE BASIC LAW

Panama ratified the Bustamante Code without reservation. Accordingly, that code provides the basic law that is relevant to the execution, in Panama, of judgments emanating from other signatory nations. The law that is otherwise applicable is found in Articles 581 through 590 of the Judicial Code:

> Article 581. Judgments rendered in foreign countries will have in the Republic of Panama such force as the relevant treaties establish.

> Article 582. If there should be no special treaty with the nation

in which the judgment was rendered, it will have the same force as is given in that country to judgments rendered in Panama.

Article 583. If the judgment was rendered in a country wherein, by judicial decision, enforcement is not granted to judgments of Panamanian courts, it will have no force in Panama.

Article 584. Unless special treaties provide otherwise, no judgment rendered outside the jurisdiction of the Republic of Panama will be executed in it, if the following requisites are not met:

1. That the judgment was rendered as a result of a personal action, except as specifically provided in the law relating to succession actions started in foreign countries;
2. That the judgment was not granted for default, meaning by that, for purposes of this article, the situation in which the defendant was not personally notified of the demand within the jurisdiction of the court in which the action was brought, unless it is the defaulting defendant himself who is seeking the execution of it;
3. That the obligation underlying the judgment is lawful in Panama;
4. That the copy of the judgment meets the requirements necessary to be considered authentic.

Article 585. The authenticity and efficacy of judgments rendered in foreign countries is to be established in conformity with Articles 431 and 432.

Article 586. The judge competent for the execution of a judgment rendered in a foreign country is the one who would be competent if the judgment [to be executed] had been rendered in Panama.

Article 587. When execution is sought for a judgment rendered in a foreign country, the court will order that the request be served on the party against whom the action is directed, and to the appropriate agent of the Public Ministry, and, if all should agree that it must be executed, will decree accordingly, if the judge himself has no substantial objection.

Article 588. If the parties do not agree, and if there are facts to be proved, the court will grant a term of fifteen working days, and after the expiration of this period, each party having had a period of three days in which to present proof, the court will decide in the following twelve days whether or not the judgment should be executed.

Article 589. The resolution issued according to the previous article, is appealable, and the appeal is to be conducted and decided like appeals of *autos*.[3]

Article 590. If the execution of the judgment is denied, it will be returned to the one who presented it; and if execution is granted, the matter will be forwarded in accordance with Panamanian law for execution as if it were a judgment rendered by a Panamanian court.

In addition to these provisions, Law 47 of 1956, which deals with the subject-matter jurisdiction of the Supreme Court, provides (Article 30.3):

The Fourth Chamber shall be competent . . .
   3. To examine judicial resolutions rendered in foreign countries in order to decide whether or not they should be enforced in Panama without prejudice to stipulations in public treaties.

The language of Article 581, like that of the laws of several other countries that copied the Spanish Civil Judgment Law of 1880[4] (among those in this study, El Salvador, Honduras, and Nicaragua), refers to "judgments rendered in foreign countries," instead of simply to "foreign judgments." In most countries of the world, this slight difference in phraseology would not be significant, but in Panama it has been the source of problems. How are the judgments of the courts in the Canal Zone to be treated? They are issued by foreign courts—that is, not by courts in the Panamanian judicial establishment—and so they cannot be executed as domestic judgments. The only provisions for enforcement of foreign judgments (except those of Bustamante Code signatories), however, are those set out above, and they do not apply to all foreign judgments, only to those "rendered in foreign countries." Panamanian policy does not recognize the Canal Zone as a foreign country: it is Panama, even though it is currently subject to the jurisdiction of the United States. Until 1948 this normally meant that Canal Zone decisions simply were not entitled to enforcement in Panama. In that year, however, the Supreme Court of Panama acknowledged that Canal Zone judgments, although they were not rendered in a foreign country, were nevertheless foreign judgments, and since the law did not expressly provide a means of dealing with them, they were enforceable, by analogy to judgments rendered in foreign countries.[5]

This particular problem will be resolved if the projected new Judicial Code, currently under discussion, is adopted.[6]

## BASIC PROCEDURE FOR RECOGNITION AND ENFORCEMENT

The Panamanian law Article 30.3 of Law 47 of 1956[7] confers upon the Fourth Chamber of the Supreme Court the jurisdiction to determine whether foreign judgments are entitled to recognition in Panama. The procedure by which this jurisdiction is exercised is not given a formal title in the law, but the term "exequatur" is the one in general use to describe it.[8]

The absence of positive legislation regulating the exequatur procedure has led to a dispute about the nature of the proceeding and whether formal pleadings are required.[9] The Supreme Court has apparently ruled that a formal pleading is not required—a simple petition will do.[10]

There has also been a dispute, which has been reflected in differing opinions by the Supreme Court itself, over the question of whether the procedural steps outlined in Articles 587 through 590 of the Judicial Code (and Articles 427 through 430 of the Bustamante Code)[11] are applicable to the exequatur proceeding in the Supreme Court or only to the later execution proceeding in case the exequatur is granted. The Supreme Court at one time indicated that those procedures were not a feature of the exequatur action, and it ruled that no one need be served with process in such an action. At that time, the judgment-recognition procedure in Panama was similar in this respect to that prescribed by the EEC Convention. Later, however, the court changed its view and recognized that those procedures are to be followed to the extent that may be applicable in the exequatur proceeding itself.[12]

In view of this, the enforcement of a foreign judgment in Panama requires the issuance of exequatur, and the basic procedure for acquiring it is that provided in Articles 426 through 430 of the Bustamante Code (in the case of judgments rendered in signatory countries) and that prescribed by Articles 587 through 590 of the Judicial Code (in the case of other foreign judgments). The Panamanian Judicial Code procedure is similar to that of the Bustamante Code, but there are some significant differences.

Both codes require that notice be given both to the party against whom the execution is sought and to a public official. The Bustamante Code allows twenty days for them to respond, but the Panamanian Judicial Code contains no time prescription. The Supreme Court of Panama has declared that the appropriate period for the other parties' response is five days.[13]

If the opposite party and the Public Ministry fail to respond, or if, in responding, they agree that the judgment should be executed, the exequatur can be granted forthwith, if the court itself has no objection.[14] If the other parties do not agree to the enforcement, on the other hand, and if facts are alleged to justify their unwillingness, a period of fifteen days will be allowed for the production of evidence on the question of whether the judgment is entitled to enforcement. Each party will also be allowed a period of three days to respond to the evidence.[15] After these periods expire, the court will decide the case within a period of twelve additional days.[16]

Both the Bustamante Code and the Panamanian Judicial Code require that the Public Ministry be notified and given an opportunity to participate in the exequatur proceeding.

Both the Bustamante Code and the Panamanian Judicial Code provide for review of the decrees granting or denying exequatur.[17] These provisions are not followed in Panama, however. Since 1946, the jurisdiction over the exequatur procedure has been lodged in the Fourth Chamber of the Supreme Court.[18] Panamanian law does not recognize any tribunal superior to the Chambers of the Supreme Court to which appeals can be taken.[19] Accordingly, no recourse is available to review the decision granting or denying exequatur, in spite of the language of the provisions of the two codes.[20]

If the exequatur is granted, the judgment can then be presented for execution to the appropriate court of the first instance, just as if it were a domestic judgment. If exequatur is denied, the judgment documents will be returned to the party who sought the exequatur.[21]

## KINDS OF JUDGMENTS ENTITLED TO RECOGNITION AND ENFORCEMENT

### PERSONAL JUDGMENTS

Article 584.1 of the Panamanian Judicial Code limits recognition to judgments resulting from a "personal action," except for foreign declarations of succession to goods.[22] The Bustamante Code does not in terms limit recognition and enforcement to personal actions, but it does specify that the defending parties must have been "personally summoned" (or "served" or "cited").[23]

Presumably, the Panamanian exception for foreign declarations of succession to goods would permit recognition of such declarations issued by courts in Bustamante Code signatory countries, even though that code might not require it.

### DEFAULT JUDGMENTS

Both the Bustamante Code and the Panamanian Judicial Code contain provisions that limit the enforceability of foreign default judgments. Article 423.2 of the Bustamante Code imposes, as a condition to enforcement, the requirement that the defendant or his personal representative must have been personally summoned or served (*citado personalmente*). The implications of this requirement have been noted previously.[24] Article 584.2 of the Panamanian Judicial Code contains different language.

Like other countries that borrowed the Spanish Civil Judgment Law,[25] Panama denies enforcement to default judgments; but unlike some others indicated in this survey (El Salvador and Honduras), it defines what is intended by the term "default judgment." In this situation, this term means that the defendant was not "personally notified of the demand within the jurisdiction of the court" which granted the judgment (except where the defendant himself is the one who is seeking enforcement in Panama). Whether "personally notified" (*personalmente notificado*) really means something different from "personally summoned" or "cited" (*citado personalmente*)—the term used in the Bustamante Code—is a question not easily answered. Some Panamanian authorities insist there is a distinction,[26] but the Panamanian standard of "personal notification" apparently is applied in order to determine the enforceability of default judgments that have been rendered even in Bustamante Code countries.[27] A default judgment, then, will be enforced in Panama only if the defendant was officially served and if either the defendant or his personal representative actually received notification within the territory of the court that rendered the judgment. It has been suggested that the application of Panama's more rigorous standard is improper and that it is productive of friction when it is applied to judgments of Bustamante Code countries,[28] but the practice apparently persists.

RESOLUTIONS OF NONJUDICIAL TRIBUNALS

The Supreme Court's jurisdictional statute that deals with foreign-judgment recognition refers to "judicial resolutions." For a time this was interpreted to mean that recognition would be denied to orders emanating from any nonjudicial tribunal—that is, a tribunal lacking "jurisdictional" status. Thus, at one time, exequatur was denied to orders of adoption that had been granted by the Patronato Nacional de la Infancia of Costa Rica, for instance, since the tribunal was not a court.[29] This particular interpretation has now been abandoned, however.[30]

Arbitration awards are regarded as "jurisdictional" in Panama, and so, foreign arbitration awards are enforceable. They can and must be submitted to the exequatur process in order to be enforced in Panama, at least if they come from countries that likewise regard such awards as "jurisdictional."[31] The Bustamante Code seems to treat such awards as being of this nature, and it declares them to be enforceable if they deal with a matter that is considered appropriate for arbitration under the law of the recognizing state.[32] Such awards obtained in signatory countries, then, are enforceable in Panama through the exequatur process.

# REQUIREMENTS FOR RECOGNITION AND ENFORCEMENT

## COMPETENCY

The Panamanian Court applies the standard provisions of the Bustamante Code to determine the competency of the rendering court when recognition is sought for the judgment of a signatory country.[33]

## NOTICE

The Panamanian Court, as noted previously,[34] insists upon compliance with the Panamanian requirement of personal notification within the territory of the rendering court, as well as the requirement of due service under the rendering court's standards, as conditions of recognition of foreign default judgments—even those emanating from Bustamante Code countries. In the case of judgments entered after the defendant's general appearance, presumably any defects in the notice will be cured by consent or waiver, as in our system.

## FINALITY

Both the Bustamante Code and the Panamanian Judicial Code use the term "judgments" (*sentencias*) to describe the orders that are entitled to recognition.[35] This term normally carries the sense of an official, final, definitive order that will put an end to the litigation. Other kinds of orders are entitled to recognition, however, and the Panamanian Supreme Court has held that the exequatur precedure is applicable to such orders. In one source the court is quoted as declaring that, in this context, the word *sentencia* "is used in the broad and general sense of a decision stemming from a judicial functionary concerning a cause submitted to him, and accordingly, including not only definitive judgments, but also interlocutory orders insofar as they recognize and declare the existence of rights."[36] This interpretation is supported by the terms of the law conferring jurisdiction on the Fourth Chamber of the Supreme Court,[37] which refers to "judicial resolutions"—not just to judgments. Relying on this language, the court held that exequatur was proper to a Liechtenstein precautionary judgment (embargo).[38] Nevertheless, the Supreme Court has sometimes construed the term *sentencia* in Articles 581 through 590 of the Judicial Code very narrowly and has denied exequatur for some interlocutory decrees because of their lack of finality.[39] The proposed new code would resolve the uncertainty about the finality requirement by specifically declaring that "by judgment [*sentencia*] is understood the resolution that puts an end to the proceedings."[40] This seems to require finality, but may permit the recognition of orders such as the "judgments of sale" that were described in connection with the Costa Rican and Nicaraguan practices.[41]

RECIPROCITY

Article 582 of the Judicial Code endorses the principle of reciprocity as a basic requirement for the enforcement of foreign judgments, in the absence of treaties dispensing with that requirement. The Bustamante Code, however, is such a treaty, and so the reciprocity rule does not apply to the judgments of other signatory nations.

The reciprocity rule has been criticized by some Panamanian writers,[42] but the projected new Judicial Code retains the requirement.[43]

PUBLIC ORDER

Article 584.3 of the Panamanian Judicial Code imposes the condition that the obligation underlying the foreign judgment must be lawful in Panama, and this is interpreted to mean that it must be "lawful" under Panamanian law. This is said to go beyond the customary "public order" exception and permits a general reexamination of the merits in the light of Panamanian legal standards.[44] However, that article does not control in the case of judgments rendered in the Bustamante Code countries. Article 423.3 of the Bustamante Code imposes the requirement that the judgment not contravene "the public policy or the public laws" of the country in which execution is sought. As was explained previously,[45] this exception applies only when the enforcement of the foreign judgment would violate some positive provisions of the forum's public law or some principle that is regarded as one of "international public order" at the forum.

## RES JUDICATA (COSA JUZGADA)

Panamanian law treats *cosa juzgada* as an irrebuttable presumption, couching the conditions that give rise to the presumption in the familiar terminology, borrowed from the Spanish Civil Judgment Law, of the three identities: namely, person, thing, and cause.[46] In the Panamanian Code, no specific mention is made of the application of the rules of *cosa juzgada* to foreign judgments, but it is clear that they do apply.[47] The Bustamante Code does treat this matter expressly, as has been noted previously.[48]

The question of whether exequatur is required before a foreign judgment can be recognized for its *cosa juzgada* effects has not been settled. I raised this question with Professor Pedro Barsallo of the University of Panama's law school.[49] His response was that the Supreme Court of Pamana had not ruled on the matter, but in his opinion, exequatur was necessary before a foreign judgment could have any effect at all in Panama. Professor Jorge Fábrega (one of the principal draftsmen of the new Judicial Code project), on the other hand, has taken the position that exequatur is necessary only for the execution of a foreign judgment; it is not necessary in order to entitle the foreign judgment to recognition as a defense or in order to establish rights or duties.[50]

## EVALUATION OF THE PANAMANIAN REGIME

Money judgments of Central American states are readily enforceable in Panama without reexamination of the merits (except where some fundamental principle of public order is violated). The participation of the Supreme Court is required (as is true in all but one of the other Central American countries), as is that of the Public Ministry also. The reciprocity requirement that is imposed in the case of judgments from non–Bustamante Code countries, does not apply to judgments of Central American states. All in all, the Panamanian law and procedure is quite similar to that of some of the other countries studied. Accordingly, the inclusion of Panama in a regional judgment-recognition arrangement should pose no peculiar problems.

# 10   Recognition and Enforcement of Judgments in Typical Actions for Money: Comparisons and Conclusions

One way to gauge the effectiveness of the regional judgment-recognition system of Central America is to examine its operation in a typical case and to compare it to the operation of the United States system and the European Common Market system in the same kind of case. For this comparison, we will use the case of a judgment that has been rendered in an ordinary action for money based on a liquidated claim. We will examine the conditions that must be satisfied for the judgment to be entitled to recognition and enforcement in the other associated states under all three regimes. From this comparison we will be able to see the relative effectiveness of the three systems in striking an appropriate balance of the individual, local, state, and association interests that are affected by the judgment-recognition decision. Finally, in the concluding chapter, we will compare the operation of the present judgment-recognition regime of Central America with the one that has been proposed by the Inter-American Juridical Committee's new convention on judgment recognition.

## BASIC PROCEDURE FOR RECOGNITION AND ENFORCEMENT

The procedural steps that must be taken in order to entitle a sister state's judgment to enforcement differ considerably between the systems we are comparing.

In the United States[1] the procedure for the enforcement of a sister state's money judgment is accomplished in an ordinary court of first instance. The law of the enforcement state governs the procedure (subject to some federal constitutional limitations), but the procedures of all states are essentially alike. In some states, enforcement is possible without an order of a court in the enforcement state: the sister state's judgment, duly authenticated, is merely registered with a designated official, usually the clerk of a general trial court. The execution process of the enforcing state can then be used to enforce the judgment. The more common (and more traditional) procedure, however, involves the initiation of an ordinary lawsuit to collect a liquidated debt—the debt being the obligation imposed by the sister state's judgment.

The procedure is a contentious one. Service of process on the defendant, which affords him an opporunity to appear in opposition to the judgment, is required before a new judgment can be rendered in the enforcing state, authorizing execution there. Although contentious, the procedure normally is not complicated. The only issues that can be raised to avoid enforcement are those relating to jurisdiction, broadly defined. No inquiry into the merits of the claim underlying the judgment is permissible. Not even the strong "public policy" of the enforcing state will provide a defense to enforcement. The federal policy of interstate enforcement of ordinary civil judgments always prevails over the local substantive policy of the enforcing state. Not even the existence of a prior inconsistent judgment in the enforcing state, or the pendency there of an action on the claim embodied in the judgment, will provide a defense to enforcement in the U.S. regime of full faith and credit. Enforcement of the judgment is the only proper way for a plaintiff to seek recovery in another state on an obligation that has been reduced to a money judgment. His original claim is said to "merge" in the judgment, and he cannot sue again on the original claim (if the opposing party brings the existence of the judgment to the attention of the court in the later action).

Appeal of the judgment granting or denying enforcement to a sister state's judgment is possible under the same conditions as appeals of other judgments. Since a federal constitutional question is involved, review may ultimately be sought in the Supreme Court of the United States to determine whether full faith and credit was properly either accorded or withheld, as the case may be.

The basic enforcement scheme of the European Economic Community is different in several respects.[2] For one thing, the European Economic Community Convention itself identifies the court that is empowered to entertain enforcement proceedings in each of the six original member states. In all except Italy, the court is the general court of first instance.[3] The procedure for enforcement is mainly governed by the local law of the enforcement state, as is the case in the United States as well, but the convention itself specifies that it is to be a noncontentious proceeding in which the defendant is not entitled to participate.[4] As such, the defendant is not entitled to notice and an opportunity to defend in that state. In this respect, the European procedure differs significantly from that of the United States and of the Central American countries. The purpose of proceeding without the defendant is to give the plaintiff a chance to prove his foreign judgment before the defendant learns about it, so as to thwart any move by the defendant to remove property from the jurisdiction—to place it out of reach of execution.[5] Protection of the plaintiff-creditor is the object. American notions of procedural fairness proceed from the opposite pole. A creditor can, sometimes, get an order that will prevent the defendant from moving property beyond the range of the court's process while the action is proceeding, but the defendant is normally entitled to some sort of prior notice and an opportunity to present countervailing contentions even then. American procedural due process places a very high importance on the defendant's right to a hearing before any official action is taken that might adversely affect his rights—even temporarily.

The European enforcement court will examine the record of the judgment to see if any of the conditions authorizing nonrecognition are apparent.[6] Nonrecognition to a money judgment is authorized only if
1. it contravenes the public policy of the enforcing state;
2. a defaulting defendant lacked adequate notice and opportunity to defend in the rendering state;
3. a prior inconsistent judgment had been rendered between the same parties in the enforcement state;
4. a prior inconsistent judgment on the same cause of action had been rendered between the same parties in a noncontracting state;
5. the convention's provisions relating to competence were not satisfied by the rendering court.[7]
In reviewing this last condition, however, the enforcing court, unlike a United States court, cannot look beyond the face of the record. The rendering court is required to pass upon the competence questions, whether they are disputed by the parties or not, and it will only be where there is a failure to comply with that requirement that lack of competence or exorbitant jurisdiction will provide grounds for nonrecognition.

The European proceeding can become a contentious one, however. The defendant can appeal from an order granting recognition, and the plaintiff can appeal from an order denying such effect. The defendant's appeal is taken to the same court that granted the enforcement order in Belgium, Italy, and the Netherlands, but to a higher court in Denmark,

France, Germany, and Luxembourg.[8] A plaintiff's appeal from an order denying enforcement is taken to a higher court in all the countries except Ireland, Italy, and the United Kingdom.[9] The appeal does not entail a second instance but merely a consideration of errors of law, and it is limited to the same questions that the enforcement court examined in the first instance. If a question of interpretation of the basic charter is raised, the question may be referred to the European Court of Justice for an authoritative ruling.[10]

As in the United States scheme, the judgment-enforcement procedure is the only mechanism through which a plaintiff can properly recover, in another member state, on a claim that has been reduced to a judgment. Suit on the original claim is barred.[11]

The existing Central American enforcement scheme, in all countries except Guatemala, involves a contentious proceeding in the highest court in the land before a judgment, even of a sister republic of Central America, can be presented to a court of first instance for enforcement. Action in two courts, then, is necessary. Moreover, the state itself is to be given the opportunity to participate in the proceeding, according to Article 426 of the Bustamante Code. Since the Bustamante Code generally leaves the enforcement procedure to the individual countries, however, the state's participation is not, in fact, required, except in Honduras and Panama.[12]

The issues that may be litigated in the enforcement proceeding include the competence of the rendering court, the adequacy of the notice that was given to the defendant in the rendering court, the "executoriness" of the judgment in the rendering state, and the conformity of the judgment to the public policy of the enforcement state. The existence of a prior inconsistent judgment in the rendering state is not an express limitation on enforceability (as it is in the EEC Convention), but in fact such a limitation is observed through the application of the public-policy exception.[13]

As is the case in the United States, the rendering court must be competent under both its own and "international" standards. The international standards to be used in judging the competency of the rendering court are basically those prescribed by the Bustamante Code. The Bustamante Code, however, declares that a state may follow its own rules in matters of competence *ratione loci,* if it so chooses;[14] therefore the enforcing court may use its own competence rule in some cases to judge the competence of the rendering court, at least if its rule makes the enforcing state exclusively competent. The competence standards that are relevant in most actions that can produce money judgments are of the type *ratione loci.* Thus, there is no such assurance that a set of

uniform competence standards will be applied to determine enforceability, as is the case in the United States (where the Fourteenth
Amendment's due-process clause and the Full Faith and Credit Clause
impose a large measure of uniformity) and in the European system
(where the convention's competency standards are applied directly in
the rendering court and may not be reexamined).

Article 425 of the Bustamante Code provides for appeal from the
ruling that either grants or withholds an enforcement decree (*exequatur,
pareatis,* or *pase de ley*), but this provision operates only in Guatemala,
since in the other Central American states the highest court in the country is the one that issues the decree in the first instance.

This comparison of the basic enforcement procedures under the
three systems indicates that the Central American procedure is much
less promotive of the association's interest in free mobility of judgments
than are the other two schemes. A judgment of the highest court in the
land based on a contentious proceeding in all the countries but one, and
in some of them the state itself participates as a party in the proceeding.
Proceedings in the high court normally will be more costly than the
same kind of proceeding in a lower court of first instance. If the state
is an active advocate in the proceeding, there is a greater likelihood that
arguments that could defeat enforcement will be made. Moreover, the
issues that may be litigated in the proceeding are more numerous than
those that are permitted to be raised in the other systems, and there is
no such assurance that the standards for resolving those issues will be
uniform throughout the region, as is true in the United States or the
EEC. And even when exequatur is granted by the high court, further
proceedings in a lower court are necessary before actual enforcement
can occur.

The basic procedure under the Central American scheme, thus, is
more costly, more complex, and less likely to produce predictable results.
The additional cost and complexity does not yield any greater protection
to the legitimate interests of the individual parties. It certainly does not
serve any interest of the plaintiff. It is perhaps advantageous to the
defendant in making enforcement more difficult to obtain, but the defendant has no legitimate interest in avoiding enforcement unless there
was some fundamental unfairness about the proceeding in the rendering
court. All three systems have provisions to protect the defendant from
enforcement of a judgment that is infected with that sort of unfairness.
It can be done at less cost to the association's interests than under the
Central American scheme.

The cost and complexity of the Central American system basically
serves some local interest of the enforcement state at the expense of the

association's interest. It is doubtful that the local interests served are really worth that cost.

No reason is apparent, other than tradition and mystical notions of sovereignty, for requiring the participation of the highest court in the land in the enforcement of every ordinary civil money judgment. Guatemala has found it possible to dispense with that requirement without suffering any apparent injury to its national dignity and sovereignty. It would surely be a step forward if the other Central American countries were to adopt a procedure like that of Guatemala, at least for the enforcement of judgments of other Central American states. Cases presenting serious questions either of interpretation of the treaty or of local public policy could be reviewed in the Supreme Court, but run-of-the-mill cases could certainly be disposed of at the level of a court of first instance with ample protection to individual and local policy interests and less sacrifice of the association's interests.

## KINDS OF JUDGMENTS ENTITLED TO RECOGNITION AND ENFORCEMENT

In the United States, every money judgment is entitled to enforcement in every other state (with the possible exception of a "penal" judgment).[15] Even money awards issued by administrative tribunals are entitled to full faith and credit.[16] Arbitration awards, however, and settlement agreements that are not embodied in official decrees are not constitutionally required to be enforced in other states (although many states do grant enforcement to such private arrangements).

The European Common Market Convention extends enforcement to all "civil and commercial" judgments, except certain kinds that are specially noted.[17] The characterization as civil or commercial turns on the nature of the cause of action, not upon the nature of the rendering tribunal. Whether or not a cause of action is of that character is to be determined, not by the law of either the rendering or the enforcing state, but by reference to a common but unwritten standard deriving from the "objectives and scheme of the convention" and from generally accepted principles.[18] Doubts are to be resolved in favor of the civil or commercial characterizations;[19] therefore, most kinds of money judgments in private actions will be enforceable under the convention, except those specifically noted. Arbitration awards are not covered by the 1968 convention, but there are other treaties and conventions that do provide for their enforcement.[20]

In Central America, too, virtually any private money judgment can be enforceable. Article 423 of the Bustamante Code declares that "[e]very civil or contentious administrative judgment . . . may be executed . . . ."

"Civil" in this passage is construed broadly; it does not refer to the character of the rendering tribunal or to the particular code that provides the substantive principles. Even penal judgments can be enforced to the extent that they include civil elements—that is, an award of damages for the victim.[21] Arbitration awards, too, are made enforceable if the subject of the arbitration was such that it could have been a subject of "compromise" under the law of the enforcing state.[22] In a few countries, it is even possible to obtain enforcement of ex parte judicial orders directing the defendant to pay money.[23]

It thus appears that the Central American system extends to more kinds of judgments and orders than either the European or the United States system.

## COMPETENCY AND JURISDICTION STANDARDS

A fundamental condition of enforcement in all the systems that we are comparing is the one relating to the competency or jurisdiction of the rendering court. The rendering court must have been competent both under its own and under "international" standards.[24]

The purpose of superimposing a requirement of competency by international standards over the requirement of competency under the rendering court's own standards is to protect the interest of the defendant in not having to defend himself in a forum that lacks the minimal connections to the parties and to the case that will satisfy general notions of fairness. It also serves to protect any interests that the enforcing state may have in providing the forum for the resolution of the issues in the underlying controversy. This latter interest is particularly strong, of course, when the enforcement state is the exclusive forum under its own law. If the enforcing state and the rendering state are members of an association of states, an association interest may also be served by the international competency standards in seeking to channel the litigation to the most convenient or the most appropriate forum, even if that is a third state.

The particular international competency standards that are recognized in all three of the regimes we are comparing do seem generally to foster these interests, but there are differences in the extent to which the systems permit these interests to prevail over competing interests: the plaintiff's interest in the choice of forum and the overall interest in the expeditious enforcement of judgments.

In the United States regime, the "international" standards of jurisdiction (those implicit in the federal Full Faith and Credit Clause) are the same as those minimal standards which are prescribed by the due-process clause of the Fourteenth Amendment. These standards focus upon the defendant's connection with the rendering state. At one time it was thought that the standards could be met by only three types of connection between the defendant and the state: he must consent to being sued there, be domiciled there, or be physically found and served with process there. Now, however, this older conception has been abandoned, leaving only a vague "fundamental fairness" standard in its place. The defendant must have such contacts with the forum state as to make it reasonable, under traditional notions of fair play and substantial justice, to require him to defend the particular lawsuit in that forum. Even under this fairness test, however, before 1977 it was generally assumed that in one situation, a state court could constitutionally exercise jurisdiction over a defendant in an in personam action that had no reasonable connection with the forum state: namely, when the defendant was physically served with process within the boundaries of that state. The United States Supreme Court in 1977, however, seemingly eliminated that possibility, declaring that all exertions of state-court jurisdiction must be judged by the "minimum contact–fundamental fairness" criteria first announced in *International Shoe Corp.* v. *State of Washington.*[25] The elimination of physical presence as a sufficient basis for personal jurisdiction means that a defendant cannot now be sued in a state with which he is not substantially related or with which he has not voluntarily formed some contact that is relevant to the action, unless he consents to such jurisdiction. If a judgment is obtained against him in a state that lacks such contacts, the judgment will not be entitled to recognition or enforcement in other states.

The U.S. standard overtly seeks to ensure basic fairness, but it is so vague that different courts can reach different conclusions in applying the standards to the same facts. This gives rise to a problem, because in the U.S. scheme the enforcing state can make an independent determination of the rendering court's jurisdiction. The vagueness of the standards means that a substantial range of review authority is lodged in the court of the enforcing state. However, this problem is relieved to a certain extent by two factors. The first is the possibility that the Supreme Court of the United States will ultimately review the rulings of a state court on the application of "international standards." The second stems from our notions of res judicata in its issue-preclusion aspect. The enforcing court can review the basis of the rendering court's jurisdiction, but if that issue was actively litigated in the rendering court, the parties may be precluded from relitigating, in the enforcing court, the ruling of the rendering court.[26] A defendant is entitled to challenge the rendering court's jurisdiction once, but only once. He may choose to challenge it in the rendering court or in the enforcing court, but if he challenges it in the rendering court and loses (or appears generally in the rendering court without challenging it), he can be precluded from making the challenge in the enforcing court. It should be noted that in the U.S. scheme, unlike that of the EEC Convention, the rendering court is under no obligation to inquire into the basis for its jurisdiction in personam unless the defendant does make an objection.

Another consequence of the broadness of the U.S. standards is that they may authorize the exercise of jurisdiction alternatively (or even simultaneously) in several states. For instance, a suit for damages for breach of contract between a resident of state A and a resident of state B that calls for performance in both states C and D could conceivably be brought in any of the four states without violating the constitutional standards. Assume that a suit has been brought in state D against a resident of state A and that a default judgment has been obtained there which is then submitted for enforcement in state A, the judgment debtor's domicile. The U.S. scheme permits the defendant to raise an objection to state D's jurisdiction in the state-A enforcement action, but the objection probably would not succeed, because state D would probably have sufficient minimal contacts. Does this scheme adequately protect the defendant's interest and the enforcing state's own interest in providing a forum for suits against its domiciliaries? The U.S. answer to that question would be yes. Our conception of fairness in the matter of the basis of personal jurisdiction consciously recognizes the need to balance the interests of the defendant and those of the plaintiff, of the forum state, and of other potential fora, and the overall interests of judicial administration in a federal system. The defendant does not have an absolute right to be sued in the state of his domicile. If there are alternative fora, the plaintiff (who must bear the burden of persuasion in the case) is generally permitted to choose the one in which the litigation is to proceed.

The U.S. system does permit the defendant to exert some influence on the selection of the forum in some kinds of cases, however; and this serves to protect the defendant against a seriously inconvenient forum choice by the plaintiff. One measure that a defendant may employ is to invoke the doctrine of *forum non conveniens*. Under that doctrine, a defendant who has been sued in a seriously inconvenient forum can move that the forum court dismiss the action. The court has discretion to do so in an appropriate case.[27] This is not a jurisdictional doctrine. The factors relevant to deciding whether dismissal for *forum non conveniens* is appropriate are the same ones that are relevant in determining whether the minimal contacts necessary for due process are present, but the jurisdictional standard may sometimes be met in a case where the forum is nevertheless seriously inconvenient. *Forum non conveniens* is not a constitutional doctrine, but it is recognized in almost every state as a common-law principle. Thus it is a means that is generally available by which the defendant can influence the choice among alternative permissible fora.

In addition to *forum non conveniens,* a defendant who has been sued outside his home state may be able to remove the action from the state court to a federal court (if the plaintiff or plaintiffs are all citizens of different states from that of the defendant and if more than $10,000 is in controversy).[28] Once the case has been removed to a federal court, the defendant may then apply for a transfer of venue of the action to another federal court where it might have been brought, if this would be convenient for the parties and for the witnesses and if it would be in the interests of justice.[29] The standards for transfer of venue from one federal court to another are not so rigorous as those that must be met under the *forum non conveniens* doctrine: the focus is upon convenience, not "serious inconvenience."

These devices work together to supply substantial protection to the defendant's interest, in spite of the very loose and permissive standards of international jurisdiction that are recognized in the United States today. The association interest in channeling the litigation to the most appropriate forum is significantly protected, although the protection depends upon the defendant's acting to invoke one of the protective measures. The enforcing state's interest in providing the exclusive forum, like the association's interest, is served if, but only if, the defendant chooses to avail himself of one of the measures to counter the plaintiff's choice of forum. Because the basic procedures are the same in all states of the United States, and because even the substantive laws are very similar in most kinds of cases that are likely to produce civil money judgments, the interest of any one state in providing the exclusive forum for a given action is not likely to be so strong as would be that of an individual state in the other systems that we are comparing; therefore, measures to protect particular states' interests in an exclusive forum are not so important in the U.S. scheme.

The jurisdictional standards that are prescribed by the EEC Convention are expressed in much more specific terms than those that are based upon the United States Constitution, and the application of these standards is quite different. Under the EEC Convention the competency standards are to be applied directly by the rendering court, and it must rule on that issue—whether or not the defendant objects—even if the defendant defaults. The determination of the rendering court is not subject to any review by the enforcing court.[30] By providing more specific standards to be directly and conclusively applied by the rendering court, the EEC Convention avoids some of the uncertainty that the U.S. system entails, but by the same token it is much more restrictive of the plaintiff's range of forum choice. The lesser importance ascribed to the plaintiff's interest no doubt reflects the different mode of trial in European civil procedure.

A defendant who is domiciled in an EEC community is subject to suit in the state of his domicile. The defendant's consent or voluntary general appearance can make a nondomiciliary court competent (unless the case is one for which the convention provides that a particular state is exclusively competent). In addition, an alternative forum is provided for certain specific kinds of cases: for example, contract cases—place of performance; tort cases—place of the tortious act; and so forth.[31] The provisions for these special cases identify countries that have particular significant contacts with the case. These contacts would undoubtedly be enough to justify requiring a nonconsenting nonresident to defend there under U.S. standards too. Thus, competency for a suit against a domiciliary of one of the member nations would not be recognized under the EEC standards in any case that would not also meet U.S. standards. U.S. standards, however, being less specific, may permit jurisdiction in some cases in states that would not be competent under the EEC standards. In most kinds of cases, however, the standards of the two systems would lead to essentially similar results. One case in which the standards of the EEC Convention may be more permissive than those of the United States, however, is the case that involves multiple defendants who reside in different countries. Under the convention, all may be sued in the domicile of any one of them.[32] The domicile of a codefendant has not been regarded as being an adequate basis for personal jurisdiction in the United States. In this situation the difference between the European conception of "competency" to entertain the *action* and the American concept that fulfills the same basic role—the basis for jurisdiction over the *person* of the defendant—is apparent.

The EEC standards, thus, although they are not expressed in terms that invite the balancing of interests, do seem to aim at striking a balance between the interests of the individual and those of the states. The defendant is protected against having to defend in a seriously inconvenient forum by the specification of only certain states in which an action can be brought without his consent. The "exorbitant" bases of jurisdiction that the laws of some of the individual countries otherwise would permit are expressly excluded when the defendant is a domiciliary of one of the contracting states.[33] The interests of individual states in providing the forum for the action are given greater weight than is true in the U.S. scheme, because the convention recognizes some states as having exclusive competence for some cases: an exclusivity that cannot be circumvented even by the defendant's consent. The greater importance that is placed on the forum interests of an individual state would not be appropriate in a federal union such as the United States, where laws and procedures of all states are very similar.

The international competency standards that are embodied in the Bustamante Code are narrower than those in the other two systems that we are comparing. For ordinary civil and commercial actions, a plaintiff has no choice of forum. If the parties expressly or impliedly consent to a particular court's competency, that will be *the* competent court if one of the parties is a domiciliary or national of that country.[34] If there is no express or implied consent or if the court that is consented to is not related to one of the parties by domicile or nationality, then the competent court is the one in which the obligation that is the subject of the action is to be performed.[35] If no place is specified or if the action does not concern an obligation to be performed, the court at the defendant's domicile (or the court of the defendant's nationality) or, as a last resort, the court at the defendant's residence will be competent.[36] All this presupposes, however, that the law of the rendering court itself also recognizes as a competent court the court that is prescribed by the Bustamante Code and that the law of the enforcing state does likewise. The jurisdictional provisions of the Bustamante Code, thus, do not really establish any firm uniform standards of international competence that will apply in all cases to determine the enforceability of a foreign judgment.

By expressly making its jurisdictional prescriptions subordinate to local law, the Bustamante Code seems to go far beyond the U.S. or EEC schemes in extending protection to the interests of the enforcing state. Under the Bustamante Code, too, the enforcing court can make its own determination of the rendering court's competency under the international standards. This permits the enforcing court to apply its own interpretation of the international competency rule, because there is no single tribunal—as there is in the United States—whose interpretation must be followed by all states. The Bustamante Code may even permit a reexamination of the facts on which the rendering court's competency rested, even though the facts were contested and specifically determined in the rendering court.[37] Thus, neither of the factors that in the U.S. system tend to eliminate the uncertainty caused by allowing the enforcing court to review the rendering court's competency is present in the regime of the Bustamante Code.

Whether this deference to the enforcing state is appropriate for a Central American regime may be questioned. In terms of basic law and procedure, the Central American states are generally more similar to each other than are the countries of the EEC. Local forum interests would seem to be relatively less important. Moreover, by thus reducing the number of cases in which automatic enforcement is prescribed, while providing no alternative fora for the plaintiff's original action, the Bustamante Code seems to favor the defendant unduly. In addition, a defendant may have two chances to challenge the rendering court's competency: once in the rendering court itself, and again in the enforcing court. In the EEC system, all challenges must be made in the rendering court. In the U.S. system a challenge may be made in one or the other, but not in both.

The Bustamante Code's scheme of competency standards, then, is significantly less conducive to the expeditious enforcement of civil judgments than are the other two systems under comparison. The individual law and practices of the particular countries of Central America apparently contain nothing to make enforcement more readily available, insofar as competency standards are concerned, than under the Bustamante Code's scheme. The only exception from that proposition might be the Nicaraguan scheme, under which a special law governs the enforcement of judgments of Central American states.[38] But I was not able to find any cases that would suggest that, in practice, there is any real difference in the way that the judgments of Central American countries and those of other signatories of the Bustamante Code are treated.

## NOTICE REQUIREMENTS AND DEFAULT JUDGMENTS

All of the systems under examination provide, in one form or another, that before a sister state's money judgment will be entitled to enforcement, it must appear that the defendant was adequately notified of the action against him in the rendering court and that he had an adequate opportunity to defend. In all of them, too, however, the defendant's voluntary participation in the action on the merits without objecting to any defect in the notice will foreclose this issue as a ground for challenging the judgment in the enforcing state.[39] Thus, the notice factor will be a defense to enforcement only in the case of a default judgment or in a case in which the defendant did unsuccessfully raise an objection to the notice element in the rendering court.

In the United States the notice requirement is combined with the requirements that relate to the bases of personal jurisdiction in the federal constitutional requirement of due process. Each state, of course, can prescribe its own procedures for notification of the defendant, but the procedures must conform to a federal standard: namely, the prescribed procedure must be such as to provide reasonable assurance that the defendant will receive actual notice in time for the adequate preparation of a defense.[40] Actual notice is in fact, however, neither necessary nor sufficient to meet the constitutional requirement. At one time, service by publication or by posting a notice was considered adequate for some kinds of cases—even for some in personam actions. Today, however, it is clear that this will not suffice for defendants whose identity and whereabouts are known. Notice by mail, sent to the defendant's last known address, is probably adequate, however, in most cases.[41]

In the United States the defense of lack of notice can only be raised to resist judgment enforcement in the case of a default judgment in which the defendant made no appearance whatsoever in the rendering court. A defendant who appeared in person in the rendering court and there unsuccessfully challenged the sufficiency of the notice or service cannot again assert the same challenge in a later enforcement action. His only recourse against an unfavorable ruling, in that case, is to appeal the resulting judgment in the rendering court, with ultimate review in the Supreme Court of the United States being possible.[42]

A defendant who made no appearance at all in the rendering court and who suffered a default judgment, however, can later, in an enforcement action, challenge the jurisdictional adequacy of the notice. He can challenge the adequacy of the process by which he was served both under the law of the rendering state itself and under federal constitutional standards. Even if the judgment formally recites that proper service and notice were effected, the enforcing court can usually make its own determination of the facts, based on an evidentiary hearing, and should it find that the facts do not show that the prescribed procedure was followed or, if it was, that the procedure did not comport with due-process standards, enforcement may be denied. The plaintiff who is seeking enforcement can, of course, appeal the denial of enforcement, with ultimate review in the Supreme Court of the United States being a possibility.

The EEC Convention contains two separate provisions recognizing the importance of adequate notice to the defendant in the rendering court. If a defendant who is domiciled in a state other than the one in which the action is brought makes no appearance—that is, if he defaults —in the action, the judge of the rendering court is required to stay the rendition of judgment until the plaintiff adequately establishes that the "defendant has been able to receive the document instituting the proceedings . . . in sufficient time to enable him to arrange for his defence, or that all necessary steps have been taken to this end" (Article 20). This means, according to the Jenard Report,[43] that the defaulting defendant must have been served personally or at his domicile in sufficient time to defend. (What constitutes sufficient time to defend is not defined in the convention itself, and so it is a factor on which judges may differ.) It is not necessary to show that the defendant actually received the notice: it is enough to show that the plaintiff took all the steps that are prescribed by the law of the rendering state (or the appropriate convention if service outside the state is required) and perhaps also those steps that are required by "good conscience and good faith."[44]

In this respect the convention's treatment of the question of competency and that of notice in a default case are similar. The rendering court must make a finding on the question, even if the defendant makes no objection. However, the convention also permits the *enforcing* court to consider the notice factor in a default case—even when the defendant was not domiciled outside the rendering state.[45]

The question arises whether this permits the enforcing court to make an independent determination of the adequacy of notice, even after the rendering court has passed on the question. Nothing in the text of the convention would preclude that interpretation. However, the Jenard Report indicates that Article 27.2 only applies in those cases in which Article 20 does not (i.e., where the defendant is domiciled in the rendering state) or in which the rendering court did not stay the proceedings as Article 20 prescribed.[46] Apparently, Article 27 does not contemplate a second, independent review by the enforcing court of the fact and the timing of notice. If the rendering court determines that notice was adequately and timely served, this will preclude consideration of that question by the enforcing court, even if the defendant did not raise his objections in the rendering court. Thus, the convention seeks to protect the defendant's right to notice and to provide him with an opportunity to defend, but it does not go so far as the U.S. scheme in granting the defendant himself a right to actively litigate that issue. This seems reasonable enough, however. If the defendant did receive notice of the action and if he had an objection to the form or timing of it, the interests of effective judicial administration would seem to require that the objection be made in the rendering court before judgment—while the proceeding is stayed for that very purpose. It is not so clearly reasonable in a case in which the defendant did not get any actual notice, but if he was duly served, he could not avoid the effect of the judgment anyway, and the rendering court will expressly examine the adequacy of service. Thus, while the EEC Convention does not in all cases guarantee the defendant a day in court on the issue of the adequacy of notice, it does seem to provide sufficient protection of his legitimate interests, and at the same time it serves the interests of interstate enforceability of judgments even better than does the U.S. scheme in this respect: namely, it eliminates the possibility of a collateral attack in the enforcing court in many kinds of cases in which the U.S. scheme would permit it.

The Bustamante Code, too, establishes as a condition of enforcement the requirement that the defendant must have been officially served, either personally or through his representative.[47] Presumably, this requirement will not be available as a defense against enforcement when the defendant participated on the merits without making an objection in the rendering court.[48]

In terms the code apparently permits the enforcement court to consider the propriety of service even when the question was raised and decided in the rendering court. Central American cases have not established a consistent position on this point, however.[49]

The code's provision for service upon a "representative" could refer not only to actual representatives but also to those fictitious representatives who are to be appointed under the "absence" procedure[50] for the defendants of unknown whereabouts. If this interpretation is proper, it could authorize enforcement in a case where the only official service upon the defendant was publication. The Central American cases that I examined, however, indicate that such a judgment will not be enforced if the enforcing court, after making an independent inquiry, determines that the defendant's location was not really unknown—at least if the defendant was a domiciliary or national of the enforcing state.[51]

It is interesting to note that the Nicaraguan Code provision relating to enforcement of judgments of Central American countries seems to authorize enforcement of judgment *without* service in some possible circumstances. It permits enforcement if "the losing party was duly served and represented or was declared in default in accordance with the laws of the place of the action."[52] However, in Nacaragua, as in the other Central American countries, due service and notice are regarded as matters of public order, and enforcement will be denied on that alternative ground if the defendant did not receive sufficient notice of the original action.[53]

The Panamanian practice also deserves special mention. Panamanian decisions have established a principle, which is applicable even to judgments of Bustamante Code countries, that denies enforcement unless the defendant was officially served *and* unless either the defendant or his personal representative actually received service of some sort *within* the *territorial* jurisdiction of the rendering court.[54] This requirement poses an obstacle to enforceability of foreign judgments that is very difficult to justify, especially in its application to judgments of Bustamante Code countries. It would surely have to be eliminated if Panama were to be an effective participant in a Central American regional scheme of judgment enforcement.

All in all, the Central American regime appears to be at least as zealous about protecting the defendant's interest in receiving adequate notice of the original action as are the U.S. and EEC systems. It apparently is less concerned, however, with promoting certainty and expeditiousness in judgment enforcement because it provides limits on the defendant's right to challenge the sufficiency of the notice in the enforcement action. A better balance of the relevant interests would seem desirable.

## FINALITY

Each of the three systems under examination extends enforceability to firm and final money judgments that could be executed in the rendering state if the defendant had any property there. There are, however, some interesting differences between the three systems in the matter of what kinds of judgments other than final judgments for a fixed single sum of money are enforceable.

In the United States, enforceability extends to "final" judgments. A judgment is not final till the trial judge has performed every judicial act that is necessary in order to entitle the judgment to be given effect in the rendering state. When it becomes "final" in the rendering state, it is subject to enforcement in a sister state, even if the judgment can still be appealed in the rendering state.[55] Enforcement will normally be stayed, however if an appeal is taken.

In the European Common Market Convention, a judgment becomes enforceable in another state as soon as it becomes enforceable in the rendering state,[56] but it will not be thus enforceable so long as appeal is possible in the rendering state.[57]

The Bustamante Code recognizes as enforceable only judgments that are "executory" in the rendering state.[58] Basically, this provision is like the EEC Convention's requirement of enforceability.

The U.S. principle of "finality" causes problems in application to judgments that call for payment in installments in the future. Such judgments are common in the areas of domestic relations—alimony and support decrees—and, in some states, worker's compensation. Although the trial judge may have done all that is required of him to make the installments collectible by execution as they fall due, still the passage of time is a condition precedent to enforceability. Are such judgments really "final" until the installments are due? The answer to that is no. Future installments are not "final" till the time for payment arrives.[59] (Some states, although they are not required to do so, nevertheless will recognize the judgments for future installments.)[60]

Most of the kinds of judgments that cause these problems for the "finality" requirement in the U.S. system are simply excluded from the coverage of the EEC Convention. Article 1 of that convention specifically excludes application to matters of status and marriage regimes and to social-security matters (which could include some kinds of what we call worker's compensation).[61] The main reason for excluding these from the convention was the recognition that in such matters the public policies of the individual states assume greater importance than they do in the case of ordinary civil and commercial judgments, and it was assumed that no judgment-recognition regime that included them and that would command uniform respect throughout the region could be adopted.[62] Thus, these matters are left up to individual state law, or to separate treaty.

In the Bustamante Code, no such express exclusion is made in the provisions relating to enforcement of judgments; but in another place,[63] each state is granted the right to recognize or not (as it sees fit) divorces that have been granted abroad with effects that are not admitted by the personal law of the parties. This, coupled with the general exception of public policy, operates to impede enforcement of alimony and support decrees that do not conform to local law (if one of the parties claims local law as his/her personal law). Where public policy is not at stake, presumably installment judgments can be enforced for accrued arrearages at least.

One other aspect of the "finality" requirement in U.S. law merits special attention. The "finality" requirement means there is no constitutional obligation upon one state to effectuate a summons, or a subpoena or attachment, or other interlocutory order that is issued by a court in another state. States will, by local law or interstate compact, often agree to serve summonses or even subpoenas that have been issued by courts in other states—but the practice is not uniform. Curiously, for reasons no doubt bound up in our former long-standing use of attachment (and quasi in rem jurisdiction) as a procedural substitute for personal jurisdiction over the defendant, states in the United States have not developed a practice of honoring attachment, garnishment, or sequestration orders issued by courts in other states against property in the enforcing state. This practice may well be under development now, however, in the wake of Justice Marshall's express invitation in *Shaffer* v. *Heitner*.[64]

The EEC Convention and the Bustamante Code both recognize the interstate enforceability of attachment orders,[65] although enforcement may be denied on public-policy grounds in some Central American states.

## RECIPROCITY

A common feature of the judgment-enforcement regimes of many individual countries is the limitation of enforcement to judgments of those countries which will reciprocally enforce the judgments issued by the courts of the enforcing state. Within the United States and the European Common Market, however, this requirement is completely eliminated with respect to the judgments of sister states. All states are bound in the same way by the same basic rules, and so there is no room for differences that might lead to a reciprocity requirement.

The fact that all the Central American countries are signatories of the Bustamante Code would seem to eliminate reciprocity as a factor to be considered in the enforcement proceeding among those states, too, even when the enforcement state's own law generally insists upon reciprocity as a condition of enforcement of foreign judgments. However, the fact that some of the countries accepted the Bustamante Code only with reservations means that the code does not operate in the same way in all countries, and so reciprocity is not ensured by the code itself. The lack of reciprocity is a defense to enforcement of a sister state's judgment in at least one Central American country (Honduras).[66] Apart from the problem of reservations, the Bustamante Code leaves several important questions up to local law, thus both opening the way for additional variation throughout the region in actual enforcement practices in the same kinds of cases and also fostering the reciprocity notion. In general, however, with the noted exception, reciprocity has not been viewed as a condition to the enforcement of judgments emanating from Bustamante Code countries. Nevertheless, the possibility of invoking it exists, and the example of Honduras shows that possibility to be a real one which other countries might emulate, perhaps in retaliation. The reciprocity factor, then is a potential obstacle to the realization in Central America of a judgment-enforcement regime that would be as effective as those of the United States and of the European Economic Community.

## PUBLIC ORDER

Nearly all judgment-enforcement schemes have recognized an exception to the obligation of enforcement when the effect would be contrary to some strongly held policy principles of the enforcing state. Since "public policy" in this context is rarely, if ever, defined, this exception introduces a potential source of unevenness and uncertainty into the judgment-recognition regime.[67] The degree to which the association interests and other interests that would be served by ready and expeditious enforcement must yield to local interests of the enforcing state through this exception depends, of course, upon how broadly or narrowly the enforcing state construes its public policy. If the exception is seen as broad enough to be applicable in any case in which the legal principles that are applied by the rendering court differ from those that would have been applied if the action had originally been brought in the enforcing court, there will be very few instances of interstate judgment enforcement unless the states have virtually identical bodies of substantive law. The problem of placing limits on the public-policy exception so that it does not virtually destroy the recognition and enforcement scheme has been a troublesome one to all regional systems.

The solution to the problem in the United States is simply to renounce local public policy as a defense to enforcement of a sister state's judgment.[68] Federal constitutional law overrides local law and policy, and the federal policy of ready and expeditious enforcement of judgments is given precedence over any local, substantive policy concerns, no matter how strong they may be. If the conditions were present for the exercise of jurisdiction by the rendering court—both in terms of the basis for jurisdiction and of the fairness of the notice and procedure— then the question of what state's policy ought to supply the substantive principles to govern the action should be raised and determined in the rendering court. Whether or not the issue is actually raised, however, once a judgment has been rendered, that question is foreclosed from collateral review.

This solution to the public-policy problem, however, gives rise to problems of its own. Because U.S. law leaves the matter of choice of law up to individual states, with very little federal constitutional restraint, there may be no corrective for a decision by the rendering court to apply rules of decision that would seriously thwart important policy interests of sister states that, in a totally rational system, ought to govern. This might lead one to believe that this feature of the U.S. system of judgment enforcement attributes excessive weight to ready interstate enforcement at the expense of local substantive policy interests of states other than the rendering state. However, in a true federal system, where state laws and policies are as similar on most subjects as they are in the United States, local policy concerns probably should be given considerably less weight than would be true in the case of a less thoroughly integrated group of states.

A "public policy" exception is operative in the EEC scheme. Article 27.1 expressly recognizes the exception. The committee that drafted the convention, however, expressed the opinion that the exception could properly be invoked only in extraordinary cases,[69] and it appears that considerable thought was given to the problem of keeping the potential scope of the exception limited. For one thing, the convention expressly excludes certain kinds of cases from its coverage. These excluded cases are kinds that are likely to provoke the enforcing court to apply the public-policy exception—cases dealing with family law, social security, and the like. Their exclusion in effect recognizes a region-wide principle that local interests are more important than association interests in interstate judgment enforcement in such cases. One state can refuse to enforce another's judgment in one of the excluded types of cases without invoking the general public-policy exception. In addition, the convention itself contains some provisions that serve to prevent the use of the public-policy exception generally as a device to permit the enforcing state to review the jurisdiction and choice-of-law rules that were applied by the rendering court. Article 28 makes it explicit that jurisdictional rules are not proper subjects of the public-policy exception, no matter how "exorbitant" they may be. Article 27.4, by expressly making the rendering court's choice of law subject to review in the enforcing court in certain kinds of cases, impliedly establishes that choice-of-law rules are not subject to review in other kinds of cases and that such rules generally are not proper subjects of the public-policy exception. The mere fact that the substantive principles that underlie the judgment are different from those that a court in the enforcing state would apply, then, will not trigger the exception. In fact, the convention's drafting committee expressed the view that it is not the foreign judgment itself that is to be examined in the light of local public policy, but the *recognition* of it.[70] It will only be where there is a strong local policy against the recognition of the judgment as such—apart from the question of the substantive principles underlying it—that the exception is warranted.

The regime of the EEC also contains a check against having a local court misinterpret the permissible scope of the public-policy exception. Provision is made in the General Treaty of the EEC for an authoritative interpretation by the European Court of Justice, which will bind all participant states.[71] Such judicial review is not compulsory, as is the United States Supreme Court's jurisdiction to interpret our constitutional scheme, but it does serve as a potential check on the public-policy exception recognized by the EEC Convention.

The public-policy exception in the Central American system, on the other hand, is free to operate virtually without restraint. Technically, however, it is not phrased as an exception but as a condition of enforceability. Article 423.3 of the Bustamante Code prescribes, as a condition to enforcement of a foreign judgment, "that the judgment does not conflict with the public policy or the public laws of the country in which its execution is sought. . . ." The term "public laws" should be read as "public law," a term that generally refers to laws that regulate relations between persons and the state. The enforcing state's "public law" can always prevent the enforcement of a sister state's judgment, then. The term "public policy" presumably refers to something different. It is generally thought to refer to that body of laws and precepts of the enforcing state that would be characterized as laws of "international public order" in Bustamante's terminology. This concept, however, is so vague and confusing as to make it nearly meaningless as a prescriptive term.[72] About all that one can say about it is that only rules that are considered pretty important to the society of the enforcing state deserve that characterization, but there is no standard for gauging importance. Family-law rules and rules relating to basic procedural fairness are common examples of matters of "public policy"; and all constitutional precepts, regardless of their content, are of that character.[73] But the concept is not limited to those. As in the EEC regime, it is not necessary to invoke the public-policy exception in order to avoid enforcing judgments that involve certain matters of family law that conflict with local policies of the enforcing state. A special provision of the Bustamante Code[74] allows each state "to permit or recognize, or not, the divorce or new marriage of persons divorced abroad, in cases, with effects or for causes which are not admitted by their personal law." In the recognition and enforcement of these cases, the local policy of the enforcing state is expressly given precedence over the association's interest. There is, then, no need to draw upon the public-policy exception in order to justify nonrecognition in such cases. Nevertheless, the Central American states that refuse recognition and enforcement to such judgments usually do so on grounds of public policy, adding unnecessarily to the freight that this concept has to carry.

The absence of any clear concept of public policy and the absence of any unifying tribunal to supply narrowing interpretations that will be binding on all states in the association means that each state is free to determine for itself what the "public policy" exception will cover. This is a potential source of great uncertainty in the Central American judgment-enforcement regime. The exception does not seem to have posed much of a threat to the enforcement of money judgments in the ordinary commercial or contract cases that have been detailed in our survey. But in the realm of labor law and in other branches of law where the public interest is more apparent, the exception poses a general inhibition to ready enforceability. In one Guatemalan case found in our survey, the public-policy exception was invoked to prevent the recognition and enforcement in Guatemala of a provisional attachment that had been issued by a Costa Rican court in a tort action against property in Guatemala belonging to a Guatemalan corporation. The Bustamante Code authorizes enforcement of such provisional attachments, but the Guatemalan appellate court ruled that to give it effect in Guatemala would violate public policy. (The Supreme Court reversed the ruling on other grounds but did not overrule the public-policy conclusion.)[75] This case illustrates the potential of the public-policy doctrine for introducing further uncertainty into the Central American judgment-enforcement regime in an area specifically covered by the code. Its scope is unpredictable.

One would think that an association of states which have as much in common as the states of the Central American isthmus—whose laws, policies, official language, and basic social institutions are more similar to one another's than are those of the states of the EEC, and which officially declare themselves to be separate elements of a single nation—could go further in subordinating local-policy interests to the association's interests in free mobility of judgments than could the nations of the European Economic Community. At present, however, the Central American regime permits the enforcing state to construe its public policy as broadly as it sees fit, with no effective check. This is a serious obstacle to the establishment of an optimally effective regime of judgment recognition.

## RES JUDICATA (COSA JUZGADA)

So far our comparisons have dealt with issues related to the enforcement of simple civil money judgments. Such judgments may have other extraterritorial consequences besides enforceability, and these should be considered in any comparative examination of the three systems. These other extraterritorial consequences are the res judicata (or *cosa juzgada*) effects of the judgments.

According to the common-law doctrine of res judicata as it is followed generally in the United States,[76] a judgment may affect future litigation between the same parties in two different ways: it may preclude a later suit on the same claim, and it may preclude relitigation of the same issues. The Full Faith and Credit Clause of the federal constitution gives these preclusive effects nationwide operation. If a judgment of state A will preclude a later suit on the same claim in state A, it will also preclude a later suit on the same claim in state B. If an adjudication in state A has conclusively established certain ultimate facts as between two parties, that same conclusive effect must be recognized in a suit between those parties in state B. Giving nationwide operation to the res judicata effects of judgments tends to conserve the judicial resources of the nation as a whole. The interests of the losing party are protected by limiting the operation of res judicata to judgments that are jurisdictionally valid (in both the existence of a proper basis for personal jurisdiction and the proper performance of service formalities that provide adequate notice) and final. This protects against a grossly unfair choice of forum and unfair procedure, and it ensures that conclusive effect will not be given to a ruling that could still be changed by the original court. Furthermore, claim preclusion will not result unless the judgment was "on the merits." Issue-preclusion effect will not be given except to issues that have actually been contested and decided and which were necessary to the judgment rendered. Some other limitations may also be imposed to assure that a proper balance be struck between the goals of the doctrine of res judicata and the protection of the losing party's interests.

No formal procedure is required to entitle a sister state's judgment to recognition for its res judicata effects. No separate judgment of the enforcing state, such as is usually required for enforcement—not even registration—is necessary for mere recognition. The sister state's judgment need only be presented in duly authenticated form to the trial court in the pending action in the recognizing state.

The U.S. system, then, ascribes to judgments of sister states conclusive effects as broad as those that a judgment would have in the rendering state, and it dispenses with all formalities for the recognition of those effects, except rudimentary requirements of proof.

The system of the EEC Convention is similar to the U.S. one in that it eliminates the need for special formalities (other than proof) when recognition, as opposed to enforcement, is sought for a sister state's judgment.[77] It is similar, too, in that the judgment that is entitled to recognition is to be accorded the same conclusive effect in the recognizing state as it has in the rendering state.[78] Its operation is different from that of the U.S. system, however, in that European law simply does not attribute such extensive effects to judgments as does the common law of the states of the United States.[79] Claim preclusion operates in a much narrower scope than in the U.S. system. It prevents the later action only when the same "object" and "cause" as were presented in the first action are involved in the second. Normally the combination of these elements will be present in fewer cases than those which would involve the "same claim or cause of action" as understood in U.S. law. Moreover, issue preclusion, except with respect to status or other juridical relations that are actually declared in the dispositive part of the judgment, is not recognized at all. Judgments may be used as evidence on issues, but not as conclusively determining them, as is the case in the United States. Although the scope of res judicata is thus limited, the EEC Convention serves to project throughout the whole community such conclusive effect as the judgment has in the state of rendition, and that effect can be realized without any special proceedings.

The scheme of the EEC Convention, unlike that of the United States, does not permit the conclusive effect of a sister state's judgment to be avoided by a collateral attack on the judgment for lack of jurisdiction (in the competency sense). Like the United State's scheme, however, it does, in some situations,[80] permit the avoidance of the conclusive effect of the sister state's judgment by a challenge in the recognizing state either to the adequacy of the service or to the notice given to the defendant in the action in the rendering state. Unlike the system of the United States, the conclusive effect of a sister state's judgment can also be challenged on grounds of the public policy of the recognizing state, although, as was noted above, the "public policy" objection does not have such a wide scope in the EEC scheme as it does in the private international-law doctrines of most individual countries.

Also, contrary to the U.S. practice, recognition for its conclusive effects need not be accorded to the sister state's judgment if there is an incompatible judgment in the rendering state between the same parties. This point will be examined at greater length in the next section.

All in all, it may be said that the interstate res judicata effects of judgments within the EEC are of lesser scope than is true within the United States. The basic doctrine of res judicata prescribes less extensive effects, and there are more instances in which even those effects can be avoided—that is, there are more grounds for nonrecognition.

Latin American law is basically the same as that of France and Italy on the question of the scope and effects of res judicata (*cosa juzgada*).[81] The effects are much more limited than is true in the U.S. scheme. The Bustamante Code's treatment of recognition of judgments for their res judicata effects is confusing at best. Two separate provisions of the code refer to the problem, and they do not fit neatly together. Article 431 declares:

> Final judgments rendered by a contracting State which by reason of their pronouncements are not to be executed shall have in the other States the effects of *res judicata* if they fulfill the conditions provided for that purpose by this Code, except those relating to their execution.

The other provision is Article 396:

> The plea of *res judicata* founded on a judgment of another contracting party shall lie only when the judgment has been rendered in the presence of the parties or their legal representatives, and no question founded on the provisions of this Code has arisen as to the competence of the foreign court.

By authorizing recognition for nonexecutable judgments, does Article 431 mean that executable judgments for which enforcement has not been sought are not to be recognized for their res judicata effects at all? If so, then a plaintiff who has once obtained a money judgment in a sister state cannot be prevented from suing again on the original claim rather than seeking enforcement in another state. The defendant would not be able to raise the defense of res judicata against such an action, because the earlier judgment would be executable. The plaintiff would have an option to sue on the original claim or to enforce the judgment in another state. This would constitute a significant difference between the regime of the Bustamante Code and those of the EEC and the United States.

Perhaps Article 431 should be read to mean that executable judgments are entitled to recognition, but that in the case of executable (as opposed to nonexecutable) judgments, *all* the conditions, including those for execution, must be satisfied. This, however, would be an anomalous requirement to impose upon a defendant who was seeking recognition for the foreign judgment to prevent a suit by the plaintiff on the original claim. Probably the most sensible reading of Article 431 is to simply ignore the reference to nonexecutable judgments as being ill-considered surplusage.

Even that, however, does not solve all the problems. What are the "conditions" that Article 431 refers to: Are they those prescribed in Article 396? Or those prescribed in Article 423 for enforcement? Or both? Most authorities have apparently assumed that both sets of conditions must be met.

Another problem is whether an order of exequatur must be obtained before a judgment can be recognized for its res judicata effects in those countries that require exequatur in connection with enforcement. In Central America (and elsewhere in Latin America) some of the states have taken the position that exequatur is required even when only recognition of the sister state's judgment is concerned.[82] Others have ruled that exequatur is necessary only when enforcement is sought.[83] In some countries of Central America, then, a formal decree of the highest court in the land is necessary before a sister state's judgment will be entitled to recognition for even the limited effects that Latin American *cosa juzgada* doctrine covers. This may be understandable in the case of recognition of divorce or other status decrees, but otherwise it is difficult to see any rational justification for this serious impairment of the association's interest in the free mobility of judgments. Does the exequatur requirement protect any local interest of the recognizing state or any individual interest of any party that is not otherwise adequately served? None is apparent, unless it be some abstract notion of sovereignty.

Apart from the inhibiting effect of the exequatur requirement, which is limited to only some of the countries, the Central American scheme contains some other impediments to ready recognition that make recognition of sister-state judgments less likely than under the U.S. and EEC regimes. All of the defenses that can be asserted to resist enforcement of a sister state's judgment (except, perhaps, lack of executoriness) can be raised against recognition: namely, lack of competence, inadequate notice, public policy, and so forth. This means basically that *both* the defenses that would be allowed in America and those that would be allowed in the European Economic Community can be asserted in Central America. Moreover, the "public policy" defense is broader than it is under the European scheme.[84] In addition, Article 396 seems to impose a stricter standard for recognition than for enforcement in its provision that "no question" must have arisen as to the competence of the rendering court. This would seem to bar recognition if a substantial question had been *raised*—whether or not it was resolved—in either the rendering or the recognizing court. Odd as it may seem, this probably is what Bustamante himself intended.[85]

From this it seems reasonably clear that the extent to which the res judicata effects of a judgment can operate throughout the region is far less in Central America than among the states of either the United States or of the European Economic Community. It would seem that judgment recognition ought to be at least as broadly effective among the Central American states as among the European ones, if not so broadly as in the United States.

## INCONSISTENT JUDGMENTS AND PENDING ACTIONS

Two common problems concerning recognition and enforcement of foreign judgments are (1) what, if any, significance should be placed on the fact that an independent action on the claim that is embodied in the judgment may be pending at the time when recognition or enforcement is sought; and (2) what, if any, significance should be placed on the fact that another judgment exists that is inconsistent with the one for which recognition or enforcement is sought. The two problems are discussed together here because of the common concern, underlying both, in the need to avoid conflicting official commands.[86]

The U.S. system generally tolerates the simultaneous pendency of two different actions on the same basic subject in different states. If the two actions are pending in the same state, local procedural rules for consolidation may be invoked, but these rules do not operate across state lines. A court in one state may seek to enjoin the prosecution of an action in another state, but the court in the second state is not bound by the Full Faith and Credit Clause to recognize or enforce such a decree. There is, then, no generally effective deterrent to concurrent litigation of the same claim in more than one state, except for practical considerations of cost and convenience.

Although actions can legally proceed simultaneously, when one of the claims is resolved in a judgment for or against the claimant, the obligation of full faith and credit arises, and the court in the second state must recognize the res judicata effect of the judgment. It can proceed no farther with the action, if the sister state's judgment is called to the court's attention through the assertion of the defense of res judicata. Even if the action that was pending in the second state had commenced before the one in the sister state that had now concluded in judgment, the pendency of that action would not be a defense to the recognition or enforcement of the sister state's judgment.

Res judicata is a defense to be asserted by a party—it is not an issue the court will raise on its own motion. It sometimes happens that the existence of the judgment is not called to the attention of the court in which another action on the same claim is pending. When this occurs, a second judgment on the same claim may be rendered. This second judgment may or may not be compatible with the first. If it is not, the system faces the problem of what to do about it. The same problem can arise if the first judgment is asserted as res judicata in the action, but the court erroneously fails to extend the recognition to it that full faith and credit requires. The solution to the problem of inconsistent judgments in the U.S. system is to treat the later one as the effective one.[87] Even though the later one could not properly have been rendered, it is effective. The remedy against this kind of erroneous judgment is the same as for erroneous judgments generally: not collateral attack, but appellate review. Review can be sought all the way to the Supreme Court of the United States, if necessary. But unless it is reversed by a higher court, the second of the two inconsistent judgments is the effective one, and it now is entitled to full faith and credit—to recognition and enforcement—even in the state in which the prior inconsistent judgment was rendered.

The treatment of these problems in the EEC Convention is quite different from that in the United States. The basic solution to the problem of concurrently pending actions on the same claim is to require the court in which the later action is brought to declare itself incompetent, leaving only the first action. Temporal priority in initiating the action determines which action is to be allowed to proceed.[88]

The convention even goes beyond the problem of concurrent actions on the *same* claim and provides also for the case when *related*[89] actions are pending. In such a case the court in which the second action is lodged *may* stay its proceedings. At the request of one of the parties, it may even yield jurisdiction of the case to permit consolidation of the two related actions in the state in which the first action is pending. This provision for dealing with interrelated actions apparently operates similarly to the doctrine of *forum non conveniens* in U.S. law. The trial court may, but is not compelled to, cede jurisdiction to a court in another state where the action might be brought in the interests of convenience (thus resulting in economy in adjudicating the actions simultaneously and avoiding incompatible results).

The convention does not declare any general rule of priority for the case in which, in spite of the rules just discussed and more general rules of res judicata, two actions do proceed to inconsistent judgments. It does, however, provide that if an incompatible judgment has been rendered in a state in which recognition or enforcement is sought, recognition may be denied.[90] This provision is not limited to inconsistent judgments on the same claim.[91] It makes no difference which judgment was rendered first. Of course, if the two actions were pending at first instance at the same time, the second one would have been stayed or dismissed in deference to the one that was commenced earlier.[92] The inconsistent-judgment defense, then, will be available only when the actions were not pending at the same time or when, in spite of the concurrent pendency, the court in which the later one was brought failed to take the steps either commanded by Articles 21 or 23 or recommended by Article 22.

It will be noted that the EEC Convention's provision for dealing with inconsistent judgments, unlike the U.S. solution, does not eliminate the inconsistency. In fact, it affirms the coexistence within the region of two incompatible judgments, each of which is valid and invulnerable in the state of its rendition. However, the U.S. solution, making the judgment that was last in time the only valid one, probably could not be imported into the European system. Basic to the "last in time" rule is the availability of appellate review in the Supreme Court of the United States to correct the second court's erroneous denial of full faith and credit to the earlier judgment. The European Court of Justice does not have such general appellate review powers. The EEC Convention could have taken the position that only the first of two inconsistent judgments could be recognized as valid, but this solution probably was rejected on the ground that it would simply be circumvented by having the recognizing court invoke the "public policy" exception when an inconsistent judgment existed in the recognizing state. The draftsmen of the convention were very concerned about keeping the public-policy exception in check, as has been noted previously. The solution that was adopted—which permits the inconsistent judgments—basically serves the local-policy interests of the recognizing state at the expense of the association's interest in uniform ready enforceability, but it does so without expanding the scope of the public-policy defense generally.

The convention provides no solution whatsover for the case in which a judgment that was inconsistent with the one for which recognition is being sought was rendered, not in the recognizing state, but in a third state. The solution to that problem must come from the local law of the recognizing state, and this means that there may be no one solution that will be uniform throughout the community.

The Bustamante Code[93] authorizes, but apparently does not require, the court of one state to dismiss the action when another action on the same claim is pending in another state. Inconsistent judgments, of course, may result. The code contains no provision for the case of inconsistent judgments. If a judgment that is inconsistent with the one for which recognition and enforcement is being sought has been rendered in the enforcing state itself, it is to be expected that recognition and enforcement will be denied on public-policy grounds.[94] If the inconsistent judgment is that of a third state, however, no single solution is apparent. The local law of the enforcing state will have to supply the solution, and this, of course, weakens the effectiveness of the code to provide a uniform region-wide scheme of judgment enforcement.

## COMPARATIVE EVALUATION

This comparison of the three systems shows that in every respect except one, the Central American one does not go as far as the others do toward providing a uniform region-wide system of expeditious recognition and enforcement of the judgments of sister states. Although the Bustamante Code regime, which prevails generally in Central America, applies in theory to more different kinds of orders than do the other two, this advantage is more than offset by numerous drawbacks. The enforcement procedure in most of the countries is more complex and cumbersome, the grounds for refusing recognition are more numerous, and the conditions upon which recognition can be denied are subject to more uncertainty and variation than is true in the U.S. and the EEC systems. The international competency standards of the Bustamante Code are really not uniform, since the code, in most ordinary cases, defers to local rules in cases where they conflict with those of the code. And even in matters for which the code does not defer to local rules, individual states may reserve the right to apply their own law, thus preventing the realization of a uniform region-wide system. The discredited reciprocity requirement does have some force even in connection with the judgments of sister states. The public-policy exception is free to operate without any effective limitation. The rules relating to recognition of judgments for their res judicata effects are confusing and ambiguous. There is not even agreement among the countries as to whether exequatur is required in connection with mere recognition. There is no provision in the Bustamante Code for the problem of inconsistent judgments.

One would not, of course, expect the Central American scheme to go so far as that of the United States in subordinating local interests to the association's interest in ready interstate enforceability of judgments. The United States is an established true federation. Central America aspires, at least verbally, to be a confederation of sorts, but it has not been seriously contemplated—at least not recently—that Central America should form a union in which the powers of the individual states would be as circumscribed as they are in the United States today.

One might, on the other hand, expect the Central American scheme to go at least as far as that of the European Economic Community in subordinating local-policy concerns to the association's interest in the free mobility of civil judgments. One would think that the common aspirations of nations with such similar legal systems as those of Central America would be conducive to the establishment of a judgment-recognition regime that would be even more promotive of association interests than is that of the EEC. These countries have a history of seeking reintegration, and they have from time to time proposed such advanced measures as uniform laws and a single tribunal with compulsory jurisdiction. The judgments of sister states should at least be accorded somewhat greater deference than the judgments of non–Central American countries.

A major obstacle to the implementation of a more effective system is the relatively greater importance that is placed upon the abstract ideal of sovereignty in Central America as compared to the United States and the countries of the EEC. This is seen in some of the cases in which the public-order exception was invoked to deny recognition to divorce judgments granted in sister states on grounds that were not authorized by the law of the recognizing state. The refusal of recognition to a divorce, valid where granted, of foreigners who had no connection to the recognizing state until later, merely because the parties had not lived apart for a period long enough to qualify as "abandoment" under the local law of the recognizing state, cannot in any meaningful sense be said to violate any of the latter state's deeply held notions of morality. If recognition to such a divorce is denied, as it may be in some Central American countries, on public-order grounds, it would seem to entail an exaggerated notion of the importance of the recognizing sovereign's legislative authority.

This attitude is also reflected in the notion, prevailing in all of Central America except Guatemala, that a ruling of the highest court in the land is necessary before any judgment of a sister state can even be presented to a lower court in a proceeding for execution. The issues that are involved in a proceeding for exequatur for an ordinary civil or commercial money judgment are usually routine questions that courts of first instance are fully capable of dealing with. Unless some seriously disputed issues are involved, there is simply no practical need for proceedings in two different courts—one of them the highest court in the land—before an ordinary money judgment is to be enforced. When the judgment comes from a country whose laws and courts and procedures are almost indistinguishable from those of the recognizing state—from a country that is officially considered to be a sister state in a nation that is seeking reintegration—the requirement of two proceedings makes even less practical sense than it might under other circumstances. Applying the requirement of the double proceeding to mere recognition of sister-state judgments is even harder to justify than is its application to enforcement, unless an extraordinary high value is placed on the abstract ideal of sovereignty.

If the Central American countries, carefully analyzing and weighing the interests affected, were to consider a new treaty that would deal with intraregional judgment recognition and enforcement, they might well find that the local sovereignty interests are not so strong as to justify continuing the present regime. They might well find that the association's interests are much more important than has heretofore been realized, and a new convention prescribing broader and more uniform region-wide effects for civil money judgments could result. They might find that a uniform procedure, which would generally permit the recognition and enforcement of sister-state judgments with no more formality than that which the Guatemalan scheme requires would be acceptable to all. Would not such a treaty be a small but important step toward reintegration? Such a step, coupled with the activation of the Central American Court of Justice, which is already provided for in the ODECA structure, with compulsory review jurisdiction to see that the treaty is given uniform interpretation and application, would seem to be a practical and relatively noncontroversial way to foster the goal of a closer, more effective union.

# 11    The Inter-American
Convention on Extraterritorial Validity of
Foreign Judgments and Arbitral Awards

We have examined the shortcomings in the existing scheme of intra-regional judgment enforcement in Central America. Before closing this study, however, we must look at the recently promulgated Inter-American Convention on Extraterritorial Validity of Foreign Judgments and Arbitral Awards. This convention was approved by the Second Inter-American Specialized Conference on Private International Law at Montevideo, 8 May 1979. It was intended for hemisphere-wide adoption, to replace the Bustamante Code and the Montevideo Treaty of 1940. It has been signed by fifteen countries,[1] including all of those of the Central American isthmus except for Nicaragua. As of 1 November 1980, however, only two of the signatories had ratified it—Peru and Uruguay. In examining this new convention, we shall not attempt to evaluate it as a general replacement for the earlier treaties. Rather, our inquiry will focus on the question of whether this convention, if ratified by the Central American states, would provide a more effective scheme for intraregional judgment recognition in Central America than does the one that presently exists.

The Governments of the Member States of the Organization of American States,

CONSIDERING that the administration of justice in the American States requires their mutual cooperation for the purpose of ensuring the extraterritorial validity of judgments and arbitral awards rendered in their respective territorial jurisdictions, have agreed as follows:

## Article 1

This Convention shall apply to judgments and arbitral awards rendered in civil commercial or labor proceedings in one of the States Parties, unless at the time of ratification it makes an express reservation to limit the Convention to compensatory judgments (sentencias de condena) involving property. In addition, any one of them may declare, when ratifying the Convention, that it also applies to rulings that end proceedings, to the decisions of authorities that exercise some jurisdictional function and to judgments in penal proceedings ordering compensation for damages resulting from an offense.

The rules of this Convention shall apply to arbitral awards in all matters not covered by the Inter-American Convention on International Commercial Arbitration, signed in Panama on January 30, 1975.

## Article 2

The foreign judgments, awards and decisions referred to in Article 1 shall have extraterritorial validity in the States Parties if they meet the following conditions:

a. They fulfill all the formal requirements necessary for them to be deemed authentic in the State of origin;

b. The judgment, award or decision and the documents attached thereto that are required under this Convention are duly translated into the official language of the State where they are to take effect;

c. They are presented duly legalized in accordance with the law of the State in which they are to take effect;

d. The judge or tribunal rendering the judgment is competent in the international sphere to try the matter and to pass judgment on it in accordance with the law of the State in which the judgment, award or decision is to take effect;

e. The plaintiff has been summoned or subpoenaed in due legal form substantially equivalent to that accepted by the law of the State where the judgment, award or decision is to take effect;

f. The parties had an opportunity to present their defense;

g. They are final or, where appropriate, have the force of *res judicata* in the State in which they were rendered;

h. They are not manifestly contrary to the principles and laws of the public policy (ordre public) of the State in which recognition or execution is sought.

## Article 3

The documents of proof required to request execution of judgments, awards and decisions are as follows:

a. A certified copy of the judgment, award or decision;
b. A certified copy of the documents proving that the provisions of items (e) and (f) of the foregoing article have been complied with; and
c. A certified copy of the document stating that the judgment, award or decision is final or has the force of *res judicata*.

## Article 4

If a foreign judgment, award or decision cannot be executed in its entirety, the judge or tribunal may agree to its partial execution at the request of an interested party.

## Article 5

A declaration *in forma pauperis* recognized in the State of origin of the judgment shall be recognized in the State of destination.

## Article 6

The procedures for ensuring the validity of foreign judgments, awards and decisions, including the jurisdiction of the respective judges and tribunals, shall be governed by the law of the State in which execution is sought.

## Article 7

This Convention shall be open for signature by the Member States of the Organization of American States.

## Article 8

This Convention is subject to ratification. The instruments of ratification shall be deposited with the General Secretariat of the Organization of American States.

## Article 9

This Convention shall remain open for accession by any other State. The instrument of accession shall be deposited with the General Secretariat of the Organization of American States.

## Article 10

Each State may, at the time of signature, ratification or accession, make reservations to this Convention, provided that each reservation concerns one or more specific provisions and is not incompatible with the object and purpose of the Convention.

## Article 11

This Convention shall enter into force on the thirtieth day

following the date of deposit of the second instrument of ratification.

For each State ratifying or acceding to the Convention after the deposit of the second instrument of ratification, the Convention shall enter into force on the thirtieth day after deposit by such State of its instrument of ratification or accession.

### Article 12

If a State Party has two or more territorial units in which different systems of law apply in relation to the matters dealt with in this Convention, it may, at the time of signature, ratification or accession, declare that this Convention shall extend to all its territorial units or only to one or more of them.

Such declaration may be modified by subsequent declarations, which shall expressly indicate the territorial unit or units to which this Convention applies. Such subsequent declarations shall be transmitted to the General Secretariat of the Organization of American States and shall become effective thirty days after the date of their receipt.

### Article 13

This Convention shall remain in force indefinitely, but any of the States Parties may denounce it. The instrument of denunciation shall be deposited with the General Secretariat of the Organization of American States. After one year from the date of deposit of the instrument of denunciation, the Convention shall no longer be in effect for the denouncing State, but shall remain in effect for the other States Parties.

### Article 14

The original instrument of this Convention, the English, French, Portuguese and Spanish texts of which are equally authentic, shall be deposited with the General Secretariat of the Organization of American States, which will forward an authenticated copy of its text to the Secretariat of the United Nations for registration and publication in accordance with Article 102 of its Charter. The General Secretariat of the Organization of American States shall notify the Member States of that Organization and the States that have acceded to the Convention of the signatures, deposits of instruments of ratification, accession and denunciation as well as of reservations, if any. It shall also transmit the declarations referred to in Article 12 of this Convention.

The text of this convention follows very closely that of a draft that was proposed in 1977. A still earlier draft convention had been proposed in 1973. The 1973 draft had consciously attempted to draw beneficial ideas from the EEC Convention and from other multi-state conventions. The 1977 draft astonishingly repudiated two of the most important features of the earlier one: the international competency standards and the elimination of an exequatur proceeding for the recognition, as contrasted with the execution, of foreign judgments. The convention, as it was ultimately approved, likewise omits these features. The elimination of such provisions seriously weakens the convention as a basis for an effective Central American judgment-recognition regime.

## KINDS OF JUDGMENTS SUBJECT TO RECOGNITION AND ENFORCEMENT

The coverage of the convention is basically the same as that of the Bustamante Code, but it eliminates the doubt expressed in some Bustamante Code countries as to whether judgments in labor cases are included. It provides comparable effect for foreign penal judgments.[2] Its application to arbitral awards is somewhat broader,[3] but it has no provision for recognition of contentious-administrative judgments.

## BASIC PROCEDURE FOR RECOGNITION AND ENFORCEMENT

The basic procedure for enforcement and recognition is left up to the law of the enforcing state.[4] This is essentially the same as the Bustamante Code's provision; by itself it would not serve to eliminate the obstacle of the separate Supreme Court proceeding that is required under the laws of all but one of the Central American states. Likewise, this leaves to individual solution by the separate states the question of whether a special exequatur procedure would be necessary for recognition as well as for enforcement of foreign judgments.[5]

## COMPETENCY

The convention prescribes, as a condition of recognition, that the rendering court must have been competent in accordance with the international competency standards of the recognizing state.[6] This provision differs significantly from its counterpart in the 1977 draft, and it differs still farther from the competency provisions of the 1973 draft. The 1973 proposal contained an elaborate statement of rules of international competency[7] that were to be applied, not directly, as in the EEC Convention, but by the recognizing court. This was rejected in the 1977 proposal, and the statement of uniform standards of international competency was replaced by a condition that the rendering court must have been competent under its own law, except where the recognizing state regarded its own courts as having exclusive competency in the matter.[8] The 1979 convention restored the notion of international competency, but instead of prescribing uniform rules, as the 1973 draft had done, it left the recognizing state free to apply its own standards. The convention, thus, permits a lack of uniformity among the signatory nations in this important condition. This fact seriously reduces its usefulness as an instrument for the kind of intraregional regime that would be promotive of integration. In this respect it appears to be even less adequate than the Bustamante Code, which at least contains some advisory standards of international competency which could be uniformly followed.[9]

## NOTICE

As with competency, so also with the notice requirement, the convention provides that this condition of recognition and enforcement is referable to the law of the recognizing state.[10] Although the laws of the Central American states are quite similar on this point, the convention's omission of an agreed standard permits a potential lack of uniformity within the region, which would not be conducive to the kind of certain, region-wide regime of judgment recognition that could positively promote the integration process.

## FINALITY

The convention is more precise than the Bustamante Code in its general provision relating to the degree of finality that the foreign judgment must have achieved in order to be entitled to recognition and enforcement.[11] Moreover, the convention deals specifically with judgments that cannot be executed in their entirety.[12] This provision may be applicable to the case of installment judgments for future support, among other kinds of judgments. It allows partial enforcement, but it does not make partial enforcement mandatory.

The convention omits any reference to the enforceability of foreign attachment orders, but the separate Convention on the Execution of Preventive Measures was approved at the same time as the Judgments Convention. This is probably a desirable development. Some states may consider it contrary to local public policy to extend enforcement to foreign attachment orders on local property. The existence of a separate treaty dealing with the matter makes it possible for such a state to express that local policy by simply refusing to ratify the separate Convention on Execution of Preventive Measures rather than expressing it through either a general reservation to the Judgments Convention or by ad hoc decisions invoking the public-policy exception (as was done in the Guatemalan appellate court decision that was referred to in chapter 6). Opposition to enforcing such precautionary orders can be expressed, in other words, without either impairing the integrity of the

Judgments Convention or expanding that convention's public-policy exception.

All in all, the convention is probably an improvement over the Bustamante Code's treatment of the factors that we examined under the rubric of Finality.

RECIPROCITY

The convention, like the Bustamante Code, contains no reference to reciprocity. The background document that was prepared in connection with the 1977 conference at which the earlier draft convention was proposed generally rejects the idea of reciprocity as a condition to the enforcement of foreign judgments[13] and declares that, in any event, the adoption of a treaty would make that condition superfluous. However, as we saw in our examination of the Honduran scheme, the mere ratification of the same treaty by two different nations does not eliminate all function from a reciprocity requirement in the local law of one of the signatory countries. If one of the two countries had ratified the convention with some reservation, as countries are permitted to do under both the Bustamante Code and the convention, cases can arise for which the treaty does not guarantee reciprocal treatment. For instance, let us assume that country A reserved the right not to follow the treaty's provisions in the recognition and enforcement of type X judgments. Assume further that country B ratified the treaty without reservation, but that in country B's own judgment-recognition law a reciprocity requirement is imposed. When a country A judgment of type X is presented for recognition or enforcement in country B, the country B court may conclude (as did the Honduran court) that no treaty exists between country A and country B which would exempt type X judgments from the requirements of country B's local judgment-enforcement law, and country B could insist on proof of reciprocity as a condition of enforcing country A's judgment.

The convention's allowance for ratification with reservation[14] is essentially the same as that of the Bustamante Code,[15] except that it adds the limitation that the reservations must not be "inconsistent with the object and purpose of the Convention." This provision, which allows reservations, was not included in the 1973 draft, and it was apparently added during the debate at the 1977 conference. The statement of the rapporteur at that conference indicates that the inclusion of the passage was responsive to the Vienna Convention on treaties.[16] The Vienna Convention, however, does not require the allowance of reservations.[17] Indeed, it could be argued that if the main purpose of a multilateral convention is to prescribe rules that will be uniformly applicable in the signatory countries, any significant reservation would be "incompatible with the object and purpose." However beneficial the reservation provision may be for securing ratification of the convention throughout the hemisphere, the allowance of reservations means that the convention cannot serve as the basis for a uniform judgment-enforcement regime for Central America any more than the Bustamante Code did, unless all the Central American states accept it without reservation.

## PUBLIC ORDER

The importance of limiting the potential scope of the public-order exception if a judgment-recognition regime is to achieve anything approaching uniform region-wide application has been noted frequently in this study. Because the concept is so vague and because it is interpreted in so many ways, it tends to subvert the association's interest in a predictable, reliable scheme of judgment recognition. Predictability—which is an essential characteristic of any regime that purports to promote the "rule of law"—would be fostered if the convention specified the particular kinds of judgments concerning which all signatories would agree that local concerns in the recognizing state should prevail over the interests favoring recognition. The general public-policy exception should be reserved for situations in which peculiar and very strong interests of the recognizing state are implicated. Devices that tend to narrow the range in which the public-order exception can be invoked are generally desirable because they foster predictability and deemphasize parochial attitudes.

The committee that prepared that 1973 Draft Convention apparently endorsed that proposition. The 1973 draft sought to eliminate the confusing ambiguity of the Bustamante Code, which referred both to the "public policy" and the "public law" of the enforcing state. The 1973 provision was basically the same as that of the EEC Convention: Judgments were to be entitled to recognition and enforcement if they did not "conflict with the public order of the country in which their recognition or enforcement is sought."[18] The 1977 Draft Convention, however, added the words "principles or laws of the [Public Order]" to that statement.[19] No reason is given in the rapporteur's statement to explain the addition of those words in the 1977 draft. The convention that was approved in 1979 retains this phrase.[20] It seems likely that the effect of this change will be to reintroduce the confusion that attended the Bustamante Code's public-order provision.

The 1977 Draft Convention made another change in the 1973 proposal that tends to broaden the scope of the public-order exception, and this change is now embodied in the convention that was approved in

1979. The 1973 proposal[21] had specifically exempted from the obligation of recognition and enforcement any foreign judgments that purported to affect real property in the enforcing state. This is a commonly recognized subject of the public-policy exception. Even in the United States' regime of full faith and credit, sister-state judgments that directly affect real property in the forum state are excepted from the general requirement of enforcement.[22] At least one Central American state expressly reserved such judgments from its ratification of the Bustamante Code.[23] By referring specifically to this kind of judgment, the 1973 draft removed this from the ambit of the public-policy execption. The 1979 convention, by omission, put it back.

Divorce judgments comprise another common subject of the public-order exception. The Bustamante Code made special reference to such judgments. The convention does not.

All in all, the convention seems to be no better than the Bustamante Code in articulating the limits of the public-order exception.

## RES JUDICATA (COSA JUZGADA)

The convention makes no distinction between the conditions that must be met for the execution of foreign judgments and for the recognition of the judgment's res judicata effects. This would correct the ambiguity in the Bustamante Code's references to this matter.[24] The rapporteur's statement in connection with the 1977 Draft Convention suggests that it aimed at expanding and strengthening the scope of the extraterritorial recognition of judgments for purposes other than execution,[25] although it nowhere says that the effect to be given is the effect that the judgment has under the law of the rendering state.

The convention, however, leaves up to local law and the enforcing state the question of whether the same procedure is required both for recognition and for enforcement.[26] The 1973 draft had sought to eliminate in all signatory countries the notion that a decree of exequatur is required in connection with the mere recognition, as opposed to the execution, of a foreign judgment.[27] This would have been an advantageous provision, particularly if one were thinking of the convention as the basis for a Central American judgment-recognition scheme. It was eliminated from the 1977 draft, however, and the 1979 convention copied it on this point. The reason that was given by the 1977 rapporteur was that having different procedures for recognition and for execution would be contrary to "principles and traditions of the Americas" and that "[i]nterational procedural law of the Americas does not contemplate *this dual regime*" (emphasis in original).[28] The stated reasons hardly justify the elimination of such a salutary provision. In the first place, it is simply not true that "international procedural law in the Americas does not contemplate this dual regime." As has been noted previously, there are two well-established viewpoints on the question of the necessity of exequatur in connection with the recognition of a foreign judgment for its res judicata effects in a collateral action. One of these viewpoints definitely holds that different procedural requirements are appropriate for such recognition, on the one hand, and for enforcement, on the other.[29] In the debates at the 1979 conference the Uruguayan representative ( Dr. Didier Opertti) noted that in his country, exequatur is not required for judgments emanating from other states that are parties to the 1940 Montevideo Treaty: such judgments go directly to the enforcing judge.[30]

It is likely that the 1977 rapporteur was thinking only of recognition of divorce judgments when he made the statement that American international procedural law does not contemplate a dual regime for recognition and enforcement.[31] In view of the strong concern about the subject of divorce in most Latin American countries, perhaps there is justification for requiring the same sort of judicial proceedings for recognition of such judgments as for enforcement of money judgments. However, the working document that was prepared before the 1977 conference makes it clear that the 1973 convention intended to dispense with the exequatur requirement (even in those countries in which it otherwise would have been required) for any case in which no execution would be necessary, including the case of divorce judgments.[32]

The 1979 convention, by eliminating this provision of the 1973 draft, leaves the exequatur requirement untouched. In some countries, then, exequatur may be required before a judgment that is covered by the convention may be recognized for purposes of the defense of res judicata as well as for divorce and for executable money judgments.

Even if the statement were true, the proposition that the traditional law in the Americas does not contemplate such a dual regime would not be much of an argument against it. The whole purpose of proposing a new convention to supplant the Bustamante Code and the Montevideo Treaty is to change—and, it is hoped, to improve—the international procedural law of the Americas. If a "dual regime" is desirable—and many of Latin America's most distinguished commentators ( including Dr. Bustamante)[33] have believed that it is—there is no reason not to provide for it in the convention, especially when the convention permits states to reserve that provision from their ratification of the convention if they do not like it.

Finally, by referring the question of procedure for both recognition and enforcement to the local law of the enforcing state, the convention in fact does approve a dual regime in those countries that already have achieved it.

## INCONSISTENT JUDGMENTS—PENDING ACTIONS

The convention contains no reference whatsoever to the problem of inconsistent judgments, nor does it deal with the situation in which an action may be pending in the enforcing state on the claim that is embodied in the foreign judgment. The Bustamante Code at least addressed the latter issue.[34] The convention leaves both these matters up to the local law of the enforcing state, which may be undesirable from the standpoint of a Central American judgment-recognition scheme.

## "ASSURED DEFENSE"

In one other noteworthy respect the convention contains a provision that is potentially deleterious to its value as the framework for a regional judgment-enforcement regime for Central America. One of the features of the 1977 Draft Convention, which apparently was added during the debate at the conference, appears in Article 1.f: as a condition to recognition and enforcement, it requires that "*se haya asegurado la defensa de las partes*" in the rendering court. This phrase was translated as requiring that "the parties be guaranteed legal counsel" in the official English version of the 1977 draft. The same Spanish words, however, are translated as "the parties had an opportunity to present their defense" in the English version of the 1979 convention. This adds another condition—of uncertain meaning—that must be met before a foreign judgment is entitled to recognition. It cannot help but be a serious impediment to the establishment of an effective enforcement regime.

The worst problem with the addition of this requirement is that its intended meaning is obscure. If it means a requirement of guaranteed counsel, does the provision limit enforcement and recognition to judgments of states whose laws guarantee free counsel for all litigants in private lawsuits? Does it limit recognition and enforcement to judgments in which free counsel was in fact provided? It seems doubtful that this could be the intended meaning, for few, if any, states generally do provide free counsel, even to indigents, in civil lawsuits. Does it mean to limit recognition to judgments of states that recognize that the parties have a right to be represented by counsel if they can secure it? If so, would any states be excluded? Does it limit recognition to cases where the parties were in fact represented by counsel? If that were the intended meaning, what would be the point in the reference to counsel being "guaranteed"?

Perhaps the phrase is intended to convey the notion, which is embodied in our conception of due process, of requiring "reasonable notice and an opportunity to defend." This interpretation is supported to some extent by the fact that the "assured defense" requirement (Article 2.f) appears next to the due-notification requirement (Article 2.e).

Curiously, no discussion of the ambiguity of this provision appears in the proceedings of the 1979 conference. In fact, by a strange oversight, article 2.f was not presented for a vote of approval to the commission of the conference that hammered out this convention. It was the only provision that was not specifically put to a vote.[35] In the proceedings, the only reference to article 2.f appears in the debate on the notice provision, article 2.e. One member suggested that the discussion of that section was to a certain extent superfluous, since the provision of article 2.f was broad enough to dispel any doubt or misunderstanding.[36]

The 1977 rapporteur's comment sheds no light on the intended meaning. The rapporteur gave this explanation for the addition of this requirement in the 1977 draft:

Subparagraph f (Working Group, paragraph 1,f) is new in this field, since it expressly requires that the defense of the parties has been ensured in the foreign judgment. Dr. Valladao showed, by citing examples from the legal practice of a number of countries, the justice of and need for this provision, which is universal in character and in accordance with natural law.[37]

Since the meaning of this requirement is far from clear, its inclusion in the treaty will provide a potential for protracted litigation over the interpretation of the requirement every time a foreign judgment is presented for recognition or enforcement. It should be noted that this provision is a requirement for the recognition of arbitration awards as well as judgments.

## IN FORMA PAUPERIS

One unusual provision appears in article 5: "A declaration in forma pauperis recognized in the State of origin of the judgment shall be recognized in the State of destination." The intention here is apparently to eliminate the need for a second proceeding to determine the poverty of a litigant in an enforcement action when the litigant had established his poverty in the original action. Whatever benefit in the form of legal assistance is extended to paupers in the enforcing state is to be extended to such a party. How this will work in practice is far from clear, but in theory it would seem to be positively promotive of the process of integration. The presence of this provision in the convention, however, may be a factor that will tend to deter widespread ratification.

This examination of the 1979 convention makes it reasonably clear that—all in all—adoption of it in its present form would not lead to a significant improvement over the regime that presently prevails in Central America. A convention that would be designed to be acceptable to all nations in the Western Hemisphere could hardly be expected to prescribe the kind of certain, ready recognition of judgments that would be required by the association interests of a group of neighboring countries that have very similar legal systems and that aspire to a high degree of economic and political integration. What is needed (in the view of an interested outsider) is a regime that would be tailored to the conditions of Central America; and this regime should be reinforced by a Central American court.

# Appendixes

## BUSTAMANTE CODE

Code of Private International Law. Annexed to the Convention adopted at Habana, February 20, 1928. In force, November 25, 1928.

[The Sixth International Conference of American States agreed that this Code should be officially called the "Bustamante Code." Addition to the Final Act of the Conference.]

### PRELIMINARY TITLE

#### GENERAL RULES

Article 1. Foreigners belonging to any of the contracting States enjoy, in the territory of the others, the same civil rights as are granted to nationals.

Each contracting State may, for reasons of public order, refuse or subordinate to special conditions, the exercise of certain civil rights by the nationals of the remaining States and any of the latter States may in such cases refuse or subordinate to special conditions the same exercise to the nationals of the former.

Art. 2. Foreigners belonging to any of the contracting States shall also enjoy in the territory of the others identical individual guarantees with those of nationals, except as limited in each of them by the Constitution and the laws.

Identical individual guarantees do not include, unless especially provided in the domestic legislation, the exercise of public functions, the right of suffrage, and other political rights.

Art. 3. For the exercise of civil rights and the enjoyment of identical individual guarantees, the laws and regulations in force in each contracting State are deemed to be divided into the three following classes:

I. Those applying to persons by reason of their domicile or their nationality and following them even when they go to another country, termed personal or of an internal public order.

II. Those binding alike upon all persons residing in the territory, whether or not they are nationals, termed territorial, local or of an international public order.

III. Those applying only through the expression, interpretation, or presumption of the will of the parties or of one of them, termed voluntary or of a private order.

Art. 4. Constitutional precepts are of an international public order.

Art. 5. All rules of individual and collective protection, established by political and administrative law, are also of an international public order, except in case of express provisions therein enacted to the contrary.

Art. 6. In all cases not provided for in this Code each one of the contracting States shall apply its own definition to the juridical institutions or relationships corresponding to the groups of laws mentioned in article 3.

Art. 7. Each contracting State shall apply as personal law that of the domicile or that of the nationality or that which its domestic legislation may have prescribed, or may hereafter prescribe.

Art. 8. The rights acquired under the rules of this Code shall have full extraterritorial force in the contracting States, except when any of their effects or consequences is in conflict with a rule of an international public order.

## BOOK I
### INTERNATIONAL CIVIL LAW
### TITLE I
#### PERSONS

### Chapter I.—Nationality and Naturalization

Art. 9. Each contracting party shall apply its own law for the determination of the nationality of origin of any individual or juristic person and of its acquisition, loss and recuperation thereafter, either within or without its territory, whenever one of the nationalities in controversy is that of the said State. In all other cases the provisions established in the remaining articles of this chapter shall apply.

Art. 10. In questions relating to nationality of origin in which the State in which they are raised is not interested, the law of that one of the nationalities in issue in which the person concerned has his domicile shall be applied.

Art. 11. In the absence of that domicile, the principles accepted by the law of the trial court shall be applied in the case mentioned in the preceding article.

Art. 12. Questions concerning individual acquisition of a new nationality shall be determined in accordance with the law of the nationality which is supposed to be acquired.

Art. 13. In collective naturalizations, in case of the independence of a State, the law of the acquiring or new State shall apply, if it has established in the territory an effective sovereignty which has been recognized by the State trying the issue, and in the absence thereof that of the old State, all without prejudice to the contractual stipulations between the two interested States, which shall always have preference.

Art. 14. In the case of loss of nationality, the law of the lost nationality should be applied.

Art. 15. Resumption of nationality is controlled by the law of the nationality which is resumed.

Art. 16. The nationality of origin of corporations and foundations shall be determined by the law of the State which authorizes or approves them.

Art. 17. The nationality of origin of associations shall be the nationality of the country in which they are constituted, and therein they shall be registered or recorded if such requisite is demanded by the local legislation.

Art. 18. Unincorporated civil, commercial, or industrial societies or companies shall have the nationality provided by the articles of association, or, in an applicable case, that of the place where its principal management or governing body is habitually located.

Art. 19. With respect to stock corporations, nationality shall be determined by the articles of incorporation or, in an applicable case, by the law of the place where the general meeting of shareholders is normally held, and in the absence thereof, by the law of the place where its principal governing or administrative board or council is located.

Art. 20. Change of nationality of corporations, foundations, associations and partnerships, except in cases of change of territorial sovereignty, should be subject to the conditions required by their old law and by the new.

In case of change in the territorial sovereignty, owing to independence, the rule established in Article 13 for collective naturalizations shall apply.

Art. 21. The provisions of Article 9, in so far as they concern juristic persons, and those of Articles 16 and 20, shall not be applied in the contracting States which do not ascribe nationality to juristic persons.

*Chapter II.—Domicile*

Art. 22. The concept, acquisition, loss and recovery of general or special domicile of natural or juristic persons shall be governed by the territorial law.

Art. 23. The domicile of diplomatic officers and that of individuals temporarily residing abroad in the employment or commission of their Government or for scientific or artistic studies, will be the last one they had in their national territory.

Art. 24. The legal domicile of the head of the family extends to the wife and children, except children who have reached their majority or have been emancipated, and that of the tutor or guardian extends to the minors or incapables under his guardianship unless otherwise provided by the personal legislation of those to whom the domicile of another is ascribed.

Art. 25. Questions relating to change of domicile of natural or juridical persons shall be determined in accordance with the law of the Court, if it is that of one of the interested States, otherwise they shall be determined by the law of the place in which it is alleged they have acquired their last domicile.

Art. 26. For persons having no domicile the place of their residence or, where they may happen to be, shall be considered as such.

*Chapter III.—Birth, extinction, and consequences of civil personality*

SECTION I. INDIVIDUAL PERSONS

Art. 27. The capacity of individual persons is governed by the personal law, with the exception of the restrictions established for its exercise by this Code or by local laws.

Art. 28. Personal law shall be applied for the purpose of deciding whether birth determines personality and whether the unborn child is to be deemed as born for all purposes favorably to him, as well as for the purpose of viability and the effects of priority of birth in the case of double or multiple childbirth.

Art. 29. The presumptions of survivorship or simultaneous death, in the absence of proof, are governed by the personal law of each of the deceased persons in so far as their respective estates are concerned.

Art. 30. Each State shall apply its own legislation for the purpose of declaring that civil personality is extinguished by the natural death of individual persons and the disappearance or official dissolution of juristic persons, as well as for the purpose of deciding whether minority, insanity or imbecility, deaf-dumbness, prodigality, and civil interdiction are only restrictions upon the status of persons permitting the existence of rights and even certain obligations.

SECTION II. JURISTIC PERSONS

Art. 31. Each contracting State, as a juristic person, has full capacity to acquire and exercise civil rights and to assume obligations of the same character within the territory of the others, without restrictions other than those expressly established by the local law.

Art. 32. The concept and recognition of juristic persons shall be governed by territorial law.

Art. 33. Excepting the restrictions provided in the two preceding articles the civil capacity of corporations is governed by the law which has created or recognized them; that of foundations by the rules of their institution, approved by the proper authority if required by their national laws; and that of associations by their constitutions upon like conditions.

Art. 34. With the same restrictions, the civil capacity of civil, commercial, or industrial partnerships is governed by the provisions relating to the contract of partnership.

Art. 35. The local law applies for the purpose of escheat in respect to the property of juristic persons which have ceased to exist, unless otherwise provided for in their by-laws, charters, or in the law in force for associations.

*Chapter IV.—Marriage and Divorce*

SECTION I. LEGAL CONDITIONS WHICH MUST PRECEDE THE CELEBRATION OF MATRIMONY

Art. 36. The parties thereto shall be subject to their personal law in so far as it relates to their capacity to celebrate the marriage, the parents' consent or advice, the impediments and their dispensation.

Art. 37. Foreigners must show, before marrying, that they have complied with the conditions provided by their personal laws in respect to the provisions of the preceding article. They may do so by a certificate issued by their diplomatic or consular officers or by any other means deemed sufficient by the local authority, which shall have full liberty of determining in every case.

Art. 38. Local legislation is applicable to foreigners in respect to the impediments which it establishes as indispensable, to the form of consent, to the bind-ing or nonbinding force of the betrothal, to the opposition to the marriage, the obligation of notifying impediments and the civil consequences of a false notice, to the form of preliminary procedure, and to the authority who may be competent to perform the ceremony.

Art. 39. The liability or nonliability for breach of promise of marriage or for the publication of banns in such case is governed by the common personal law of the parties and in the absence thereof by the local law.

Art. 40. The contracting States are not obliged to recognize a marriage celebrated in any one of them, by their nationals or by foreigners, which is in conflict with their provisions relative to the necessity of dissolution of a former marriage, to the degree of consanguinity or affinity, in respect to which there exists an absolute impediment, to the prohibition of marriage established in respect to those guilty of adultery by reason of which the marriage of one of them has been dissolved, to the same prohibition in respect to the one guilty of an attempt against the life of one of the spouses for the purpose of marrying the survivor, and to any other inexcusable grounds of annulment.

SECTION II. THE FORM OF MARRIAGE

Art. 41. A marriage shall be held valid everywhere in respect to its form if it has been celebrated in the manner prescribed as valid by the laws of the country where it has taken place. However, the States whose legislation prescribes a religious ceremony may refuse to recognize the validity of marriages entered into by their nationals abroad without the observance of that form.

Art. 42. In the countries where the law admits thereof, marriages entered into by foreigners before the diplomatic or consular agents of both contractants shall be subject to their personal law, without prejudice to the application thereto of the provisions of Article 40.

SECTION III. EFFECTS OF MARRIAGE IN
RESPECT TO THE PERSONS OF THE
SPOUSES

Art. 43. The personal law of the
spouses shall be applied, and, if different,
that of the husband, in what concerns
the respective duties of protection and
obedience, the obligation or nonobliga-
tion of the wife to follow the husband
when he changes his residence, the disposal and administration of their joint
property and all other special effects of
marriage.

Art. 44. The personal law of the wife
will govern the disposal and administration of her own property and her appearance in trial.

Art. 45. The obligation of the spouses
to live together and be faithful to and
help each other is subject to the territorial law.

Art. 46. A local law which deprives
the marriage of a bigamist of civil effects
is also imperatively applied.

SECTION IV. NULLITY OF MARRIAGE
AND ITS EFFECTS

Art. 47. The nullity of marriage should
be governed by the law to which the
intrinsic or extrinsic condition which
gives rise to it is subject.

Art. 48. Coercion, fear, and abduction
as causes of nullity of marriage are governed by the law of the place of sol-
emnization.

Art. 49. The personal law of the
spouses if it is the same, otherwise that
of the spouse who acted in good faith,
and in the absence of both conditions
that of the male, shall apply in respect
to the rules regarding the care of the
children of void marriages in cases in
which the parents can not or do not wish
to stipulate anything on the subject.

Art. 50. The same personal law shall
be applied to all other civil effects of a
void marriage, except those which it must
produce in respect to the property of the
spouses, which shall follow the law of
the matrimonial economic régime.

Art. 51. The rules fixing the judicial
effects of the action of nullity are of an
international public order.

SECTION V. SEPARATION AND DIVORCE

Art. 52. The right to separation and
divorce is regulated by the law of the
matrimonial domicile, but it can not be
founded on causes prior to the acquisition of said domicile if they are not
authorized with equal effect by the personal law of both spouses.

Art. 53. Each contracting State has
the right to permit or recognize, or not,
the divorce or new marriage of persons
divorced abroad, in cases, with effects or
for causes which are not admitted by
their personal law.

Art. 54. The causes of divorce and
separation shall be subject to the law of
the place in which they are sought, if
the married couple is domiciled there.

Art. 55. The law of the court before
which the litigation is pending determines the judicial consequences of the
action and terms of the judgment in respect to the spouses and the children.

Art. 56. Separation and divorce, obtained in conformity with the preceding
articles, produce their civil effects in
accordance with the legislation of the
court which grants them, in the other
contracting States, saving the provisions
of Article 53.

Chapter V.—Paternity and Filiation

Art. 57. Rules concerning the presumption of legitimacy and its conditions,
those conferring the right to the name,
and those which determine the evidence
of filiation and regulate the inheritance
of the child are rules of an internal
public order, the personal law of the
child if different from that of the father
being applied.

Art. 58. The rules granting rights of
inheritance to legitimated children partake of the same character, but in this
case the personal law of the father is
applied.

Art. 59. The rule which gives the legitimate child the right to maintenance is of an international public order.

Art. 60. The capacity to legitimate is governed by the personal law of the father, and the capacity to be legitimated by the personal law of the child, legitimation requiring the concurrence of the conditions prescribed by both.

Art. 61. A prohibition against legitimation of children not simply natural is of an international public order.

Art. 62. The consequences of legitimation and the action to impugn it are subject to the personal law of the child.

Art. 63. Investigation of paternity, maternity and prohibition thereof are regulated by territorial law.

Art. 64. The rules prescribing the required conditions for acknowledgment, compelling it in certain cases, establishing the actions necessary for the purpose, granting or refusing the family name, and fixing the causes of nullity, are subject to the personal law of the child.

Art. 65. The inheritance rights of illegitimate children are subject to the personal law of the father, and those of illegitimate parents are subject to the personal law of the child.

Art. 66. The form and circumstances of acknowledging illegitimate children are subordinated to the territorial law.

### Chapter VI.—Maintenance among relatives

Art. 67. The legal concept of maintenance, the order in which it is to be provided, the manner of furnishing it, and the extinction of that right shall be subject to the personal law of the one to be maintained.

Art. 68. The provisions establishing the duty to provide maintenance, its quantity, reduction or increase, the time at which it is due, and the manner in which it is to be provided, as well as those forbidding the renunciation and the assignment of that right, are of an international public order.

### Chapter VII.—Paternal power

Art. 69. The existence and general extent of paternal power in respect to person and property, as well as the cause of its extinction and recovery, and the limitation, by reason of a new marriage, of the right to punish, are subject to the personal law of the child.

Art. 70. The existence of the right of usufruct and all other rules applicable to the different classes of his private property are also subject to the personal law of the child, whatever the nature of the property or the place where it is situated may be.

Art. 71. The provisions of the preceding article are to be applied in foreign territory without prejudice to the rights of third parties which may be granted by local law and the local provisions in respect to publicity and specialty of mortgage securities.

Art. 72. Provisions which determine the kind and limits of the right of the father to correct and punish and his recourse to the authorities, as well as provisions depriving him of power by reason of incapacity, absence or by judgment of a court, are of an international public order.

### Chapter VIII.—Adoption

Art. 73. The capacity to adopt and to be adopted and the conditions and limitations of adoption are subject to the personal law of each of the interested persons.

Art. 74. The effects of adoption are regulated by the personal law of the adopting party in so far as his estate is concerned, and by that of the adopted one in respect to the name, the rights and duties which he retains regarding his natural family, as well as to his estate in regard to the adopting person.

Art. 75. Either one of the interested persons may repudiate the adoption in accordance with the provisions of his personal law.

Art. 76. Provisions regulating in this

matter the right to maintenance, as well as provisions establishing solemn forms for the act of adoption, are of an international public order.

Art. 77. The provisions of the four preceding articles will not apply to States whose legislations do not recognize adoption.

### Chapter IX.—Absence

Art. 78. Provisional measures in the case of absence are of an international public order.

Art. 79. Notwithstanding the provisions of the preceding article, the representation of the person whose absence is presumed shall be designated in accordance with his personal law.

Art. 80. The personal law of the absentee determines who is competent to institute an action requesting such declaration and establishes the order and conditions of the administrators.

Art. 81. The local law shall be applied for the purpose of deciding when the declaration of absence is made and takes effect and when and how the administration of the property of the absentee shall terminate as well as the obligation and manner of rendering accounts.

Art. 82. Everything relating to the presumption of death of the absentee and his eventual right is regulated by his personal law.

Art. 83. A declaration of absence or of its presumption as well as its cessation and that of presumption of death of the absentee have extraterritorial force, including what has reference to the appointment and powers of the administrators.

### Chapter X.—Guardianship

Art. 84. The personal law of the minor or incapacitated person shall be applied to what concerns the object of the guardianship or curatorship, its organization, and its different classes.

Art. 85. The same law is to be observed in respect to the appointment of an ancillary guardian.

Art. 86. To incapacities and excuses concerning guardianship, curatorship, and ancillary guardianship must be simultaneously applied the personal laws of the guardian, curator, or ancillary guardian and of the minor or incapacitated person.

Art. 87. The security to be furnished by the guardian or curator and the rules for the exercise of guardianship are subject to the personal law of the minor or incapacitated person. If the security is a mortgage or a pledge, it is to be furnished in the manner prescribed by the local law.

Art. 88. Obligations relating to accountings, except responsibilities of a penal nature, which are territorial, are also governed by the personal law of the minor or incapacitated person.

Art. 89. In respect to registration of guardianships, the local and the personal laws of the guardian or curator and of the minor or incapacitated person shall be simultaneously applied.

Art. 90. The precepts which compel the public prosecutor or any other local functionary to request the declarations of incapacity of insane and deaf-mutes and those fixing the procedure to be followed for that declaration are of an international public order.

Art. 91. Rules establishing the consequences of interdiction are also of an international public order.

Art. 92. The declaration of incapacity and interdiction have extraterritorial force.

Art. 93. Local law shall be applied to the obligation of the guardian or curator to support the minor or incapacitated person and to the power to correct the latter only to a moderate degree.

Art. 94. The capacity to be a member of a family council is regulated by the personal law of the interested person.

Art. 95. The special incapacities and the organization, functioning, rights and duties of the family council, are subject to the personal law of the ward.

Art. 96. The proceedings and resolutions of the family council shall in all cases conform with the forms and solemnities prescribed by the law of the place in which it meets.

Art. 97. Contracting States which have as personal law that of domicile, may demand, on transferring the domicile of incapacitated persons from one country to another, that the guardianship or curatorship be ratified or that the guardian or tutor be reappointed.

### Chapter XI.—Prodigality

Art. 98. A spendthrift decree and its effects are subject to the personal law of the spendthrift.

Art. 99. Notwithstanding the provisions of the preceding article, the law of the domicile shall not be applied to a spendthrift decree respecting parties whose national law ignores this institution.

Art. 100. A spendthrift decree made in one of the contracting States shall have extraterritorial force in respect to the others in so far as the local law may permit it.

### Chapter XII.—Emancipation and majority

Art. 101. The rules applicable to emancipation and majority are the ones established by the personal legislation of the interested persons.

Art. 102. However, the local legislation may be declared applicable to majority as a requisite for electing the nationality of said legislation.

### Chapter XIII.—Civil registry

Art. 103. Provisions relating to the civil registry are territorial, except in respect to the register kept by consular or diplomatic agents. The stipulations of this article do not affect the rights of another State in legal relations under international public law.

Art. 104. A literal and formal certificate of each inscription relating to a national of any of the contracting States, made in the civil registry of another, shall be sent gratuitously and through diplomatic channels to the country of the interested person.

### Title II

#### PROPERTY

#### Chapter I.—Classification of property

Art. 105. All property of whatever description, is subject to the law of the place where it is situated.

Art. 106. For the purposes of the preceding article, as regards personal property of a corporal nature, and of all titles representative of debts of any kind, account shall be taken of the place of their ordinary or normal situation.

Art. 107. The situation of debts is determined by the place in which they should be paid, and, if that is not fixed, by the domicile of the debtor.

Art. 108. Industrial property, copyrights, and all other similar rights of an economic nature which authorize the exercise of certain activities granted by law, are considered to be situated where they have been formally registered.

Art. 109. Concessions are deemed to be situated where they have been legally acquired.

Art. 110. In the absence of any other rule and also in the cases not provided for in this Code, it shall be understood that personal property of every kind is situated in the domicile of its owner, or if he be absent, in that of the property holder.

Art. 111. From the provision of the preceding article are excepted things given as pledge, which are considered as situated in the domicile of the person in whose possession they have been placed.

Art. 112. The territorial law shall be always applied for the purpose of distinguishing between personal and real property, without prejudice to rights acquired by third parties.

Art. 113. The other legal classifications

and qualifications of property are subject to the same territorial law.

## Chapter II.—Possession

Art. 114. Inalienable family property exempt from encumbrances and attachments is governed by the law of the place.

However, the nationals of a contracting State in which that kind of property is not admitted or regulated shall not be able to hold it or organize it in another, except in so far as it does not injure their necessary heirs.

Art. 115. Copyrights and industrial property shall be governed by the provisions of the special international conventions at present in force or concluded in the future.

In the absence thereof, their acquisition, registration, and enjoyment shall remain subject to the local law which grants them.

Art. 116. Each contracting State has the power to subject to special rules as respects foreigners, property in mines, in fishing and coasting vessels, in industries in territorial waters and in the maritime zone, and the acquisition and enjoyment of concessions and works of public utility and public service.

Art. 117. The general rules relating to property and the manner of acquiring it or alienating it *inter vivos,* including those applicable to treasure trove, as well as those governing the waters of public and private domain and the use thereof, are of an international public order.

## Chapter III.—Community of property

Art. 118. The community of property is governed in general by the agreement or will of the parties and in the absence thereof by the law of the place. Its place shall be the domicile of the community in the absence of an agreement to the contrary.

Art. 119. The local law shall be always applied, exclusively, to the right of requesting a division of the thing held in common and to the forms and conditions of its exercise.

Art. 120. Provisions relative to surveying and marking and the right to inclose rural properties, as well as those relating to ruined buildings and trees threatening to fall, are of an international public order.

## Chapter IV.—Possession

Art. 121. Possession and its effects are governed by local law.

Art. 122. The modes of acquiring possession are governed by the law applicable to each in accordance with its nature.

Art. 123. The means and procedure to be employed in order to maintain the possession of a holder, disquieted, disturbed, or dispossessed by judicial measures or resolution or in consequence thereof are determined by the law of the court.

## Chapter V.—Usufruct, use, and habitation

Art. 124. When the usufruct is established by mandate of the law of a contracting State, the said law shall govern it obligatorily.

Art. 125. If it has been established by the will of private persons as manifested in acts *inter vivos* or *mortis causa,* the law of the act or that of the succession shall be respectively applied.

Art. 126. If it springs from prescription, it shall be subject to the local law which establishes it.

Art. 127. The precept which does or does not excuse the usufructuary father from furnishing security depends upon the personal law of the child.

Art. 128. The requiring of security by the surviving spouse for the hereditary usufruct and the obligation of the usufructuary to pay certain legacies or hereditary debts are subordinated to the law of the succession.

Art. 129. The rules defining the usufruct and the forms of its establishment, those fixing the legal causes which extinguish it, and that which limits it to a certain number of years for peoples, corporations, or partnerships are of an international public order.

Art. 130. Use and habitation are governed by the will of the party or parties who establish them.

### Chapter VI.—Servitudes

Art. 131. The local law shall be applied to the concept and classification of servitudes, to the noncontractual ways of acquiring them and extinguishing them, and to the rights and obligations in this case of the owners of the dominant and servient lands.

Art. 132. The servitudes of a contractual or voluntary origin are subject to the law of the instrument or juridical relationship which creates them.

Art. 133. From the provision of the preceding article are excepted community of pasturage on public lands and the redemption of the use of wood and all other products of the mountains of private ownership which are subject to the territorial law.

Art. 134. The rules applicable to legal servitudes imposed in the interest or for the use of private persons are of a private order.

Art. 135. Territorial law should be applied to the concept and enumeration of legal servitudes and to the nonconventional regulation of those relating to waters, passage, party walls, light and prospect, drainage of buildings, and distances and intermediate works for constructions and plantations.

### Chapter VII.—Registries of property

Art. 136. Provisions establishing and regulating them and imposing them as necessary as regards third persons are of an international public order.

Art. 137. There shall be recorded in the registries of property of each of the contracting States the recordable documents or titles executed in another and having valid force in the former in ac-

cordance with this Code, and executory judgments which under this Code are given effect in the State to which the registry belongs, or which have in it the force of res adjudicata.

Art. 138. Provisions relating to legal mortgages in favor of the State, provinces, or towns are of an international public order.

Art. 139. The legal lien which some laws concede in benefit of certain individual persons, shall be enforceable only when the personal law agrees with the law of the place in which the property thereby affected is situated.

### TITLE III
#### VARIOUS MODES OF ACQUISITION
### Chapter I.—General rule

Art. 140. The local law is applied to the modes of acquisition regarding which there are no provisions to the contrary in this Code.

### Chapter II.—Gifts

Art. 141. Whenever they are of contractual origin they shall remain subject for their perfection and effects inter vivos to the general rules of contracts.

Art. 142. The capacity of both the donor and donee shall be subject to the respective personal law of each of them.

Art. 143. Gifts which are to take effect on the death of the donor shall partake of the nature of testamentary provisions and shall be governed by the international rules established in this Code for testamentary succession.

### Chapter III.—Successions in general

Art. 144. Successions, both intestate and testamentary, including the order of descent, the quantum of the rights of descent and the intrinsic validity of the provisions, shall be governed, except as hereinafter provided, by the personal law of the person from whom the rights are derived, whatever may be the nature of the estate and the place where it is found.

Art. 145. The precept by which the rights to the estate of a person are transmitted from the moment of his death is of an international public order.

### Chapter IV.—Wills

Art. 146. The capacity to devise by will is regulated by the personal law of the testator.

Art. 147. The territorial law shall be applied to the rules established by each State for the purpose of showing that an insane testator acted in a lucid interval.

Art. 148. Provisions forbidding a joint or a holographic or a nuncupative will, and those which declare it to be a purely personal act are of an international public order.

Art. 149. Rules relating to the form of private papers relating to wills and concerning the nullity of a will made under duress of force, deceit, or fraud, are also of an international public order.

Art. 150. The rules on the form of wills are of an international public order, except those concerning a will made in a foreign country, and military and maritime wills, when made abroad.

Art. 151. The procedure, conditions, and effects of the revocation of a will are subject to the personal law of the testator, but the presumption of revocation is determined by the local law.

### Chapter V.—Inheritance

Art. 152. The capacity to inherit by will or without it is regulated by the personal law of the heir or legatee.

Art. 153. Notwithstanding the provision of the preceding article, the incapacities to inherit which contracting States consider as such, are of an international public order.

Art. 154. The appointment and substitution of heirs shall be according to the personal law of the testator.

Art. 155. The local law shall, nevertheless, be applied to the prohibition of fideicommissary substitutions beyond the second degree, or those made in favor of persons not living at the time of the death of the testator, and of those involving a perpetual prohibition against alienation.

Art. 156. The appointment and powers of testamentary executors depend upon the personal law of the deceased and should be recognized in each one of the contracting States in accordance with that law.

Art. 157. In case of intestate estates, in which the law designates the State as heir in the absence of others, the personal law of the person from which the right is derived shall be applied; but if it is designated as occupant of res nullius the local law shall be applied.

Art. 158. The precautions which are to be taken when the widow is pregnant shall be in accordance with the provisions of the legislation of the place where she happens to be.

Art. 159. The formalities required in order to accept the inheritance with benefit of inventory or for the purpose of using the right of deliberating shall be subject to the law of the place where the succession is opened; and this is sufficient to produce their extraterritorial effects.

Art. 160. The rule referring to the unlimited undivided preservation of the inheritance or establishing a provisional partition, is of an international public order.

Art. 161. The capacity to solicit and carry into effect a division is subject to the personal law of the heir.

Art. 162. The appointment and powers of the auditor or partitioner depend upon the personal law of the person from whom the title is derived.

Art. 163. The payment of hereditary debts is subordinated to the same law. However, the creditors who have security of a real nature may realize on it in accordance with the law controlling said security.

## TITLE IV

### OBLIGATIONS AND CONTRACTS

*Chapter I.—Obligations in general*

Art. 164. The concept and classification of obligations are subject to the territorial law.

Art. 165. Obligations arising from the operation of law are governed by the law which has created them.

Art. 166. Those obligations arising from contracts have force of law as between the contracting parties and should be discharged in accordance with the terms thereof with the exception of the limitations established by this Code.

Art. 167. Those arising from crimes or offenses are subject to the same law as the crime or offense from which they arise.

Art. 168. Those arising from actions or omissions involving guilt or negligence not punishable by law shall be governed by the law of the place in which the negligence or guilt giving rise to them was incurred.

Art. 169. The nature and effect of the various classes of obligations, as well as the extinction thereof, are governed by the law of the obligation in question.

Art. 170. Notwithstanding the provisions of the preceding article, the local law regulates the conditions of payment and the money in which payment shall be made.

Art. 171. The law of the place also determines who is to cover the judicial costs for enforcing payment and regulates them.

Art. 172. The evidence relative to obligations is subject, so far as its admission and value is concerned, to the law governing the obligation itself.

Art. 173. Objection to the certainty of the place where a private instrument was executed, if having any bearing on its validity, may be made at any time by a third party prejudiced thereby, and the burden of proof shall be on him who makes it.

Art. 174. The presumption of *res judicata* by a foreign judgment shall be admissible whenever the judgment fulfils the necessary requirements for its execution within the territory, in conformity with the present Code.

*Chapter II.—Contracts in general*

Art. 175. The rules which prevent the conclusion of contracts, clauses, and conditions in conflict with the law, morality, and public policy, and the one which forbids the taking of an oath and regards the latter as void, are of an international public order.

Art. 176. The rules which determine the capacity or incapacity to give consent depend upon the personal law of each contracting party.

Art. 177. The territorial law shall be applied to mistake, violence, intimidation, and fraud, in connection with consent.

Art. 178. Every rule which prohibits as the subject matter of contracts, services contrary to law and good morals and things placed outside the field of trade, is also territorial.

Art. 179. Provisions which refer to unlawful matters in contracts are of an international public order.

Art. 180. The law of the place of the contract and that of its execution shall be applied simultaneously to the necessity of executing a public indenture or document for the purpose of giving effect to certain agreements and to that of reducing them to writing.

Art. 181. The rescission of contracts by reason of incapacity or absence is determined by the personal law of the absentee or incapacitated person.

Art. 182. The other causes of rescission and the form and effects thereof are subordinated to the territorial law.

Art. 183. Provisions relating to the nullity of contracts shall be subject to the law upon which the cause of nullity depends.

Art. 184. The interpretation of contracts should be effected, as a general rule, in accordance with the law by which they are governed.

However, when that law is in dispute and should appear from the implied will of the parties, the legislation provided for in that case in Articles 186 and 187 shall be presumptively applied, although it may result in applying to the contract a different law as a consequence of the interpretation of the will of the parties.

Art. 185. Aside from the rules already established and those which may be hereafter laid down for special cases, in contracts of accession, the law of the one proposing or preparing them is presumed to be accepted, in the absence of an expressed or implied consent.

Art. 186. In all other contracts and in the case provided for in the preceding article, the personal law common to the contracting parties shall be first applied, and in the absence of such law there shall be applied that of the place where the contract was concluded.

### Chapter III.—Contracts relating to property in respect to marriage

Art. 187. This contract is governed by the personal law common to the parties, and in the absence thereof, by that of the first matrimonial domicile.

The same laws determine, in that order, the supplemental legal control in the absence of stipulation.

Art. 188. The precept which forbids the making of marriage settlements during wedlock or modification of same, or which alters the control of property by changes of nationality or of domicile after marriage are of an international public order.

Art. 189. Those relating to the enforcement of laws and good morals, to the effects of marriage settlements affecting third parties, and to the solemn form thereof are of the same character.

Art. 190. The will of the parties regulates the law applicable to gifts by reason of marriage, except in respect to their capacity, to the safeguard of lawful rights of heirship, and to the nullity thereof during wedlock, all of which is subordinated to the general law governing marriage as long as it does not affect international public order.

Art. 191. Provisions regarding dowry and paraphernalia depend on the personal law of the wife.

Art. 192. The rule which repudiates the inalienableness of dowries is of an international public order.

Art. 193. A prohibition against renouncing the conjugal partnership during marriage is of an international public order.

### Chapter IV.—Sale, assignment, and exchange

Art. 194. Provisions relating to compulsory alienation for purposes of public utility are of an international public order.

Art. 195. It is the same with provisions fixing the effects of possession and registration among various acquirers and those referring to the right of legal redemption.

### Chapter V.—Leases

Art. 196. In respect to leases of things, the territorial law should be applied to such measures as are intended to protect the interest of third parties and the rights and duties of the purchaser of leased real estate.

Art. 197. In so far as the contract for services is concerned, the rule which prevents the making of such contracts for life or for more than a certain time, is of an international public order.

Art. 198. Legislation relating to accidents of labor and social protection of the laborer is also territorial.

Art. 199. Special and local laws and regulations are territorial as regards carriers by water, land, and air.

### Chapter VI.—Annuities

Art. 200. The territorial law is applied to the determination of the concept and classes of annuities, the redeemable character and prescription thereof, and the real action arising therefrom.

Art. 201. In respect to emphyteutic annuities (*censos enfitéuticos*), provisions fixing the conditions and formalities thereof, prescribing an acknowledgment every certain number of years, and forbidding subemphyteusis, are also territorial.

Art. 202. In case of transferable annuities (*censos consignativos*), the rule forbidding that payment in fruits may consist of an aliquot part of the products of the land subject to the annuity is of an international public order.

Art. 203. The same is the character of the demand that the land subject to the annuity be appraised, in the case of reservative annuities.

### Chapter VII.—Partnership

Art. 204. Laws requiring a lawful object, solemn forms, and an inventory when there is real estate, are territorial.

### Chapter VIII.—Loans

Art 205. Local law is applied to the necessity of an express agreement for interest and the rate thereof.

### Chapter IX.—Bailment

Art. 206. Provisions relating to necessary bailments and attachments are territorial.

### Chapter X.—Aleatory contracts

Art. 207. The effects of capacity in actions arising out of gambling contracts are determined by the personal law of the interested party.

Art. 208. The local law defines lottery contracts and determines the games of chance and the betting which are permitted or forbidden.

Art. 209. A provision which declares null and void an annuity constituted on the life of a person deceased at the time of its creation, or at a time when he was suffering from an incurable disease, is territorial.

### Chapter XI.—Compromise and arbitration

Art. 210. Provisions forbidding compromise or arbitration of certain matters are territorial.

Art. 211. The extent and effects of the arbitration and the authority of *res judicata* of the compromise also depend upon the territorial law.

### Chapter XII.—Security

Art. 212. A rule forbidding the surety to assume a greater liability than that of the principal debtor is of an international public order.

Art. 213. To the same class belong the provisions relating to legal or judicial security.

### Chapter XIII.—Pledge, mortgage, and antichresis

Art. 214. The provision forbidding the creditor to appropriate to himself the chattels received by him as pledge or mortgage is territorial.

Art. 215. The precepts fixing the essential requirements of the pledge contract are also territorial, and they must be complied with when the thing which is pledged is taken to a place where such requirements are different from those required when the contract was executed.

Art. 216. The provisions by virtue of which the pledge is to remain in the possession of the creditor or of a third party, the one which requires as against strangers that a certain date be expressed in a public instrument, and the one which fixes the procedure for the alienation of the pledge, are also territorial.

Art. 217. The special rules and regulations of pawn shops and analogous public establishments are territorially binding in respect to all transactions made with them.

Art. 218. The provisions fixing the objects, conditions, requisites, extent, and recording of the mortgage contract are territorial.

Art. 219. A prohibition against the creditor acquiring the property of the real estate involved in the antichresis, for default in payment of the debt, is also territorial.

### Chapter XIV.—Quasi contracts

Art. 220. The conduct of another's business is regulated by the law of the place in which it is effected.

Art. 221. The collection of that which is not due is subject to the common personal law of the parties and, in the absence thereof, to that of the place in which the payment was made.

Art. 222. The other quasi-contracts are subject to the law which regulates the legal institution which gives rise to them.

### Chapter XV.—Concurrence and preference of debts

Art. 223. When concurrent obligations have no real character and are subject to one and the same law, the latter shall also regulate the preference of said obligations.

Art. 224. In respect to those which are guaranteed by a real action, the law of the place of the guaranty shall apply.

Art. 225. Aside from the cases provided for in the preceding articles, the law of the trial court should be applied to the preference of debts.

Art. 226. When the question is simultaneously presented in more than one court of different States, it shall be determined in accordance with the law of that one which actually has under its jurisdiction the property or money which is to render the preference effective.

### Chapter XVI.—Prescription

Art. 227. Acquisitive prescription of both real and personal property is governed by the law of the place where they are situated.

Art. 228. If personal property should change situation during the period of prescription, the latter shall be governed by the law of the place where it is at the moment the period required is completed.

Art. 229. Extinctive prescription of personal actions is governed by the law to which the obligation which is to be extinguished is subject.

Art. 230. Extinctive prescription of real actions is governed by the law of the place where the object to which it refers is situated.

Art. 231. If in the case provided for in the preceding article personal property has changed its location during the period of prescription, the law of the place where the property is found at the completion of the time there specified for prescription shall apply.

### BOOK II
### International Commercial Law
#### Title I
##### MERCHANTS AND COMMERCE IN GENERAL

### Chapter I.—Merchants

Art. 232. The capacity to engage in commerce and to become party to commercial acts and contracts, is regulated by the personal law of each interested person.

Art. 233. To the same personal law are subordinated incapacities and their cessation.

Art. 234. The law of the place where the business is carried on should be applied in the measures for publicity necessary to the effect that persons incapacited therefor may engage in it through their representatives, and married women by themselves.

Art. 235. The local law should be applied to the incompatibility to engage in commerce of public servants and of commercial agents and brokers.

Art. 236. Every incompatibility for commerce resulting from laws or special provisions in force in any territory shall be governed by the law of the same.

Art. 237. The said incompatibility, in so far as diplomatic and consular agents are concerned, shall be measured by the law of the State appointing them. The country where they reside has also the right to forbid them to engage in commerce.

Art. 238. The partnership contract or, in an applicable case, the law to which such contract may be subject, is applied to the prohibition against general or silent partners engaging in commercial transactions, or in certain classes of them, on their own account or on that of others.

### Chapter II.—The quality of merchants and acts of commerce

Art. 239. For all purposes of a public character, the quality of merchants is governed by the law of the place where the act has taken place or where the trade in question has been carried on.

Art. 240. The form of contracts and commercial acts is subject to the territorial law.

### Chapter III.—Commercial registry

Art. 241. Provisions relating to the recording in the commercial registry of foreign merchants and partnerships are territorial.

Art. 242. Rules fixing the effect of recording in said registry the credits or rights of third parties have the same character.

### Chapter IV.—Places and houses of commercial traffic and official quotation of public securities and commercial paper payable to bearer

Art. 243. Provisions relating to the places and exchanges for the official quotation of public securities and documents payable to bearer are of an international public order.

### Chapter V.—General provisions relating to commercial contracts

Art. 244. The general rules provided for civil contracts in Chapter II, Title IV, Book I, of this Code shall be applied to commercial contracts.

Art. 245. Contracts by correspondence shall be complete only when the conditions prescribed for the purpose by the legislation of all the contracting parties have been duly complied with.

Art. 246. Provisions relating to unlawful contracts and terms of grace, courtesy, and others of a similar nature are of an international public order.

### TITLE II
#### SPECIAL COMMERCIAL CONTRACTS
### Chapter I.—Commercial companies

Art. 247. The commercial character of a collective or silent partnership is determined by the law to which the articles of partnership are subject, and in the absence thereof, by the law of the place where it has its commercial domicile.

If those laws do not distinguish between commercial and civil societies, the law of the country where the question is submitted to the courts shall be applied.

Art. 248. The commercial character of a corporation depends upon the law provided in the articles of association; in the absence of such provision, upon the law of the place where the general meetings of shareholders are held, and in the absence thereof, the law of the place where its board of directors is normally located.

If the said laws should not distinguish between commercial and civil societies, the said corporation shall have either character according to whether it is or not registered in the commercial registry of the country where the question is to be judicially determined. In the absence of a commercial registry the local law of the latter country shall be applied.

Art. 249. Questions relative to the constitution and manner of operation of commercial societies and the liability of the members thereof are subject to the articles of association or, in an applicable case, to the law governing such articles.

Art. 250. The issue of shares and obligations in one of the contracting States, the forms and guarantees of publicity and the liability of managers of agencies and branch offices in respect to third persons are subject to the territorial law.

Art. 251. Laws subordinating the partnership to a special régime by reason of its transactions are also territorial.

Art. 252. Commercial partnerships duly constituted in a contracting State will enjoy the same juristic personality in the other contracting States except for the limitations of territorial law.

Art. 253. Provisions referring to the creation, operation, and privilege of banks of issue and discount, general warehouse companies, and other similar companies, are territorial.

*Chapter II.—Commercial commission*

Art. 254. Provisions relating to the form of an urgent sale by a commission merchant to save as far as possible the value of the articles of the commission are of an international public order.

Art. 255. The obligations of the factor are subject to the law of the commercial domicile of the principal.

*Chapter III.—Commercial deposit and loans*

Art. 256. The noncivil liabilities of a depositary are governed by the law of the place where the deposit is made.

Art. 257. The rate or freedom of commercial interests is of an international public order.

Art. 258. Provisions relating to loans upon collateral of quotable securities made in the exchange, through the intervention of a duly authorized broker or official functionary, are territorial.

*Chapter IV.—Land transportation*

Art. 259. In cases of international transportation there is only one contract, governed by the proper law corresponding to it according to its nature.

Art. 260. Time limits and formalities for the exercise of actions arising out of this contract but not provided for therein are governed by the law of the locality where the facts took place.

*Chapter V.—Contracts of insurance*

Art. 261. The contract of fire insurance is governed by the law of the place where the thing insured is located at the time of its execution.

Art. 262. All other contracts of insurance follow the general rule, being regulated by the personal law common to the parties, or in the absence thereof, by the law of the place where the contract of insurance was executed; but the external formalities for proving facts or omissions necessary to the exercise or preservation of actions or rights are subject to the law of the locality where the act or omission which gives rise to them took place.

*Chapter VI.—Contracts and bills of exchange and similar commercial instruments*

Art. 263. The forms of the order, indorsement, suretyship, intervention for honor, acceptance, and protest of a bill of exchange, are subject to the law of the locality in which each one of those acts takes place.

Art. 264. In the absence of expressed or implied agreement, the legal relations between the drawer and the payee are governed by the law of the place where the bill is drawn.

Art. 265. Likewise, the obligations and rights existing between the acceptor and the holder are regulated by the law of the place in which the acceptance was made.

Art. 266. In the same hypothesis, the legal effects produced by indorsement between indorser and indorsee depend upon the law of the place where the bill has been indorsed.

Art. 267. The greater or lesser extent of the obligations of each indorser does not alter the original rights and duties of the drawer and the payee.

Art. 268. Guaranty (*aval*), in the same conditions, is governed by the law of the place in which it is furnished.

Art. 269. The legal effects of acceptance by intervention are regulated, in the absence of agreement, by the law of the place in which the third party intervenes.

Art. 270. The time limits and formalities for acceptance, payment, and protest, are subject to the local law.

Art. 271. The rules of this chapter are applicable to local drafts (*libranzas*), duebills, promissory notes, and orders or checks.

*Chapter VII.—Forgery, robbery, larceny, or loss of public securities and negotiable instruments*

Art. 272. Provisions relating to the forgery, robbery, theft or loss of credit documents and bonds payable to bearer, are of an international public order.

Art. 273. The adoption of the measures established by the law of the locality in which the fact takes place does not excuse the interested parties from taking all other measures established by the law of the place in which those documents and securities are negotiated, and by that of the place of their payment.

## TITLE III

### MARITIME AND AIR COMMERCE

*Chapter I.—Ships and aircraft*

Art. 274. The nationality of ships is proved by the navigation license and the certificate of registration and has the flag as an apparent distinctive symbol.

Art. 275. The law of the flag governs the forms of publicity required for the transfer of property in a ship.

Art. 276. The power of judicial attachment and sale of a ship, whether or not it is loaded and cleared, should be subject to the law of the place where it is situated.

Art. 277. The rights of the creditors after the sale of the ship, and their extinguishment, are regulated by the law of the flag.

Art. 278. Maritime hypothecation, privileges, and real guaranties, constituted in accordance with the law of the flag, have extraterritorial effect even in those countries the legislation of which does not recognize nor regulate such hypothecation.

Art. 279. The powers and obligations of the master and the liability of the proprietors and ship's husbands for their acts are also subject to the law of the flag.

Art. 280. The recognition of the ship, the request for a pilot, and the sanitary police depend upon the territorial law.

Art. 281. The obligations of the officers and seamen and the internal order of the vessel are subject to the law of the flag.

Art. 282. The preceding provisions of this chapter are also applicable to aircraft.

Art. 283. The rules on nationality of the proprietors of ships and aircraft and ship's husbands, as well as of officers and crew, are of an international public order.

Art. 284. Provisions relating to the nationality of ships and aircraft for river, lake, and coastwise commerce, or commerce between certain points of the territory of the contracting States, as well as for fishing and other submarine exploitations in the territorial sea, also are of an international public order.

*Chapter II.—Special contracts of maritime and aerial commerce*

Art. 285. The charter party, if not a contract of adhesion, shall be governed by the law of the place of departure of the merchandise.

The acts of execution of the contract shall be subject to the law of the place where they are performed.

Art. 286. The powers of the captain in respect to loans on bottomry bond are determined by the law of the flag.

Art. 287. The contract of a bottomry bond, except as otherwise provided by agreement, is subject to the law of the place in which the loan is made.

Art. 288. In order to determine

whether the average is particular or general and the proportion in which the vessel and cargo are to contribute therefor, the law of the flag is applied.

Art. 289. A fortuitous collision in territorial waters or in the national air is subject to the law of the flag if common to colliding vessels.

Art. 290. In the same case, if the flags are different the law of the place is applied.

Art. 291. The same local law is in every case applied to wrongful collisions in territorial waters or in the national air.

Art. 292. To a fortuitous or wrongful collision in the open sea or air is applied the law of the flag if all the ships or aircraft carry the same one.

Art. 293. If that is not the case, the collision shall be regulated by the flag of the ship or aircraft struck if the collision has been wrongful.

Art. 294. In the cases of fortuitous collision on the high sea or in the open air between vessels or aircraft of different flags, each shall bear one half of the sum total of the damage apportioned in accordance with the law of one of them, and the other half apportioned in accordance with the law of the other.

### Title IV

#### PRESCRIPTION

Art. 295. Prescription of actions arising from contracts and commercial acts shall be subject to the rules established in this Code in respect to civil actions.

### BOOK III

#### International Penal Law
#### Chapter I.—Penal laws

Art. 296. Penal laws are binding on all persons residing in the territory, without other exceptions than those established in this chapter.

Art. 297. The head of each of the contracting States is exempt from the penal laws of the others when he is in the territory of the latter.

Art. 298. The diplomatic representatives of the contracting States in each of the others, together with their foreign personnel, and the members of the families of the former who are living in his company enjoy the same exemption.

Art. 299. Nor are the penal laws of the State applicable to offenses committed within the field of military operations when it authorizes the passage of an army of another contracting State through its territory, except offenses not legally connected with said army.

Art. 300. The same exemption is applied to offenses committed on board of foreign war vessels or aircraft while in territorial waters or in the national air.

Art. 301. The same is the case in respect to offenses committed in territorial waters or in the national air, on foreign merchant vessels or aircraft, if they have no relation with the country and its inhabitants and do not disturb its tranquillity.

Art. 302. When the acts of which an offense is composed take place in different contracting States, each State may punish the act committed within its jurisdiction, if it by itself constitutes a punishable act.

In the contrary case, preference shall be given to the right of the local sovereignty where the offense has been committed.

Art. 303. In case of related offenses committed in the territories of more than one contracting State, only the one committed in its own territory shall be subject to the penal law of each.

Art. 304. No contracting State shall apply in its territory the penal laws of the others.

#### Chapter II.—Offenses committed in a foreign contracting State

Art. 305. Those committing an offense against the internal or external security of a contracting State or against its public credit, whatever the nationality or domicile of the delinquent person, are subject in a foreign country to the penal laws of each contracting State.

Art. 306. Every national of a contracting State or every foreigner domiciled therein who commits in a foreign country an offense against the independence of that State remains subject to its penal laws.

Art. 307. Moreover, those persons are subject to the penal laws of the foreign State in which they are apprehended and tried who have committed outside its territory an offense, such as white slavery, which said contracting State has bound itself by an interational agreement to repress.

*Chapter III.—Offenses committed outside the national territory*

Art. 308. Piracy, trade in negroes and slave traffic, white slavery, the destruction or injury of submarine cables, and all other offenses of a similar nature against international law committed on the high sea, in the open air, and on territory not yet organized into a State, shall be punished by the captor in accordance with the penal laws of the latter.

Art. 309. In cases of wrongful collision on the high sea or in the air, between ships or aircraft carrying different colors, the penal law of the victim shall be applied.

*Chapter IV.—Sundry questions*

Art. 310. For the legal concept of reiteration or recidivism will be taken into account the judgment rendered in a foreign contracting State, with the exception of the cases in which same is contrary to local law.

Art. 311. The penalty of civil interdiction shall have effect in each of the other States upon the previous compliance with the formalities of registration or publication which may be required by the legislation of such State.

Art. 312. Prescription of an offense is subordinated to the law of the State having cognizance thereof.

Art. 313. Prescription of the penalty is governed by the law of the State which has imposed it.

## BOOK IV

### INTERNATIONAL LAW OF PROCEDURE

#### TITLE I

##### GENERAL RULES

Art. 314. The law of each contracting State determines the competence of courts, as well as their organization, the forms of procedure and of execution of judgments, and the appeals from their decisions.

Art. 315. No contracting State shall organize or maintain in its territory special tribunals for members of the other contracting States.

Art. 316. Competence *ratione loci* is subordinated, in the order of international relations, to the law of the contracting State which establishes it.

Art. 317. Competence *ratione materiae* and *ratione personae,* in the order of international relations should not be based by the contracting States on the status as nationals or foreigners of the interested parties, to the prejudice of the latter.

#### TITLE II

##### COMPETENCE

*Chapter I.—General rules concerning competence in civil and commercial matters*

Art. 318. The judge competent in the first place to take cognizance of suits arising from the exercise of civil and commercial actions of all kinds shall be the one to whom the litigants expressly or impliedly submit themselves, provided that one of them at least is a national of the contracting State to which the judge belongs or has his domicile therein, and in the absence of local laws to the contrary.

The submission in real or mixed actions involving real property shall not be possible if the law where the property is situated forbids it.

Art. 319. The submission can be made only to a judge having ordinary jurisdiction to take cognizance of a similar class of cases in the same degree.

Art. 320. In no case shall the parties be able to submit themselves expressly or impliedly for relief to any judge or court other than that to whom is subordinated according to local laws the one who took cognizance of the suit in the first instance.

Art. 321. By express submission shall be understood the submission made by the interested parties in clearly and conclusively renouncing their own court and unmistakably designating the judge to whom they submit themselves.

Art. 322. Implied submission shall be understood to have been made by the plaintiff from the fact of applying to the judge in filing the complaint, and by the defendant from the fact of his having, after entering his appearance in the suit, filed any plea unless it is for the purpose of denying jurisdiction. No submission can be implied when the suit is proceeded with as in default.

Art. 323. Outside the cases of express or implied submissions, without prejudice to local laws to the contrary, the judge competent for hearing personal causes shall be the one of the place where the obligation is to be performed, and in the absence thereof the one of the domicile or nationality of the defendants and subsidiarily that of their residence.

Art. 324. For the exercise of real actions in respect to personal property, the judge of the place where the property is situated shall be competent, and if it is not known by the plaintiff, then the judge of the domicile, and in the absence thereof, the one of the residence of the defendant.

Art. 325. For the exercise of real actions in respect to real property, and for that of mixed actions to determine boundary and partition of common property, the competent judge shall be the one where the property is situated.

Art. 326. If in the cases to which the two preceding articles refer there is any property situated in more than one of the contracting States, recourse may be had to the judges of any of them, unless prohibited, as to immovables, by the law of their situation.

Art. 327. In cases relating to the probate of wills or to intestate estates, the competent court will be that of the place in which the deceased had his last domicile.

Art. 328. In insolvency and bankruptcy proceedings, when the debtor has acted voluntarily, the judge of the domicile of the latter shall be the one competent.

Art. 329. In insolvency or bankruptcy proceedings brought by the creditors the competent judge shall be the one of any of the places who has cognizance of the claim which gives rise to them, preference being given, if among them, to that of the domicile of the debtor if he or the majority of the creditors demand it.

Art. 330. In respect to acts of voluntary jurisdiction, saving also the case of submission without prejudice to local laws to the contrary, the competent judge shall be the one of the place where the person instituting it has or has had his domicile, or if none, his residence.

Art. 331. Respecting acts of voluntary jurisdiction in commercial matters, apart from the case of submission, without prejudice to local laws to the contrary, the competent judge shall be the one of the place where the obligation should be performed or, in the absence thereof, the one of the place where the event giving rise to them occurred.

Art. 332. Within each contracting State, the preferable competence of several judges shall be in conformity with their national law.

Chapter II.—Exceptions to the General rules of competence in respect to civil and commercial matters

Art. 333. The judges and courts of

each contracting State shall be incompetent to take cognizance of civil or commercial cases to which the other contracting States or their heads are defendant parties, if the action is a personal one, except in case of express submission or of counterclaims.

Art. 334. In the same case and with the same exception, they shall be incompetent when real actions are exercised, if the contracting State or its head has acted on the case as such and in its public character, when the provisions of the last paragraph of Article 318 shall be applied.

Art. 335. If the foreign contracting State or its head has acted as an individual or private person, the judges or courts shall be competent to take cognizance of the cases where real or mixed actions are brought, if such competence belongs to them in respect to foreign individuals in conformity with this Code.

Art. 336. The rule of the preceding article shall be applicable to universal causes (*juicios universales, e.g.,* distribution of a bankrupt's or decedent's effects), whatever the character in which the contracting foreign State or its head intervenes in them.

Art. 337. The provisions established in preceding articles shall be applied to foreign diplomatic agents and to the commanders of war vessels or aircraft.

Art. 338. Foreign consuls shall not be exempt from the civil jurisdiction of the judges and courts of the country in which they act, except in respect to their official acts.

Art. 339. In no case can judges or courts adopt coercive or other measures which have to be executed within the legations or consulates or their archives, nor in respect to diplomatic or consular correspondence, without the consent of the respective diplomatic or consular agents.

*Chapter III.—General rules of competence in penal matters*

Art. 340. The judges and courts of the contracting State in which crimes or misdemeanors have been committed are competent to take cognizance of and pass judgment upon them.

Art. 341. Competence extends to all other crimes and misdemeanors to which the penal law of the State is to be applied in conformity with the provisions of this Code.

Art. 342. It also extends to crimes or misdemeanors committed in a foreign country by national officials enjoying the benefit of immunity.

*Chapter IV.—Exceptions to the general rules of competence in penal matters*

Art. 343. Persons and crimes and misdemeanors to which the penal law of the respective State does not extend are not subject, in penal matters, to the competence of the judges and courts of the contracting States.

## TITLE III

### EXTRADITION

Art. 344. In order to render effective the international judicial competence in penal matters each of the contracting States shall accede to the request of any of the others for the delivery of persons convicted or accused of crime, if in conformity with the provisions of this title, subject to the dispositions of the international treaties and conventions containing a list of penal infractions which authorize the extradition.

Art. 345. The contracting States are not obliged to hand over their own nationals. The nation which refuses to give up one of its citizens shall try him.

Art. 346. Whenever before the receipt of the request, a person accused or convicted has committed an offense in the country from which his delivery is requested, the said delivery may be postponed until he is tried and has served sentence.

Art. 347. If various contracting States should request the extradition of a delinquent for the same offense, he should be delivered to that one in whose territory the offense has been committed.

Art. 348. In case the extradition is requested for different acts, the preference shall belong to the contracting State in whose territory the most grievous offense has been committed, according to the legislation of the State upon which the request was made.

Art. 349. If all the acts imputed should be equally grave, the preference shall be given to the contracting State which first presents the request for extradition. If all have applied simultaneously, the State upon which the request was made shall decide, but the preference should be given to the State of origin, or in the absence thereof to that of the domicile, of the accused, if such State is among those requesting extradition.

Art. 350. The foregoing rules in respect to preference shall not be applicable if the contracting State is obligated toward a third one, by reason of treaties in force prior to the adoption of this Code, to establish a different method.

Art. 351. In order to grant extradition it is necessary that the offense has been committed in the territory of the State requesting it, or that its penal laws are applicable to it in accordance with the provisions of Book III of this Code.

Art. 352. Extradition extends to persons accused or convicted as principals, accomplices, or abettors of a consummated offense.

Art. 353. It is necessary that the act which gives rise to the extradition be a criminal offense in the legislation of the State making the request and in that upon which it is made.

Art. 354. It shall be likewise necessary that the penalty attached to the alleged acts, according to their provisional or final description by the competent judge or court of the State requesting the extradition, is not less than one year of deprivation of liberty, and that the arrest or detention of the accused has been ordered or decided upon, in case final sentence has not been delivered. The sentence should be deprivation of liberty.

Art. 355. Political offenses and acts related thereto, as defined by the requested State, are excluded from extradition.

Art. 356. Nor shall it be granted, if it is shown that the request for extradition has been in fact made for the purpose of trying or punishing the accused for an offense of a political character in accordance with the same definition.

Art. 357. Homicide or murder of the head of a contracting State or of any other person who exercises authority in said State, shall not be deemed a political offense nor an act related thereto.

Art. 358. Extradition shall not be granted if the person demanded has already been tried and acquitted, or served his sentence, or is awaiting trial, in the territory of the requested State for the offense upon which the request is based.

Art. 359. Nor should extradition be granted if the offense or the penalty is already barred by limitation by the laws of the requesting or requested State.

Art. 360. In all cases in which the legislation of the requested State prevents extradition it is an indispensable requirement that such legislation be enacted before the commission of the crime.

Art. 361. Consuls general, consuls, vice consuls, or consular agents may request the arrest and delivery on board of a vessel or aircraft of their country of the officers, sailors, or members of the crew of its war or merchant ships or aircraft who may have deserted therefrom.

Art. 362. For the purposes of the preceding article, they shall exhibit to the proper local authority, delivering also to it an authenticated copy thereof, the register of the ship or aircraft, the crew list, or any other official document upon which the request is founded.

Art. 363. In adjoining countries special rules may be agreed upon for extradition in the regions or localities of the boundary.

Art. 364. The request for extradition should be made through agents duly authorized for this purpose by the laws of the petitioning State.

Art. 365. Together with the final request for extradition the following should be submitted:

1. A sentence of conviction or a warrant or order of arrest or a document of equal force, or one which obliges the interested party to appear periodically before the criminal court together with such parts of the record in the case as furnish proof or at least some reasonable evidence of the guilt of the person in question.

2. The filiation of the person whose extradition is requested, or such marks or circumstances as may serve to identify him.

3. An authenticated copy of the provisions establishing the legal definition of the act which gives rise to the request for extradition, describing the participation imputed therein to the defendant, and prescribing the penalty applicable.

Art. 366. The extradition may be requested by telegraph and, in that case, the documents mentioned in the preceding article shall be presented to the requesting country or to its legation or consulate general in the requesting country, within two months following the detention of the accused. Otherwise he shall be set at liberty.

Art. 367. Moreover, if the requesting State does not dispose of the person demanded within three months following his being placed at its disposal, he shall be set at liberty.

Art. 368. The person detained may use, in the State to which the request for extradition is made, all legal means provided for its nationals for the purpose of regaining their freedom, basing the exercise thereof on the provisions of this Code.

Art. 369. The person detained may also thereafter use the legal remedies which are considered proper in the State which requests the extradition, against the qualifications and resolutions upon which the latter is founded.

Art. 370. The delivery should be made together with all the effects found in the possession of the person demanded, whether as proceeds of the alleged crime, or whether to be used as evidence, in so far as practicable in accordance with the laws of the State effecting the delivery and duly respecting the rights of third persons.

Art. 371. The delivery of the effects referred to in the preceding article can be made, if requested by the State requesting the extradition, even though the detained person dies or escapes before it is effected.

Art. 372. The expenses of detention and delivery shall be borne by the requesting State, but the latter shall not, in the meanwhile, have to defray any expenses for the services rendered by the public paid employees of the government from which extradition is requested.

Art. 373. The charge for the services of such public employees or officers as receive only fees or perquisites shall not exceed their customary fees for their acts or services under the laws of the country in which they reside.

Art. 374. All liability arising from the fact of a provisional detention shall rest upon the requesting State.

Art. 375. The passage of the extradited person and his custodians through the territory of a third contracting State shall be permitted upon presentation of the original document which allows the extradition, or of an authenticated copy thereof.

Art. 376. A State which obtains extradition of an accused who is afterwards acquitted shall be obliged to communicate to the State which granted it an authenticated copy of the judgment.

Art. 377. The person delivered can not be detained in prison nor tried by the contracting State to which he is delivered for an offense different from the one giving rise to the extradition and committed prior thereto, unless it is done with the consent of the requested State, or unless the extradited person remains free in the territory of the former for three months after his trial and acquittal for the offense which gave rise to the extradition, or after having served the sentence of deprivation of liberty imposed upon him.

Art. 378. In no case shall the death penalty be imposed or executed for the offense upon which the extradition is founded.

Art. 379. Whenever allowance for temporary detention is proper, it shall be computed from the time of the detention of the extradited person in the State to which the request was made.

Art. 380. The detained person shall be set free if the requesting State does not present the request for extradition in a reasonable period, within the least time possible after temporary arrest, taking into account the distance and facilities of postal communication between the two countries.

Art. 381. If the extradition of a person has been refused, a second request on account of the same crime cannot be made.

## Title IV

### THE RIGHT TO APPEAR IN COURT AND ITS MODALITIES

Art. 382. The nationals of each contracting State shall enjoy in each of the others the benefit of having counsel assigned to them upon the same conditions as natives.

Art. 383. No difference shall be made between nationals and foreigners in the contracting States in respect to giving security for judgment.

Art. 384. Aliens belonging to a contracting State may exercise in the others public rights of action in matters of a penal nature upon the same conditions as the nationals.

Art. 385. Nor shall those aliens be required to furnish security when exercising a private right of action in cases in which it is not required from nationals.

Art. 386. None of the contracting States shall require from the nationals of another the security *judicio sisti* nor the *onus probandi* in cases where they are not required from its own nationals.

Art. 387. No provisional attachments, bail, or any other measures of a similar nature shall be authorized in respect to the nationals of the contracting States by reason merely of their being foreigners.

## Title V

### LETTERS REQUISITORIAL OR LETTERS ROGATORY

Art. 388. Every judicial step which a contracting State has to take in another shall be effected by means of letters requisitorial or letters rogatory, transmitted through the diplomatic channel. Nevertheless, the contracting States may agree upon or accept as between themselves any other form of transmission in respect to civil or criminal matters.

Art. 389. The judge issuing the letters requisitorial is to decide as to his own competence and the legality and propriety of the act or evidence, without prejudice to the jurisdiction of the judge to whom said letters are addressed.

Art. 390. The judge to whom such letters requisitorial are sent shall decide as to his own competence *ratione materiae* in respect to the act which he is requested to perform.

Art. 391. The one receiving the letters requisitorial or letters rogatory should comply, as to the object thereof, with the law of the one issuing the same, and as to the manner of discharging the request he should comply with his own law.

Art. 392. The letters requisitorial will be written in the language of the State which sent them and will be accompanied by a translation in the language of the State to which they are addressed, said translation to be duly certified by a sworn public translator.

Art. 393. Parties interested in the execution of letters requisitorial and rogatory of a private nature should give powers of attorney, being responsible for the expenses incurred by the same and by the investigations made.

## TITLE VI

### EXCEPTIONS HAVING AN INTERNATIONAL CHARACTER

Art. 394. *Litispendencia* by reason of a suit in another of the contracting States may be pleaded in civil matters when the judgment rendered in one of them is to take effect in the other as *res judicata*.

Art. 395. In criminal cases the plea of *litispendencia* by reason of a cause pending in another contracting state shall not lie.

Art. 396. The plea of *res judicata* founded on a judgment of another contracting party shall lie only when the judgment has been rendered in the presence of the parties or their legal representatives, and no question founded on the provisions of this Code has arisen as to the competence of the foreign court.

Art. 397. In all cases of juridical relations subject to this Code questions of competence founded on its precepts may be addressed to the jurisdiction of the Court.

## TITLE VII

### EVIDENCE

*Chapter I.—General provisions in respect to evidence*

Art. 398. The law governing the offense or the legal relation constituting the subject of the civil or commercial suit determines upon whom the burden of proof rests.

Art. 399. In order to determine the modes of proof which may be used in each case, the law of the place in which the act or fact to be proved has taken place shall apply, except those which are not authorized by the law of the place in which the suit is instituted.

Art. 400. The form of the evidence is regulated by the law in force in the place where it is taken.

Art. 401. The weight of the evidence depends on the law of the judge.

Art. 402. Documents executed in each of the contracting States shall have in the others the same value in court as those executed therein, if they fulfil the following requirements:

1. That the subject matter of the act or contract in question is lawful and permitted by the laws of the country where it is executed and of that where it is used.

2. That the contracting parties have ability and capability to bind themselves in conformity with their personal law.

3. That in the execution thereof the forms and formalities established in the country where the acts or contracts have been executed have been observed.

4. That the document is authenticated and contains the other requisites necessary to this authenticity in the place where it is used.

Art. 403. The executory force of a document is subordinated to the local law.

Art. 404. The capacity of witnesses and challenging thereof depend upon the law to which the legal relation constituting the object of the suit is subject.

Art. 405. The form of the oath shall conform to the law of the judge or court before whom it is administered, and its validity is subject to the law governing the fact in respect to which the oath is taken.

Art. 406. The presumptions derived from an act are subject to the law of the place where the act giving rise to them occurs.

Art. 407. Circumstantial evidence is subject to the law of the judge or court.

*Chapter II.—Special rules on evidence of foreign laws*

Art. 408. The judge and courts of each contracting State shall apply *ex officio,* in suitable cases, the laws of the others, without prejudice to the means of proof referred to in this chapter.

Art. 409. The party invoking the application of the law of any contracting State in one of the others, or dissenting from it, may show the text thereof, force and sense, by means of a certificate subscribed by two practicing lawyers of the country whose legislation is in question, which certificate shall be duly authenticated.

Art. 410. In the absence of proof, or if the judge or the court deems it insufficient for any reason, they may request ex officio before deciding, through the diplomatic channel, that the State whose legislation is in question furnish a report on the text, force, and sense of the applicable law.

Art. 411. Each contracting State binds itself to furnish to the others, as soon as possible, the information referred to in the preceding article, which information should come from its Supreme Court, or from some one of its divisions or sections, or from the State Attorney, or from the Department or Ministry of Justice.

### TITLE VIII

#### APPEAL FOR ANNULMENT

Art. 412. In every contracting State where the appeal for annulment or other similar institution exists, it may be interposed for the infraction, erroneous interpretation, or improper application of a law of another contracting State, upon the same conditions and in the same cases as in respect to the national law.

Art. 413. The rules established in Chapter II of the preceding title shall be applicable to the appeal for annulment although the inferior judge or the lower court may have already applied them.

### TITLE IX

#### BANKRUPTCY OR INSOLVENCY

*Chapter I.—Unity of bankruptcy or insolvency*

Art. 414. If the insolvent or bankrupt creditor has only one civil or commercial domicile, there can be only one preventive proceeding in insolvency or bankruptcy, or one suspension of payments, or a composition ( *quita y espera* ) in respect of all his assets and his liabilities in the contracting States.

Art. 415. If one and the same person or partnership should have in more than one contracting State various commercial establishments entirely separate economically, there may be as many suits for preventive proceeding in bankruptcy as there are commercial establishments.

*Chapter II.—Universality of bankruptcy or insolvency, and their effects*

Art. 416. A decree establishing the capacity of the bankrupt or insolvent, has extraterritorial effect in each of the contracting States, upon the previous compliance with the formalities of registration or publication which may be required by the legislation of each State.

Art. 417. A decree of bankruptcy or insolvency, rendered in one of the contracting States, shall be executed in others in the cases and manner established in this code in respect to judicial resolutions; but it shall have the effect of *res judicata* from the moment it is made final, as to the persons which it is to affect.

Art. 418. The powers and functions of the trustees appointed in one of the contracting States in accordance with the provisions of this code shall have extraterritorial effect in the others, without the necessity of any local proceeding.

Art. 419. The retroactive effect of a

declaration of bankruptcy or insolvency and the annulment of certain acts in consequence of those judgments shall be determined by the law thereof and shall be applicable to the territory of all the other contracting States.

Art. 420. Real actions and rights of the same nature shall continue to be subject, notwithstanding the declaration in bankruptcy or insolvency, to the law of the situation of the things affected thereby and to the competence of the judges of the place in which they are found.

### Chapter III.—Agreement and rehabilitation

Art. 421. The agreement among the creditors and the bankrupt or insolvent shall have extraterritorial effect in the other contracting States, saving the right to a real action by the creditors who may not have accepted.

Art. 422. The rehabilitation of the bankrupt has also extraterritorial validity in the other contracting States, as soon as the judicial resolution by which it is ordered becomes final, and in conformity with its terms.

### TITLE X

#### EXECUTION OF JUDGMENTS RENDERED BY FOREIGN COURTS

### Chapter I.—Civil matters

Art. 423. Every civil or contentious administrative judgment rendered in one of the contracting States shall have force and may be executed in the others if it combines the following conditions:

1. That the judge or the court which has rendered it have competence to take cognizance of the matter and to pass judgment upon it, in accordance with the rules of this Code.

2. That the parties have been summoned for the trial either personally or through their legal representative;

3. That the judgment does not conflict with the public policy or the public

laws of the country in which its execution is sought;

4. That it is executory in the State in which it was rendered.

5. That it be authoritatively translated by an official functionary or interpreter of the State in which it is to be executed, if the language employed in the latter is different.

6. That the document in which it is contained fulfils the requirements necessary in order to be considered as authentic in the State from which it proceeds, and those which the legislation of the State in which the execution of the judgment is sought requires for authenticity.

Art. 424. The execution of the judgment should be requested from a competent judge or tribunal in order to carry it into effect, after complying with the formalities required by the internal legislation.

Art. 425. In the case referred to in the preceding article, every recourse against the judicial resolution granted by the laws of that State in respect to final judgments rendered in a declarative action of greater import shall be granted.

Art. 426. The judge or tribunal from whom the execution is requested shall, before decreeing or denying it, and for a term of twenty days, hear the party against whom it is directed as well as the prosecuting attorney.

Art. 427. The summons of the party who should be heard shall be made by means of letters requisitorial or letters rogatory, in accordance with the provisions of this Code if he has his domicile in a foreign country and lacks sufficient representation in the country, or in the form established by the local law if he has his domicile in the requested State.

Art. 428. After the term fixed for appearance by the judge or the court, the case shall be proceeded with whether or not the party summoned has appeared.

Art. 429. If the execution is denied,

the judgment shall be returned to the party who presented it.

Art. 430. When the execution of judgment is granted, the former shall be subject to the procedure determined by the law of the judge or the court for its own judgments.

Art. 431. Final judgments rendered by a contracting State which by reason of their pronouncements are not to be executed shall have in the other States the effects of *res judicata* if they fulfill the conditions provided for that purpose by this Code, except those relating to their execution.

Art. 432. The procedure and effects regulated in the preceding articles shall be applied in the contracting States to awards made in any of them by arbitrators or friendly compositors, whenever the case to which they refer can be the subject of a compromise in accordance with the legislation of the country where the execution is requested.

Art. 433. The same procedure shall be also applied in respect to civil judgments rendered in any of the contracting States by an international tribunal when referring to private persons or interests.

### Chapter II.—Acts of voluntary jurisdiction

Art. 434. The provisions made in acts of voluntary jurisdiction regarding commercial matters by judges or tribunals of a contracting State or by its consular agents shall be executed in the others in accordance with the procedure and the manner indicated in the preceding article.

Art. 435. The resolutions adopted in acts of voluntary jurisdiction in civil matters in a contracting State shall be accepted by the others if they fulfill the conditions required by this Code for the validity of documents executed in a foreign country and were rendered by a competent judge or tribunal, and they shall in consequence have extraterritorial validity.

### Chapter III.—Penal matters

Art. 436. No contracting State shall execute the judgments rendered in one of the others in penal matters in respect to the sanctions of that class which they impose.

Art. 437. They may, however, execute the said judgments in respect to civil liability and the effects thereof upon the property of the convicted person if they have been rendered by a competent judge or tribunal in accordance with this Code and upon a hearing of the interested party and if the other conditions of form and procedure established by the first chapter of this title have been complied with.

### Declaration of the Delegations of Colombia and of Costa Rica

The Delegations of Colombia and of Costa Rica subscribe to the Code of Private International Law as a whole with the express reservation as to everything which may be in contradiction with the Colombian or Costa Rican legislations.

With respect to juristic persons, our view is that they should be subject to the local law as regards everything relating to their "concept and recognition", as wisely provided by Article 32 of the Code, in contradiction,—at least apparently—with other provisions thereof, such as Articles 16 to 21.

For the undersigned Delegations, juristic persons can not have any nationality either under scientific principles or in the view of the highest and most permanent interests of America. It would have been preferable that in this Code which we are going to enact, there should have been omitted everything which might serve to assert that juristic persons, particularly those with capital stock, have nationality.

The undersigned Delegations, upon accepting the compromise set forth in Article 7 between the European doctrine of the personality of the law and the genuinely American doctrine of domicile for regulating the civil status and capacity of persons in private international law, declare that they accept this compromise in order not to delay the issuance of this Code, to which all the nations of America are looking forward as one of the most transcendental accomplishments of this Conference; but the subscribing Delegations emphatically assert that such a compromise should be transitory because juridical unity must be accomplished in the continent around the law of the domicile, the only one which effectively safeguards the sovereignty and independence of the peoples of America. Immigration countries, as these Republics are or will be, cannot but regard with the greatest concern that European immigrants should bring with them the pretension of invoking in America their own laws of origin, to determine here their civil status as to contractual capacity. To accept this possibility (which is sanctioned by the principle of national law, partially acknowledged in the Code), amounts to creating in America a State within a State and to placing ourselves almost under the capitulation régime which Europe imposed during centuries on the nations of Asia, which she considered as inferior in their international relations. The undersigned Delegations earnestly hope that very soon there will disappear from the American legislations all traces of theories (more political than legal) favored by Europe in order to preserve here jurisdiction over her nationals, who have established themselves in these free lands of America, and they hope that the legislation of the Continent will be unified in accordance with the principles that subject alien immigrants to the unrestricted force of the local laws. With the hope, therefore, that very soon the doctrine of the domicile will be the one to regulate in America the civil status and capacity of persons, and feeling assured that it will constitute one of the most characteristic aspects of juridical Pan-

Americanism, which we are all anxious to create, the undersigned Delegations vote in favor of the Code of Private International Law and accept the doctrinary compromise on which it is inspired.

As regards the provisions relative to divorce, the Delegation of Colombia formulates its unqualified reservation to the regulation of divorce by the law of the matrimonial domicile, because it considers that for such purpose and in view of the exceptionally transcendental and sacred character of marriage (basis of society and of the State itself) Colombia can not accept the application within her territory of alien laws.

The subscribing Delegations also desire to record their enthusiastic admiration for the fruitful efforts of Dr. Sanchez de Bustamante which the Code embodies in its five hundred articles, formulated in clear-cut phrases, which can well serve as models for the legislators of all countries. From this day on Dr. Sanchez de Bustamante will not only be one of the most eminent sons of Cuba, but also one of the foremost citizens of the great American fatherland which can justly feel proud of raising egregious scientists and statesmen like the author of the Code of Private International Law which we have considered, and which the Sixth International Conference of American States is about to sanction on behalf of all the Americas.

### Declaration of the Delegation of Guatemala

Guatemala has incorporated into its civil legislation the doctrine of domicile, but even if such were not the case, the conciliatory articles of the Code harmonize perfectly any conflict which might arise between different States due to their affiliation with diverse schools.

In consequence, therefore, the Delegation of Guatemala is in perfect accord with the method which, with so much wisdom, caution, ingenuity, and scientific judgment, is set forth in the Project of Code of Private International Law, and it desires to leave express record of its absolute acceptance of the latter without reservations of any kind.

### RESERVATIONS OF THE DELEGATION OF SALVADOR

*First Reservation:* Especially applicable to Articles 44, 146, 176, 232, and 233.

With respect to the incapacities to which aliens may be subjected in accordance with their personal law for disposing by will, for entering into contracts, for appearing in court, and for engaging in commerce or participating in commercial transactions or contracts, the reservation is made that said incapacities will not be acknowleged in Salvador in cases where the transactions or contracts in question have been executed in Salvador without contravention of the Salvadorean law and to take effect within its national territory.

*Second Reservation:* Applicable to Article 187, last paragraph.

As to community of property imposed upon spouses by their personal law under the legislation of a foreign state, it will be recognized in Salvador only if confirmed by contract between the interested parties and all requirements which the Salvadorean law now provides or may hereafter provide with respect to property located in Salvador are complied with.

*Third Reservation:* Especially applicable to Articles 327, 328, and 329.

The Delegation of Salvador makes the reservation that in so far as Salvador is concerned the jurisdiction of foreign judges or tribunals in inheritance hearings and proceedings and in creditors' suits and bankruptcy cases affecting immovables located in Salvador, will be unacceptable.

### DECLARATION OF THE DELEGATION OF NICARAGUA

The Republic of Nicaragua will be unable to apply the provisions of the Code of Private International Law which may be in conflict with the Canon Law in matters which now or in the future Nicaragua may consider to be subject to such Canon Law.

The Nicaraguan Delegation declares, as it has previously done several times verbally throughout the discussions, that some of the provisions of the approved Code are in disagreement with express provisions of the legislation of Nicaragua or with principles which form the basis of such legislation; but, as deserved homage to the notable work of the illustrious author of this Code, it chooses, instead of formulating the corresponding reservations, to make these declarations and to leave to the public authorities of Nicaragua the formulation of such reservations or the modification, as far as possible, of the national legislation, in cases of conflict.

### DECLARATION OF THE DELEGATION OF PANAMÁ

When casting its vote in favor of the Project of Code of Private International Law at the meeting of the Committee held on January 27th ultimo, the Delegation of the Republic of Panamá stated that at an opportune time it would present such reservations as it might deem necessary, should the need arise. This attitude of the Delegation of Panamá was due to certain doubts it entertained with reference to the meaning and scope of some of the provisions contained in the Project, particularly as regards the application of the national law to foreigners residing in the country, as this would have given rise to a real conflict, because in the Republic of Panamá ever since its establishment as an independent nation, the system of the territorial law has been in force. However, the Delegation of Panamá considers that all the difficulties which could possibly arise in this delicate matter have been foreseen and wisely obviated by Article 7 of the Project, in accordance with which "each contracting State shall apply as personal law that of the domicile or that of the nationality, or that which its domestic legislation may have prescribed or may hereafter prescribe." As in the case of all other States subscribing and ratifying the Convention, Panamá, therefore, will be at full liberty to apply its own law, which is the territorial law.

With matters so understood, it is highly gratifying for the Delegation of Panamá to declare, as it does, that it extends its approval without reservations of any kind to the Project of Code of Private International Law, or Bustamante Code, as it should be called in honor of its author.

## EUROPEAN ECONOMIC COMMUNITY CONVENTION ON JURISDICTION AND THE ENFORCEMENT OF JUDGMENTS IN CIVIL AND COMMERCIAL MATTERS

[Text as amended by the Convention of Accession]

### PREAMBLE

THE HIGH CONTRACTING PARTIES TO THE TREATY ESTABLISHING THE EUROPEAN ECONOMIC COMMUNITY,

Desiring to implement the provisions of Article 220 of that Treaty by virtue of which they undertook to secure the simplification of formalities governing the reciprocal recognition and enforcement of judgments of courts or tribunals;

Anxious to strengthen in the Community the legal protection of persons therein established;

Considering that it is necessary for this purpose to determine the international jurisdiction of their courts, to facilitate recognition and to introduce an expeditious procedure for securing the enforcement of judgments, authentic instruments and court settlements;

Have decided to conclude this Convention. . . .

### TITLE I: SCOPE

*Article 1.* This Convention shall apply in civil and commercial matters whatever the nature of the court or tribunal. It shall not extend, in particular, to revenue, customs or administrative matters.

The Convention shall not apply to:
1. the status or legal capacity of natural persons, rights in property arising out of a matrimonial relationship, wills and succession;
2. bankruptcy, proceedings relating to the winding-up of insolvent companies or other legal persons, judicial arrangements, compositions and analogous proceedings;
3. social security;
4. arbitration.

### TITLE II: JURISDICTION

Section 1: General provisions

*Article 2.* Subject to the provisions of this Convention, persons domiciled in a Contracting State shall, whatever their nationality, be sued in the courts of that State.

Persons who are not nationals of the State in which they are domiciled shall be governed by the rules of jurisdiction applicable to nationals of that State.

*Article 3.* Persons domiciled in a Contracting State may be sued in the courts of another Contracting State only by virtue of the rules set out in Sections 2 to 6 of this Title.

In particular the following provisions shall not be applicable as against them:
— in Belgium: Article 15 of the civil code (Code civil — Burgerlijk Wetboek) and Article 638 of the judicial code (Code judiciaire — Gerechtelijk Wetboek),
— in Denmark: Article 248 (2) of the law on civil procedure (Lov om rettens pleje) and Chapter 3, Article 3 of the Greenland law on civil procedure (Lov for Grønland om rettens pleje),
— in the Federal Republic of Germany: Article 23 of the code of civil procedure (Zivilprozeßordnung),
— in France: Articles 14 and 15 of the civil code (Code civil),
— in Ireland: the rules which enable jurisdiction to be founded on the document instituting the proceedings having been served on the defendant during his temporary presence in Ireland,
— in Italy: Articles 2 and 4, Nos 1 and 2 of the code of civil procedure (Codice di procedura civile),
— in Luxembourg: Articles 14 and 15 of the civil code (Code civil),
— in the Netherlands: Articles 126 (3) and 127 of the code of civil procedure (Wetboek van Burgerlijke Rechtsvordering),
— in the United Kingdom: the rules which enable jurisdiction to be founded on:
  (a) the document instituting the proceedings having been served on the defendant during his temporary presence in the United Kingdom; or
  (b) the presence within the United

Kingdom of property belonging to the defendant; or
  (c) the seizure by the plaintiff of property situated in the United Kingdom.

*Article 4.* If the defendant is not domiciled in a Contracting State, the jurisdiction of the courts of each Contracting State shall, subject to the provisions of Article 16, be determined by the law of that State.

As against such a defendant, any person domiciled in a Contracting State may, whatever his nationality, avail himself in that State of the rules of jurisdiction there in force, and in particular those specified in the second paragraph of Article 3, in the same way as the nationals of that State.

Section 2: Special jurisdiction

*Article 5.* A person domiciled in a Contracting State may, in another Contracting State, be sued:
1. in matters relating to a contract, in the courts for the place of performance of the obligation in question;
2. in matters relating to maintenance, in the courts for the place where the maintenance creditor is domiciled or habitually resident or, if the matter is ancillary to proceedings concerning the status of a person, in the court which, according to its own law, has jurisdiction to entertain those proceedings, unless that jurisdiction is based solely on the nationality of one of the parties;
3. in matters relating to tort, delict or quasi-delict, in the courts for the place where the harmful event occurred;
4. as regards a civil claim for damages or restitution which is based on an act giving rise to criminal proceedings, in the court seised of those proceedings, to the extent that that court has jurisdiction under its own law to entertain civil proceedings;
5. as regards a dispute arising out of the

operations of a branch, agency or other establishment, in the courts for the place in which the branch, agency or other establishment is situated;

6. as settlor, trustee or beneficiary of a trust created by the operation of a statute, or by a written instrument, or created orally and evidenced in writing, in the courts of the Contracting State in which the trust is domiciled;

7. as regards a dispute concerning the payment of remuneration claimed in respect of the salvage of a cargo or freight, in the court under the authority of which the cargo or freight in question:
   (a) has been arrested to secure such payment, or
   (b) could have been so arrested, but bail or other security has been given;
   provided that this provision shall apply only if it is claimed that the defendant has an interest in the cargo or freight or had such an interest at the time of salvage.

*Article 6.* A person domiciled in a Contracting State may also be sued:

1. where he is one of a number of defendants, in the courts for the place where any one of them is domiciled;

2. as a third party in an action on a warranty or guarantee or in any other third party proceedings, in the court seised of the original proceedings, unless these were instituted solely with the object of removing him from the jurisdiction of the court which would be competent in his case;

3. on a counter-claim arising from the same contract or facts on which the original claim was based, in the court in which the original claim is pending.

*Article 6a.* Where by virtue of this Convention a court of a Contracting State has jurisdiction in actions relating to liability arising from the use or operation of a ship, that court, or any other court

substituted for this purpose by the internal law of that State, shall also have jurisdiction over claims for limitation of such liability.

Section 3: Jurisdiction in matters relating to insurance

*Article 7.* In matters relating to insurance, jurisdiction shall be determined by this Section, without prejudice to the provisions of Articles 4 and 5 (5).

*Article 8.* An insurer domiciled in a Contracting State may be sued:

1. in the courts of the State where he is domiciled, or

2. in another Contracting State, in the courts for the place where the policyholder is domiciled, or

3. if he is a co-insurer, in the courts of a Contracting State in which proceedings are brought against the leading insurer.

An insurer who is not domiciled in a Contracting State but has a branch, agency or other establishment in one of the Contracting States shall, in disputes arising out of the operations of the branch, agency or establishment, be deemed to be domiciled in that State.

*Article 9.* In respect of liability insurance or insurance of immovable property, the insurer may in addition be sued in the courts for the place where the harmful event occurred. The same applies if movable and immovable property are covered by the same insurance policy and both are adversely affected by the same contingency.

*Article 10.* In respect of liability insurance, the insurer may also, if the law of the court permits it, be joined in proceedings which the injured party has brought against the insured.

The provisions of Articles 7, 8 and 9 shall apply to actions brought by the injured party directly against the insurer, where such direct actions are permitted.

If the law governing such direct actions provides that the policy-holder or the insured may be joined as a party to the action, the same court shall have jurisdiction over them.

*Article 11.* Without prejudice to the provisions of the third paragraph of Article 10, an insurer may bring proceedings only in the courts of the Contracting State in which the defendant is domiciled, irrespective of whether he is the policy-holder, the insured or a beneficiary.

The provisions of this Section shall not affect the right to bring a counter-claim in the court in which, in accordance with this Section, the original claim is pending.

*Article 12.* The provisions of this Section may be departed from only by an agreement on jurisdiction:
1. which is entered into after the dispute has arisen, or
2. which allows the policy-holder, the insured or a beneficiary to bring proceedings in courts other than those indicated in this Section, or
3. which is concluded between a policy-holder and an insurer, both of whom are domiciled in the same Contracting State, and which has the effect of conferring jurisdiction on the courts of that State even if the harmful event were to occur abroad, provided that such an agreement is not contrary to the law of that State, or
4. which is concluded with a policy-holder who is not domiciled in a Contracting State, except in so far as the insurance is compulsory or relates to immovable property in a Contracting State, or
5. which relates to a contract of insurance in so far as it covers one or more of the risks set out in Article 12a.

*Article 12a.* The following are the risks referred to in Article 12 (5):
1. Any loss of or damage to
   (a) sea-going ships, installations situated off-shore or on the high seas, or aircraft, arising from perils which relate to their use for commercial purposes,
   (b) goods in transit other than passengers' baggage where the transit consists of or includes carriage by such ships or aircraft;
2. Any liability, other than for bodily injury to passengers or loss of or damage to their baggage,
   (a) arising out of the use or operation of ships, installations or aircraft as referred to in (1) (a) above in so far as the law of the Contracting State in which such aircraft are registered does not prohibit agreements on jurisdiction regarding insurance of such risks,
   (b) for loss or damage caused by goods in transit as described in (1) (b) above;
3. Any financial loss connected with the use or operation of ships, installations or aircraft as referred to in (1) (a) above, in particular loss of freight or charter-hire;
4. Any risk or interest connected with any of those referred to in (1) to (3) above.

Section 4: Jurisdiction over consumer contracts

*Article 13.* In proceedings concerning a contract concluded by a person for a purpose which can be regarded as being outside his trade or profession, hereinafter called 'the consumer', jurisdiction shall be determined by this Section, without prejudice to the provisions of Articles 4 and 5 (5), if it is:
1. a contract for the sale of goods on instalment credit terms, or
2. a contract for a loan repayable by instalments, or for any other form of credit, made to finance the sale of goods, or
3. any other contract for the supply of goods or a contract for the supply of services, and

(a) in the State of the consumer's domicile the conclusion of the contract was preceded by a specific invitation addressed to him or by advertising, and

(b) the consumer took in that State the steps necessary for the conclusion of the contract.

Where a consumer enters into a contract with a party who is not domiciled in a Contracting State but has a branch, agency or other establishment in one of the Contracting States, that party shall, in disputes arising out of the operations of the branch, agency or establishment, be deemed to be domiciled in that State.

This Section shall not apply to contracts of transport.

*Article 14.* A consumer may bring proceedings against the other party to a contract either in the courts of the Contracting State in which that party is domiciled or in the courts of the Contracting State in which he is himself domiciled.

These provisions shall not affect the right to bring a counter-claim in the court in which, in accordance with this Section, the original claim is pending.

*Article 15.* The provisions of this Section may be departed from only by an agreement:

1. which is entered into after the dispute has arisen, or

2. which allows the consumer to bring proceedings in courts other than those indicated in this Section, or

3. which is entered into by the consumer and the other party to the contract, both of whom are at the time of conclusion of the contract domiciled or habitually resident in the same Contracting State, and which confers jurisdiction on the courts of that State, provided that such an agreement is not contrary to the law of that State.

Section 5: Exclusive jurisdiction

*Article 16.* The following courts shall

have exclusive jurisdiction, regardless of domicile:

1. in proceedings which have as their object rights *in rem* in, or tenancies of, immovable property, the courts of the Contracting State in which the property is situated;

2. in proceedings which have as their object the validity of the constitution, the nullity or the dissolution of companies or other legal persons or associations of natural or legal persons, or the decisions of their organs, the courts of the Contracting State in which the company, legal person or association has its seat;

3. in proceedings which have as their object the validity of entries in public registers, the courts of the Contracting State in which the register is kept;

4. in proceedings concerned with the registration or validity of patents, trade marks, designs, or other similar rights required to be deposited or registered, the courts of the Contracting State in which the deposit or registration has been applied for, has taken place or is under the terms of an international convention deemed to have taken place;

5. in proceedings concerned with the enforcement of judgments, the courts of the Contracting State in which the judgment has been or is to be enforced.

Section 6: Prorogation of jurisdiction

*Article 17.* If the parties, one or more of whom is domiciled in a Contracting State, have agreed that a court or the courts of a Contracting State are to have jurisdiction to settle any disputes which have arisen or which may arise in connection with a particular legal relationship, that court or those courts shall have exclusive jurisdiction. Such an agreement conferring jurisdiction shall be either in writing or evidenced in writing or, in international trade or commerce, in a form which accords with practices in that trade or commerce of which the parties are or ought to have been aware. Where such an agreement is concluded by parties, none of whom is domiciled in a Contracting State, the courts of other Contracting States shall have no jurisdiction over their disputes unless the court or courts chosen have declined jurisdiction.

The court or courts of a Contracting State on which a trust instrument has conferred jurisdiction shall have exclusive jurisdiction in any proceedings brought against a settlor, trustee or beneficiary, if relations between these persons or their rights or obligations under the trust are involved.

Agreements or provisions of a trust instrument conferring jurisdiction shall have no legal force if they are contrary to the provisions of Article 12 or 15, or if the courts whose jurisdiction they purport to exclude have exclusive jurisdiction by virtue of Article 16.

If an agreement conferring jurisdiction was concluded for the benefit of only one of the parties, that party shall retain the right to bring proceedings in any other court which has jurisdiction by virtue of this Convention.

*Article 18.* Apart from jurisdiction derived from other provisions of this Convention, a court of a Contracting State before whom a defendant enters an appearance shall have jurisdiction. This rule shall not apply where appearance was entered solely to contest the jurisdiction, or where another court has exclusive jurisdiction by virtue of Article 16.

Section 7: Examination as to jurisdiction and admissibility

*Article 19.* Where a court of a Contracting State is seised of a claim which is principally concerned with a matter over which the courts of another Contracting State have exclusive jurisdiction by virtue of Article 16, it shall declare of its own motion that it has no jurisdiction.

*Article 20.* Where a defendant domiciled in one Contracting State is sued in a court of another Contracting State and does not enter an appearance, the court shall declare of its own motion that it has no jurisdiction unless its jurisdiction is derived from the provisions of this Convention.

The court shall stay the proceedings so long as it is not shown that the defendant has been able to receive the document instituting the proceedings or an equivalent document in sufficient time to enable him to arrange for his defence, or that all necessary steps have been taken to this end.

The provisions of the foregoing paragraph shall be replaced by those of Article 15 of the Hague Convention of 15 November 1965 on the service abroad of judicial and extrajudicial documents in civil or commercial matters, if the document instituting the proceedings or notice thereof had to be transmitted abroad in accordance with that Convention.

Section 8: Lis Pendens — related actions

*Article 21.* Where proceedings involving the same cause of action and between the same parties are brought in the courts of different Contracting States, any court other than the court first seised shall of its own motion decline jurisdiction in favour of that court.

A court which would be required to decline jurisdiction may stay its proceedings if the jurisdiction of the other court is contested.

*Article 22.* Where related actions are brought in the courts of different Contracting States, any court other than the court first seised may, while the actions are pending at first instance, stay its proceedings.

A court other than the court first seised may also, on the application of one of the parties, decline jurisdiction if the law of that court permits the consolidation of related actions and the court first seised has jurisdiction over both actions.

For the purposes of this Article, actions are deemed to be related where they are so closely connected that it is expedient to hear and determine them together to avoid the risk of irreconcilable judgments resulting from separate proceedings.

*Article 23.* Where actions come within the exclusive jurisdiction of several courts, any court other than the court first seised shall decline jurisdiction in favour of that court.

### Section 9: Provisional, including protective, measures

*Article 24.* Application may be made to the courts of a Contracting State for such provisional, including protective, measures as may be available under the law of that State, even if, under this Convention, the courts of another Contracting State have jurisdiction as to the substance of the matter.

### TITLE III: RECOGNITION AND ENFORCEMENT

*Article 25.* For the purposes of this Convention, 'judgment' means any judgment given by a court or tribunal of a Contracting State, whatever the judgment may be called, including a decree, order, decision or writ of execution, as well as the determination of costs or expenses by an officer of the court.

### Section 1: Recognition

*Article 26.* A judgment given in a Contracting State shall be recognized in the other Contracting States without any special procedure being required.

Any interested party who raises the recognition of a judgment as the principal issue in a dispute may, in accordance with the procedures provided for in Sections 2 and 3 of this Title, apply for a decision that the judgment be recognized.

If the outcome of proceedings in a court of a Contracting State depends on the determination of an incidental question of recognition that court shall have jurisdiction over that question.

*Article 27.* A judgment shall not be recognized:

1. if such recognition is contrary to public policy in the State in which recognition is sought;
2. where it was given in default of appearance, if the defendant was not duly served with the document which instituted the proceedings or with an equivalent document in sufficient time to anable him to arrange for his defence;
3. if the judgment is irreconcilable with a judgment given in a dispute between the same parties in the State in which recognition is sought;
4. if the court of the State in which the judgment was given, in order to arrive at its judgment, has decided a preliminary question concerning the status or legal capacity of natural persons, rights in property arising out of a matrimonial relationship, wills or succession in a way that conflicts with a rule of the private international law of the State in which the recognition is sought, unless the same result would have been reached by the application of the rules of private international law of that State;
5. if the judgment is irreconcilable with an earlier judgment given a a non-Contracting State involving the same cause of action and between the same parties, provided that this latter judgment fulfils the conditions necessary for its recognition in the State addressed.

*Article 28.* Moreover, a judgment shall shall not be recognized if it conflicts with the provisions of Section 3, 4 or 5 of Title II, or in a case provided for in Article 59.

In its examination of the grounds of jurisdiction referred to in the foregoing paragraph, the court or authority applied to shall be bound by the findings of fact on which the court of the State in which the judgment was given based its jurisdiction.

Subject to the provisions of the first paragraph, the jurisdiction of the court of the State in which the judgment was given may not be reviewed; the test of public policy referred to in Article 27 (1) may not be applied to the rules relating to jurisdiction.

*Article 29.* Under no circumstances may a foreign judgment be reviewed as to its substance.

*Article 30.* A court of a Contracting State in which recognition is sought of a judgment given in another Contracting State may stay the proceedings if an ordinary appeal against the judgment has been lodged.

A court of a Contracting State in which recognition is sought of a judgment given in Ireland or the United Kingdom may stay the proceedings if enforcement is suspended in the State in which the judgment was given by reason of an appeal.

### Section 2: Enforcement

*Article 31.* A judgment given in a Contracting State and enforceable in that State shall be enforced in another Contracting State when, on the application of any interested party, the order for its enforcement has been issued there.

However, in the United Kingdom, such a judgment shall be enforced in England and Wales, in Scotland, or in Northern Ireland when, on the application of any interested party, it has been registered for enforcement in that part of the United Kingdom.

*Article 32.* The application shall be submitted:
— in Belgium, to the tribunal de première instance or rechtbank van eerste aanleg,
— in Denmark, to the underret,
— in the Federal Republic of Germany,

to the presiding judge of a chamber of the Landgericht,
— in France, to the presiding judge of the tribunal de grande instance,
— in Ireland, to the High Court,
— in Italy, to the corte d'appello,
— in Luxembourg, to the presiding judge of the tribunal d'arrondissement,
— in the Netherlands, to the presiding judge of the arrondissementsrechtbank,
— in the United Kingdom:
  1. in England and Wales, to the High Court of Justice, or in the case of a maintenance judgment to the Magistrates' Court on transmission by the Secretary of State;
  2. in Scotland, to the Court of Session, or in the case of a maintenance judgment to the Sheriff Court on transmission by the Secretary of State;
  3. in Northern Ireland, to the High Court of Justice, or in the case of a maintenance judgment to the Magistrates' Court on transmission by the Secretary of State.

The jurisdiction of local courts shall be determined by reference to the place of domicile of the party against whom enforcement is sought. If he is not domiciled in the State in which enforcement is sought, it shall be determined by reference to the place of enforcement.

*Article 33.* The procedure for making the application shall be governed by the law of the State in which enforcement is sought.

The applicant must give an address for service of process within the area of jurisdiction of the court applied to. However, if the law of the State in which enforcement is sought does not provide for the furnishing of such an address, the applicant shall appoint a representative *ad litem.*

The documents referred to in Articles 46 and 47 shall be attached to the application.

*Article 34.* The court applied to shall give its decision without delay; the party against whom enforcement is sought shall not at this stage of the proceedings be entitled to make any submissions on the application.

The application may be refused only for one of the reasons specified in Articles 27 and 28.

Under no circumstances may the foreign judgment be reviewed as to its substance.

*Article 35.* The appropriate officer of the court shall without delay bring the decision given on the application to the notice of the applicant in accordance with the procedure laid down by the law of the State in which enforcement is sought.

*Article 36.* If enforcement is authorized, the party against whom enforcement is sought may appeal against the decision within one month of service thereof.

If that party is domiciled in a Contracting State other than that in which the decision authorizing enforcement was given, the time for appealing shall be two months and shall run from the date of service, either on him in person or at his residence. No extension of time may be granted on account of distance.

*Article 37.* An appeal against the decision authorizing enforcement shall be lodged in accordance with the rules governing procedure in contentious matters:
— in Belgium, with the tribunal de première instance or rechtbank van eerste aanleg,
— in Denmark, with the landsret,
— in the Federal Republic of Germany, with the Oberlandesgericht,
— in France, with the cour d'appel,
— in Ireland, with the High Court,
— in Italy, with the corte d'appello,
— in Luxembourg, with the Cour supérieure de justice sitting as a court of civil appeal,
— in the Netherlands, with the arrondissementsrechtbank,
— in the United Kingdom:

1. in England and Wales, with the High Court of Justice, or in the case of a maintenance judgment with the Magistrates' Court;
2. in Scotland, with the Court of Session, or in the case of a maintenance judgment with the Sheriff Court;
3. in Northern Ireland, with the High Court of Justice, or in the case of a maintenance judgment with the Magistrates' Court.

The judgment given on the appeal may be contested only:
— in Belgium, France, Italy, Luxembourg and the Netherlands, by an appeal in cassation,
— in Denmark, by an appeal to the højesteret, with the leave of the Minister of Justice,
— in the Federal Republic of Germany, by a Rechtsbeschwerde,
— in Ireland, by an appeal on a point of law to the Supreme Court,
— in the United Kingdom, by a single further appeal on a point of law.

*Article 38.* The court with which the appeal under the first paragraph of Article 37 is lodged may, on the application of the appellant, stay the proceedings if an ordinary appeal has been lodged against the judgment in the State in which that judgment was given or if the time for such an appeal has not yet expired; in the latter case, the court may specify the time within which such an appeal is to be lodged.

Where the judgment was given in Ireland or the United Kingdom, any form of appeal available in the State in which it was given shall be treated as an ordinary appeal for the purposes of the first paragraph.

The court may also make enforcement conditional on the provision of such security as it shall determine.

*Article 39.* During the time specified for an appeal pursuant to Article 36 and until any such appeal has been determined, no measures of enforcement may be taken other than protective measures taken against the property of the party against whom enforcement is sought.

The decision authorizing enforcement shall carry with it the power to proceed to any such protective measures.

*Article 40.* If the application for enforcement is refused, the applicant may appeal:
— in Belgium, to the cour d'appel or hof van beroep,
— in Denmark, to the landsret,
— in the Fèderal Republic of Germany, to the Oberlandesgericht,
— in France, to the cour d'appel,
— in Ireland, to the High Court,
— in Italy, to the corte d'appello,
— in Luxembourg, to the Cour supérieure de justice sitting as a court of civil appeal,
— in the Netherlands, to the gerechtshof,
— in the United Kingdom:
  1. in England and Wales, to the High Court of Justice, or in the case of a maintenance judgment to the Magistrates' Court;
  2. in Scotland, to the Court of Session, or in the case of a maintenance judgment to the Sheriff Court;
  3. in Northern Ireland, to the High Court of Justice, or in the case of a maintenance judgment to the Magistrates' Court.

The party against whom enforcement is sought shall be summoned to appear before the appellate court. If he fails to appear, the provisions of the second and third paragraphs of Article 20 shall apply even where he is not domiciled in any of the Contracting States.

*Article 41.* A judgment given on an appeal provided for in Article 40 may be contested only:
— in Belgium, France, Italy, Luxembourg and the Netherlands, by an appeal in cassation,
— in Denmark, by an appeal to the

højesteret, with the leave of the Minister of Justice,
— in the Federal Republic of Germany, by a Rechtsbeschwerde,
— in Ireland, by an appeal on a point of law to the Supreme Court,
— in the United Kingdom, by a single further appeal on a point of law.

*Article 42.* Where a foreign judgment has been given in respect of several matters and enforcement cannot be authorized for all of them, the court shall authorize enforcement for one or more of them.

An applicant may request partial enforcement of a judgment.

*Article 43.* A foreign judgment which orders a periodic payment by way of a penalty shall be enforceable in the State in which enforcement is sought only if the amount of the payment has been finally determined by the courts of the State in which the judgment was given.

*Article 44.* An applicant who, in the State in which the judgment was given, has benefited from complete or partial legal aid or exemption from costs or expenses, shall be entitled, in the procedures provided for in Articles 32 to 35, to benefit from the most favourable legal aid or the most extensive exemption from costs or expenses provided for by the law of the State addressed.

However, an applicant who requests the enforcement of a decision given by an administrative authority in Denmark in respect of a maintenance order may, in the State addressed, claim the benefits referred to in the first paragraph if he presents a statement from the Danish Ministry of Justice to the effect that he fulfils the economic requirements to qualify for the grant of complete or partial legal aid or exemption from costs or expenses.

*Article 45.* No security, bond or deposit, however described, shall be required of a party who in one Contracting State applies for enforcement of a judgment given in another Contracting State on the ground that he is a foreign national or that he is not domiciled or resident in the State in which enforcement is sought.

### Section 3: Common provisions

*Article 46.* A party seeking recognition or applying for enforcement of a judgment shall produce:

1. a copy of the judgment which satisfies the conditions necessary to establish its authenticity;

2. in the case of a judgment given in default, the original or a certified true copy of the document which establishes that the party in default was served with the document instituting the proceedings or with an equivalent document.

*Article 47.* A party applying for enforcement shall also produce:

1. documents which establish that, according to the law of the State in which it has been given, the judgment is enforceable and has been served;

2. where appropriate, a document showing that the applicant is in receipt of legal aid in the State in which the judgment was given.

*Article 48.* If the documents specified in Article 46(2) and Article 47(2) are not produced, the court may specify a time for their production, accept equivalent documents or, if it considers that it has sufficient information before it, dispense with their production.

If the court so requires, a translation of the documents shall be produced; the translation shall be certified by a person qualified to do so in one of the Contracting States.

*Article 49.* No legalization or other similar formality shall be required in respect of the documents referred to in Articles 46, 47, or the second paragraph of Article 48, or in respect of a document appointing a representative *ad litem.*

### TITLE IV: AUTHENTIC INSTRUMENTS AND COURT SETTLEMENTS

*Article 50.* A document which has been formally drawn up or registered as an authentic instrument and is enforceable in one Contracting State shall, in another Contracting State, have an order for its enforcement issued there, on application made in accordance with the procedures provided for in Article 31 *et seq.* The application may be refused only if enforcement of the instrument is contrary to public policy in the State in which enforcement is sought.

The instrument produced must satisfy the conditions necessary to establish its authenticity in the State of origin.

The provisions of Section 3 of Title III shall apply as appropriate.

*Article 51.* A settlement which has been approved by a court in the course of proceedings and is enforceable in the State in which it was concluded shall be enforceable in the State in which enforcement is sought under the same conditions as authentic instruments.

### TITLE V: GENERAL PROVISIONS

*Article 52.* In order to determine whether a party is domiciled in the Contracting State whose courts are seised of a matter, the court shall apply its internal law.

If a party is not domiciled in the State whose courts are seised of the matter, then, in order to determine whether the party is domiciled in another Contracting State, the court shall apply the law of that State.

The domicile of a party shall, however, be determined in accordance with his national law if, by that law, his domicile depends on that of another person or on the seat of an authority.

*Article 53.* For the purposes of this Convention, the seat of a company or other legal person or association of natural or legal persons shall be treated as its domicile. However, in order to determine that seat, the court shall apply its rules of private international law.

In order to determine whether a trust is domiciled in the Contracting State whose courts are seised of the matter, the court shall apply its rules of private international law.

### TITLE VI: TRANSITIONAL PROVISIONS

*Article 54.* The provisions of this Convention shall apply only to legal proceedings instituted and to documents formally drawn up or registered as authentic instruments after its entry into force.

However, judgments given after the date of entry into force of this Convention in proceedings instituted before that date shall be recognized and enforced in accordance with the provisions of Title III if jurisdiction was founded upon rules which accorded with those provided for either in Title II of this Convention or in a convention concluded between the State of origin and the State addressed which was in force when the proceedings were instituted.

### TITLE VII: RELATIONSHIP TO OTHER CONVENTIONS

*Article 55.* Subject to the provisions of the second paragraph of Article 54, and of Article 56, this Convention shall, for the States which are parties to it, supersede the following conventions concluded between two or more of them:
— the Convention between Belgium and France on jurisdiction and the validity and enforcement of judgments, arbitration awards and authentic instruments, signed at Paris on 8 July 1899,
— the Convention between Belgium and the Netherlands on jurisdiction, bankruptcy, and the validity and enforcement of judgments, arbitration awards and authentic instruments, signed at Brussels on 28 March 1925,

— the Convention between France and Italy on the enforcement of judgments in civil and commercial matters, signed at Rome on 3 June 1930,
— the Convention between the United Kingdom and the French Republic providing for the reciprocal enforcement of judgments in civil and commercial matters, with Protocol, signed at Paris on 18 January 1934,
— the Convention between the United Kingdom and the Kingdom of Belgium providing for the reciprocal enforcement of judgments in civil and commercial matters, with Protocol, signed at Brussels on 2 May 1934,
— the Convention between Germany and Italy on the recognition and enforcement of judgments in civil and commercial matters, signed at Rome on 9 March 1936,
— the Convention between the Federal Republic of Germany and the Kingdom of Belgium on the mutual recognition and enforcement of judgments, arbitration awards and authentic instruments in civil and commercial matters, signed at Bonn on 30 June 1958,
— the Convention between the Kingdom of the Netherlands and the Italian Republic on the recognition and enforcement of judgments in civil and commercial matters, signed at Rome on 17 April 1959,
— the Convention between the United Kingdom and the Federal Republic of Germany for the reciprocal recognition and enforcement of judgments in civil and commercial matters, signed at Bonn on 14 July 1960,
— the Convention between the Kingdom of Belgium and the Italian Republic on the recognition and enforcement of judgments and other enforceable instruments in civil and commercial matters, signed at Rome on 6 April 1962,
— the Convention between the Kingdom of the Netherlands and the Fed-

eral Republic of Germany on the mutual recognition and enforcement of judgments and other enforceable instruments in civil and commercial matters, signed at The Hague on 30 August 1962,

— the Convention between the United Kingdom and the Republic of Italy for the reciprocal recognition and enforcement of judgments in civil and commercial matters, signed at Rome on 7 February 1964, with amending Protocol signed at Rome on 14 July 1970,

— the Convention between the United Kingdom and the Kingdom of the Netherlands providing for the reciprocal recognition and enforcement of judgments in civil matters, signed at The Hague on 17 November 1967,

and, in so far as it is in force:

— the Treaty between Belgium, the Netherlands and Luxembourg on jurisdiction, bankruptcy, and the validity and enforcement of judgments, arbitration awards and authentic instruments, signed at Brussels on 24 November 1961.

*Article 56.* The Treaty and the conventions referred to in Article 55 shall continue to have effect in relation to matters to which this Convention does not apply.

They shall continue to have effect in respect of judgments given and documents formally drawn up or registered as authentic instruments before the entry into force of this Convention.

*Article 57.* This Convention shall not affect any conventions to which the Contracting States are or will be parties and which, in relation to particular matters, govern jurisdiction or the recognition or enforcement of judgments.

This Convention shall not affect the application of provisions which, in rela-

tion to particular matters, govern jurisdiction or the recognition or enforcement of judgments and which are or will be contained in acts of the institutions of the European Communities or in national laws harmonized in implementation of such acts.

*Article 58.* This Convention shall not affect the rights granted to Swiss nationals by the Convention concluded on 15 June 1869 between France and the Swiss Confederation on Jurisdiction and the enforcement of judgments in civil matters.

*Article 59.* This Convention shall not prevent a Contracting State from assuming, in a convention on the recognition and enforcement of judgments, an obligation towards a third State not to recognize judgments given in other Contracting States against defendants domiciled or habitually resident in the third State where, in cases provided for in Article 4, the judgment could only be founded on a ground of jurisdiction specified in the second paragraph of Article 3.

However, a Contracting State may not assume an obligation towards a third State not to recognize a judgment given in another Contracting State by a court basing its jurisdiction on the presence within that State of property belonging to the defendant, or the seizure by the plaintiff of property situated there:

1. if the action is brought to assert or declare proprietary or possessory rights in that property, seeks to obtain authority to dispose of it, or arises from another issue relating to such property, or,

2. if the property constitutes the security for a debt which is the subject-matter of the action.

[Articles 60–68 omitted]

In witness whereof, the undersigned Plenipotentiaries have signed this Convention.

Done at Brussels this twenty-seventh day of September in the year one thousand nine hundred and sixty-eight.

PROTOCOL

[Text as amended by the Convention of Accession]

The High Contracting Parties have agreed upon the following provisions, which shall be annexed to the Convention:

*Article II*. Without prejudice to any more favourable provisions of national laws, persons domiciled in a Contracting State who are being prosecuted in the criminal courts of another Contracting State of which they are not nationals for an offence which was not intentionally committed may be defended by persons qualified to do so, even if they do not appear in person.

However, the court seised of the matter may order appearance in person; in the case of failure to appear a judgment given in the civil action without the person concerned having had the opportunity to arrange for his defence need not be recognized or enforced in the other Contracting States.

*Article III*. In proceedings for the issue of an order for enforcement, no charge, duty or fee calculated by reference to the value of the matter in issue may be levied in the State in which enforcement is sought.

*Article IV*. Judicial and extrajudicial documents drawn up in one Contracting State which have to be served on persons in another Contracting State shall be transmitted in accordance with the procedures laid down in the conventions and agreements concluded between the Contracting States.

Unless the State in which service is to take place objects by declaration to the Secretary-General of the Council of the European Communities, such documents may also be sent by the appropriate public officers of the State in which the document has been drawn up directly to the appropriate public officers of the State in which the addressee is to be found. In this case the officer of the State of origin shall send a copy of the document to the officer of the State applied to who is competent to forward it to the addressee. The document shall be forwarded in the manner specified by the law of the State applied to. The forwarding shall be recorded by a certificate sent directly to the officer of the State of origin.

[Articles I, V, Va, Vb, Vc, Vd, and VI omitted]

# Notes

CHAPTER 1

1. Panama was part of Colombia until 1903; hence, it does not share the common political history of the other five.
2. KARNES, THE FAILURE OF UNION: CENTRAL AMERICA, 1824–1960 9 (1961).
3. The designation Federal Republic of Central America also was used in the 1824 Constitution. The national flag, however, retained the title United Provinces of Central America, as did the national seal. A thorough account of the various attempts at unification of the Central American states is GALLARDO, LAS CONSTITUCIONES DE LA REPÚBLICA DE CENTRO-AMÉRICA (1958).
4. Some commentators have suggested that the constitution borrowed too heavily from that of the United States and that this was a major cause of the ultimate failure of the Central American Union. "The governing regime wanted to imitate to the letter the form of government of the United States of North America, and forgot that the reality of Central America was very different. By imitating the foreign, the failure of the constitution was total, since, far from uniting Central America, it was one of the causes of future ruptures," MATÁ GAVIDIA, ANOTACIONES DE HISTORIA PATRIA CENTROAMERICANA 332 (1953). However, an examination of the document itself makes it clear that it is certainly not a slavish copy of the United States Constitution. For instance, unlike the president of the United States, the president of Central America had no veto power. The power was lodged in the Senate, which had no power to initiate legislation. There were many other major differences as well. The text of the 1824 Constitution is reproduced in ORTEZ COLINDRES, LA INTEGRACIÓN POLÍTICA DE CENTROAMÉRICA 357–94 (1975).
5. The lack of good roads, as well as the difficulty of constructing and maintaining them in the mountain-

ous terrain and tropical climate, has remained a major problem in the development of Central America.

6. Karnes, *supra* note 2, at 126.

7. *Id.* at 136–38.

8. Instituto Interamericano de Estudios Jurídicos Internacionales, Derecho comunitario centroamericano 160 (1968).

9. *Id.* at 160.

10. Memoria de las relaciones exteriores, 1886–1887, 24–25 (Guatemala).

11. This commission was apparently the source of a document called the Central American Procedural Convention of 1892, which still survives in the Nicaraguan Code of Civil Procedure, Articles 9–20. *See infra* chap. 8, section "The Basic Law." It contained, among other matters, provisions relating to judgment recognition.

12. The translation is taken from work accomplished by the Interamerican Juridical Committee during its regular meeting from 26 July to 27 August 1973 (CJI-17) (OEA/Ser. Q/IV. 7), pp. 113–14.

13. Karnes, *supra* note 2, at 165.

14. *Id.* at 166.

15. *See supra* note 11.

16. Instituto, *supra* note 8, at 161–62.

17. Karnes, *supra* note 2, at 183–85.

18. 2 Malloy, Treaties, Conventions, International Acts, Protocols and Agreements between the United States and Other Powers, 1776–1909, at 2395–96 (1910). This provision was reaffirmed in treaties of 1923 and 1934.

19. Bustamante, The World Court 68 (1925).

20. Karnes, *supra* note 2, at 200–201.

21. Herrarte, La Union de Centroamérica: Tragedia y esperanza 253 (1955).

22. Karnes, *supra* note 2, at 197.

23. *Id.* at 212–21.

24. Herrarte, *supra* note 21, at 275 & 279.

25. Karnes, *supra* note 2, at 234–35.

26. Instituto Interamericano de Estudios Jurídicos Internacionales, Derecho de la integración latinoamericana 664–65 (1969).

27. Referred to as CEPAL in Spanish writings.

28. *See* Ereli, *The Central American Common Market: Integration in Practice* 43 Tul. L. Rev. 1, at 4–6 (1968). The institutional structure of the Organization of Central American States and the plethora of institutions that are active in the process of economic integration are dealt with at length in Instituto, *supra* note 8, at 148–278. *See also* Barbante, *Estructura institucional del Mercado Común Centroamericano* 42 Lecciones y Ensayos 123 (1970).

29. *See* Barbante, *supra* note 28, at 142.

30. Ereli, *supra* note 28, at 6; Barbante, *supra* note 28, at 145.

31. For a statement of the extremely complex institutional structure of the Common Market and ODECA and of how they relate to each other, *see* Simmonds, *The Central American Common Market: An Experiment in Regional Integration,* 16 Int. & Comp. L. Q. 911 (1967).

32. Art. 33.

33. Art. 24.

34. Art. 26.

35. *See* Barbante, *supra* note 28, at 159. *See also* Soto Jimenez, *Sobre la justicia en la integración regional,* 20 & 21 Revista de Ciencias Jurídicas 285 (1972).

36. Inter-American Institute of International Legal Studies, Instruments Relating to the Economic Integration of Latin America 199–200 (1968).

37. Arts. 14–16.

38. *See supra* note, text at notes 18–20.

39. Soto Jimenez, *supra* note 35, at 287.

40. Simmonds, *International Economic Organisations in Central and Latin America and the Caribbean: Regionalism and Sub-Regionalism in* *the Integration Process,* 19 INT. & COMP. L. Q. 376, at 379 (1970).

41. *Id.* at 380.

42. CLINE & DELGADO, ECONOMIC INTEGRATION IN CENTRAL AMERICA 35 and 41 (1978).

CHAPTER 2

1. Convention of 27 September 1968 on Jurisdiction and the Enforcement of Civil and Commercial Judgments, 2 ENCYCLOPEDIA OF EUROPEAN COMMUNITY LAW B11044. This treaty will be discussed at greater length below, at pp. 35 *et seq.*

2. *See* Hay & Walker, *The Proposed Recognition-of-Judgments Convention between the United States and the United Kingdom,* 11 TEX. INT. L. J. 421 (1976). A draft of the proposed convention appears in the article cited, at pp. 452–59.

3. Hilton v. Guyot, 159 U.S. 113, at 163–64, 16 S. Ct. 139, 40 L. Ed. 95 (1895). *See also* Barry, *Comity,* 12 VA. L. REV. 353 (1926).

4. *See* EHRENZWEIG, CONFLICT OF LAWS 162 (1962). *See also* READ, RECOGNITION AND ENFORCEMENT OF FOREIGN JUDGMENTS IN THE COMMON LAW UNITS OF THE BRITISH COMMONWEALTH 111 (1938).

5. *See* LAZCANO, . . . DERECHO INTERNACIONAL PRIVADO 648 (1965); BUSTAMANTE, TRES CONFERENCIAS SOBRE DERECHO INTERNACIONAL PRIVADO 54 (1929).

6. *See, e.g.,* 2 BEALE, A TREATISE ON THE CONFLICT OF LAWS 1377 (1935).

7. *Supra* note 4.

8. Von Mehren & Trautman, *Recognition of Foreign Adjudications: A Survey and a Suggested Approach,* 81 HARV. L. REV. 1601, at 1603 (1968).

9. Von Mehren & Trautman, *supra* note 8, at 1603–4.

10. *Id.* at 1610.

11. *See* discussion of jurisdictional bases in the United States, *infra* at note 32.

12. *See, e.g.,* the discussion of the French rules of competence in HERZOG, CIVIL PROCEDURE IN FRANCE 170 *et seq.* (1967).

13. *See* von Mehren & Trautman, *supra* note 8, at 1659.

14. *Id.* at 1636.

15. *Id.* at 1637.

16. *See* Hilton v. Guyot, *supra* note 3. GOODRICH AND SCOLES, HANDBOOK OF THE CONFLICT OF LAWS (4th ed.) 392–93 (1964).

17. *See, e.g.,* Johnston v. Compagnie Generale Transatlantique, 242 N.Y. 381, 152 N.E. 121 (1926).

18. The discussions of the judgment-recognition regimes of the Central American countries that follow in succeeding chapters reveal that in all but two of those countries (Costa Rica and El Salvador) there is a general reciprocity requirement. None of them, however (except, to a limited extent, Honduras), applies the requirement to judgments of other signatories of the Bustamante Code.

19. *See* MANN, THE FUNCTION OF JUDICIAL DECISION IN EUROPEAN ECONOMIC INTEGRATION 49–89 (1972), and GREEN, POLITICAL INTEGRATION BY JURISPRUDENCE 57 *et seq.* (1970).

20. General Treaty, Art. 26. Barbante, *Estructura institucional del Mercado Común Centroamericano* 42

LECCIONES Y ENSAYOS 133, at 154
(1970).

21. See Soto Jimenez, *Sobre la justicia en la integración regional* 20 & 21 REVISTA DE CIENCIAS JURÍDICAS 285 (1972). The cited work contains a draft of a plan for the creation of a fully functional Central American Superior Court, pp. 302–5.

22. Unfortunately, in the Central American region, judicial decisions are not regularly published and are not circulated widely even in the country where they are rendered, much less throughout the region. The role of courts in refining and clarifying association policy, thus, has been severely limited.

23. U.S. CONSTITUTION, Art. 3.

24. *Id.*, Art. 6.

25. *Id.*, Art. 4, § 1.

26. This, at least, is assumed to be one of the purposes served by the diversity jurisdiction of the federal courts. See WRIGHT, HANDBOOK OF THE LAW OF FEDERAL COURTS (3d ed.) 91–92 (1976).

27. 1 Stat. 122 (1790).

28. Mills v. Duryea, 11 U.S. (7 Cranch.) 481 (1813).

29. See McElmoyle v. Cohen, 38 U.S. (13 Pet.) 312 (1839).

30. See RESTATEMENT (SECOND) OF CONFLICT OF LAWS § 92 (p. 273) (1971).

31. The national standards developed under the Full Faith and Credit Clause were determined to be the criteria of due process under the Fourteenth Amendment as well in the leading case of Pennoyer v. Neff, 95 U.S. 714 (1877).

32. See RESTATEMENT OF JUDGMENTS § 14, comment a, p. 77 (1942): "It has long been established that certain relations are sufficient as bases for the exercise of jurisdiction by the State. Thus, jurisdiction may be exercised over persons pres-

ent within the State or domiciled there or consenting to the exercise of jurisdiction."

33. See Kurland, *The Supreme Court, the Due Process Clause and the In Personam Jurisdiction of State Courts: From Pennoyer to Denckla: A Review*, U. CHI. L. REV. 569, at 577 (1958).

34. 326 U.S. 310 (1945).

35. *Id.* at 316 (1945).

36. *Id.* at 319.

37. The voluntariness of the contact and the foreseeability of its jurisdictional significance became elements of the due-process standard after *Hanson v. Denckla*, 357 U.S. 235 (1958), where the majority opinion declared that there must be "some act by which the defendant purposefully avails itself of the privilege of conducting activities within the forum state . . ." (at p. 253).

38. See Perkins v. Benguet Consolidated Mining Co., 342 U.S. 437 (1952).

39. 97 S. Ct. 2569 (1977).

40. *Id.* at 2584–85.

41. See Casad, *Shaffer v. Heitner: An End to Ambivalence in Jurisdiction Theory?* 26 U. KAN L. REV. 61, at 73 (1977).

42. "An elementary and fundamental requirement of due process in any proceeding which is to be accorded finality is notice reasonably calculated, under all the circumstances, to apprise interested parties of the pendency of the action and afford them an opportunity to present their objections . . . and it must afford a reasonable time for those interested to make their appearance," Mullane v. Central Hanover Bank and Trust Co., 339 U.S. 306, at 314 (1950).

43. See RESTATEMENT (SECOND) OF CONFLICT OF LAWS § 115, comment d, pp. 333–34 (1971).

44. *Id.* at 334.
45. *See* Thompson v. Whitman, 85 U.S. (18 Wall.) 457 (1873).
46. *Cf.* York v. Texas, 137 U.S. 15 (1890).
47. *See* Baldwin v. Iowa State Travelling Men's Assn., 283 U.S. 522 (1931).
48. *See* Chicot County Drainage District v. Baxter State Bank, 308 U.S. 371 (1940).
49. *See* Durfee v. Duke, 375 U.S. 106 (1963).
50. *See* Johnson v. Muelberger, 340 U.S. 581 (1951). *See also* RESTATEMENT OF JUDGMENTS § 10 (1942).
51. *See* RESTATEMENT (SECOND) OF CONFLICT OF LAWS § 107 (p. 230) (1971).
52. *See* Barber v. Barber, 323 U.S. 77 (1944); Sistare v. Sistare, 218 U.S. 1 (1910).
53. *See, e.g.,* Worthley v. Worthley, 44 Cal. 2d 465, 283 P. 2d 19 (1955); Light v. Light, 12 Ill. 2d 502, 147 N.E. 2d 34 (1957).
54. 9c UNIFORM LAWS ANNOTATED.
55. *See* RESTATEMENT (SECOND) OF CONFLICT OF LAWS § 102, Reporter's note to comment c, p. 311 (1971).
56. The act extends to any "judgment, decree or order . . . which is entitled to full faith and credit . . ." (section 1). Nonmoney decrees are "entitled to full faith and credit" as conclusive adjudications. Thus, the act presumably permits their enforcement by proceedings that would be appropriate for domestic judgments of the same nature (section 2).
57. Fall v. Eastin, 215 U.S. 1 (1907).
58. *See, e.g.,* McCrary v. McCrary, 228 N.C. 714, 47 S.E. 2d 27 (1948); Clouse v. Clouse, 185 Tenn. 666, 207 S.W. 2d 576 (1948).
59. *See* EHRENZWEIG, CONFLICT OF LAWS 211 (1962), and cases cited therein.
60. *See* VON MEHREN & TRAUTMAN, THE LAW OF MULTISTATE PROBLEMS 886–88 (1965).
61. *See, e.g.,* De Brimont v. Penniman, 7 F. Cas. 309 (no. 3715) (1873).
62. Hilton v. Guyot, 159 U.S. 113 (1895).
63. 210 U.S. 230 (1908).
64. Milwaukee County v. M. E. White Co., 296 U.S. 268 (1935).
65. Huntington v. Attrill, 146 U.S. 657 (1892).
66. *See, e.g.,* Arkansas v. Bowen, 3 App. D.C. 537 (1894).
67. *See, e.g.,* Schuler v. Schuler, 209 Ill. 522, 71 N.E. 16 (1904).
68. Huntington v. Attrill, *supra* note 65, at 673–74.
69. *See* RESTATEMENT (SECOND) OF CONFLICT OF LAWS § 120, comment d, p. 346 (1971) and cases cited.
70. McElmoyle v. Cohen, 38 U.S. (13 Pet.) 312 (1839); Watkins v. Conway, 385 U.S. 188 (1966).
71. *See* Treinies v. Sunshine Mining Co., 308 U.S. 66 (1939). *See generally* Ginsburg, *Judgments in Search of Full Faith and Credit: The Last-in-Time Rule for Conflicting Judgments,* 82 HARV. L. REV. 798 (1969).
72. Treinies v. Sunshine Mining Co., *id.* at 77.
73. McElmoyle v. Cohen, 38 U.S. (13 Pet.) 312 (1839).
74. 28 U.S.C. § 1738.
75. 28 U.S.C. § 1963.
76. 9c UNIFORM LAWS ANNOTATED.
77. *See* reporter's note to § 61.2 RESTATEMENT (SECOND) OF JUDGMENTS (tent. draft 1), pp. 139–43 (1973).
78. *See id.* at 144–45.
79. *See id.* at 150.
80. *See* RESTATEMENT (SECOND) OF CONFLICT OF LAWS § 94, comment b, pp. 279–80 (1971).

81. *Id.*
82. Restatement of Judgments § 96 (1943).
83. The leading case is *Bernhard v. Bank of America,* 19 Cal. 2d 807, 122 P. 2d 892 (1942).
84. *See* Restatement (Second) of Conflict of Laws § 95 (1971).
85. In *Hart v. American Airlines, Inc.,* 61 Misc. 2d 41, 304 N.Y.S. 2d 810 (1969), the New York court permitted a non-party to invoke the issue-preclusion effect of a Texas judgment even though Texas would not have done so.
86. *See, e.g.,* Constitution of the United States of Mexico, Art. 121; Constitution of Argentina, Art. 7; Constitution of Australia, Art. 118.
87. Constitution of 1824, Art. 193: "The legal and juridical acts of one State will be recognized in all the others," Ortez Colindres, La integración política de Centroamérica 389 (1975). Convention of 27 July 1842, Art. 5: "[The States] recognize reciprocally their juridical and civil acts," Montúfar, Reseña histórica de Centroamérica 267 (1881).
88. Treaty of Rome, 25 March 1957, Art. 220.
89. Report of the Convention on Jurisdiction and the Enforcement of Judgments in Civil and Commercial Matters, Bulletin of the European Communities, Supplement 12/72 ("Jenard Report").
90. *See* Bartlett, *Full Faith and Credit Comes to the Common Market: An Analysis of the Provisions of the Convention on Jurisdiction and Enforcement of Judgments in Civil and Commercial Matters* 24 Int. & Comp. L. Q. 44 (1975).
91. Art. 1.
92. Jenard Report, p. 17.
93. *Id.* and *see* Bartlett, *supra* note 90, at 48.
94. Lufttransportunternehmen Gmbh.

& Co. K.G. v. Orgnisation Europeenne Pour la Securite de la Navigation Aerienne (Eurocontrol), Case 29/76 European Court of Justice, 14 October 1976.
95. Hay, *The Common Market Preliminary Draft Convention of the Recognition and Enforcement of Judgments—Some Considerations of Policy and Interpretation,* 16 Am. J. Comp. L. 149, at 154 (1968).
96. Case 29/76, *supra* note 94. The Convention of Accession of 9 October 1978 made this point clearly by adding to the text of Article 1 that "[i]t shall not extend, in particular, to revenue, customs or administrative matters."
97. Art. 1.
98. Jenard Report, p. 19. *See also* Weser, *Some Reflections on the Draft Treaty on Execution of Judgments in the E.E.C.,* in La Fave & Hay, eds., International Trade, Investment, and Organization 377, at 381 (1967).
99. Weser, *id.* at 382.
100. *Id.*
101. Jenard Report, p. 19.
102. Art. 1.
103. Jenard Report, p. 24.
104. Art. 26.
105. Jenard Report, p. 74.
106. Von Mehren & Trautman, *supra* note 8, at 1674–75, and authorities cited.
107. *Id.*
108. "The party relying on recognition or applying for enforcement of a judgment must produce: 1. A copy of the judgment meeting the conditions necessary for authenticity; 2. in the case of a judgment by default, the original or a certified true copy of the document establishing that the summons has been served on the defaulting party."
109. Arts. 31–49.
110. Arts. 31 & 34. *See* Arts. 27 & 38,

discussed below, for grounds for nonrecognition.

111. Art. 46.1.
112. Jenard Report, p. 94.
113. Art. 46.2.
114. Art. 34.
115. Jenard Report, p. 86.
116. Art. 45.
117. Art. 34.
118. Art. 36. If one is domiciled outside the community, local law of the rendering state controls. Jenard Report, p. 87.
119. Art. 38.
120. Art. 37.
121. Art. 41.
122. Jenard Report, p. 75.
123. This is implicit in the express provision in Art. 27.4 for a choice-of-law test in certain specific cases.
124. Jenard Report, p. 76.
125. Arts. 3 & 4.
126. Art. 27.2.
127. Art. 27.3.
128. Art. 21.
129. Art. 27.4.
130. Arts. 2–18.
131. Art. 2. The law of the forum is to be applied in determining domicile, Art. 52.
132. Art. 5.1. The Court of Justice of the European Communities has ruled that the place of performance is to be determined in accordance with the law applicable to the obligation under the conflict-of-laws law of the forum, Industrie Tessili Italiana v. Dunlop A.G. XIX C.M.L.R. 26 (1977).
133. Art. 5.3. The place where the harmful event occurred can be either the place where the wrongful act or omission took place or the place where the injury was sustained, Reinwater Foundation v. Mines de Potasse d'Alsace S.A. (Court of Justice of the European Communities) XIX C.M.L.R. 284 (1977).
134. Art. 5.4.

135. Art. 5.2.
136. Art. 5.5.
137. Art. 6.1.
138. Arts. 7–12a.
139. Arts. 13–15.
140. Art. 16.
141. Art. 17.
142. Art. 18.
143. Art. 3.
144. Bartlett, *supra* note 90, at 44.
145. Code Civil, Art. 14.
146. Bartlett, *supra* note 90, at 53.
147. ZPO (Code of Civil Procedure), Art. 23.
148. Code of Civil Procedure, Art. 120.3.
149. Art. 4.
150. *See* Nadelmann, *The Common Market Judgments Convention and a Hague Conference Recommendation: What Steps Next?* 82 HARV. L. REV. 1282 (1969), and *Jurisdictionally Improper Fora in Treaties on Recognition of Judgments: The Common Market Draft* 67 COL. L. REV. 995 (1967). *See also* Hay, *supra* note 95; and Carl, *The Common Market Judgments Convention—Its Threat and Challenge to Americans*, 8 INT. LAWYER 446 (1974).
151. Convention, Art. 28.
152. Convention, Art. 59.
153. *Reprinted in* 15 AM. J. COMP. L. 362 (1967).
154. *See* Hay & Walker, *supra* note 2, at 421.
155. 97 S. Ct. 2569 (1977). *See* Casad, *supra* note 41.
156. The Court of Justice of the European Communities (Luxembourg, 1975), at 14.
157. *See* cases cited *supra* at notes 94, 132, & 133. *See generally* Giardina, *The European Court and the Brussels Convention on Jurisdiction and Judgments* 27 INT. & COMP. L. Q. 263 (1978).
158. *See* Soto Jimenez, *supra* note 21, at 292.

159. COUTURE, FUNDAMENTOS DEL DE-
RECHO PROCESAL CIVIL (3d ed.) 27
(1958).
160. See 2 ALSINA, TRATADO TEÓRICO
PRÁCTICO DE DERECHO PROCESAL
CIVIL Y COMERCIAL (2d ed.) 418
(1957), describing jurisdiction as
"the power conferred by the state
upon certain organs to resolve in a
judgment litigious questions submitted to them, and to enforce
those resolutions."
161. Supra note 159, at 40–41.
162. See, e.g., RESTATEMENT OF JUDG-
MENTS § 7 (1942); RESTATEMENT
(SECOND) OF CONFLICT OF LAWS
§ 105 (1971). The RESTATEMENT
(SECOND) OF JUDGMENTS tent.
draft no. 5, § 14 (p. 11), rejects
the use of "competency" in this
context, replacing it with "subject
matter jurisdiction."
163. COUTURE, supra note 159, at 29.
164. 2 ALSINA, supra note 160, at 512.
165. See MUÑOZ, CAMEY, & HALL,
DERECHO INTERNACIONAL PRIVADO
214 (1953); 1 AGUIRRE, DERECHO
PROCESAL CIVIL DE GUATEMALA 92

(1973); 2 ALSINA, supra note 160,
at 514–18.
166. COUTURE, supra note 159, at 401.
167. See COUTURE, id. at 402; 4 AL-
SINA, supra note 160, at 124.
168. 4 ALSINA, id.
169. Virtually any Latin American treatise on civil procedure could be
cited for this point. The "three
identities" are traceable to Article
1351 of the Code Napoléon.
170. COUTURE, supra note 159, at 424.
171. See COUTURE, id. at 426–32; 4
ALSINA, supra note 160, at 167–74.
The scope of the conclusive effect
is comparable to that described
above in relation to German and
French law. See supra, at note
106.
172. The procedures for execution in the
case of judgments requiring the
defendant to do or refrain from
doing a specific act, other than
transference of property, however,
are significantly different from those
used in Anglo-American jurisdictions to enforce equitable decrees.
See COUTURE, supra note 159, at
457–64.

## CHAPTER 3

1. See Lorenzen, The Pan-American
Code of Private International Law,
4 TUL. L. REV. 499 (1930).
2. E.g., Brazil and Chile.
3. Bustamante Code, Art. 7.
4. Id. Art. 3.
5. Argentina, Colombia, Mexico, Paraguay, Uruguay, and the United
States refused to sign. See Lorenzen, supra note 1, at 500.
6. See 4 HUDSON, INTERNATIONAL
LEGISLATION 2352 (1932).
7. Id. at 2348.
8. Id. at 2350–51.
9. The Organization of American
States Inter-American Council of
Jurists has, for over twenty years,

been debating from time to time a
resolution seeking to harmonize the
Bustamante Code with the Montevideo Treaties of 1940 (on Commercial Navigation Law, Procedural Law, Penal Law, and Civil
Law) and with the U.S. RESTATE-
MENT OF CONFLICT OF LAWS.
10. Arts. 314–449, 382–87.
11. Arts. 423–35.
12. Art. 396.
13. E.g., BUSTAMANTE, EL ORDEN
PÚBLICO (1893), and LA AUTAR-
QUIA PERSONAL (1914).
14. With certain exceptions: see Lorenzen, supra note 1, at 525.
15. Id. at 499.

16. *Id.* at 527.
17. Muñoz, Camey, & Hall, Derecho internacional privado 124 (1953; my translation).
18. Arellano, Derecho internacional privado 640–54 (1974).
19. *Id.* at 652.
20. *Id.* (my translation).
21. Lorenzen, *supra* note 1, at 526–27.
22. *Cf.* Art. 434, specifically authorizing enforcement of "acts of voluntary jurisdiction regarding commercial matters."
23. *Cf.* the "competency" restrictions in such cases, Arts. 333–39. Arellano boldly declares: 'The only judgments capable of being executed in conformity with rules [relating to execution of foreign judgments] are civil judgments, broadly speaking—that is, those that deal with civil or mercantile matters." There can be exceptions based on treaties, however, and the Codigo Bustamante apparently is such an exception. Arellano, *supra* note 18, at 711.
24. *See* Working Document, Second Inter-American Specialized Conference on Private International Law, "Recognition and Execution of Foreign Judicial Judgments" (OEA/Ser. K./XXI.2) (June 1977), at 17–18.
25. Art. 436.
26. Art. 437.
27. *See* chap. 2 *supra* at note 4.
28. *See* Muñoz et al., *supra* note 17, at 214.
29. Aguirre, 1 Derecho procesal civil de Guatemala 92 (1973). Aguirre indicates that this is true even in cases where the territorial connection is the location of things —not just where it is the residence or domicile of a party.
30. *But see* 2 Alsina, Tratado teórico práctico de derecho procesal civil y comercial (2d ed.) 514–18 (1957), treating competence *ratione personae* and *ratione loci* as both resting on territorial concepts. That is surely not what Bustamante had in mind, however.
31. *See also* Arts. 1 & 2 of the code.
32. *Cf.* Ortiz Martin, El derecho internacional privado de Costa Rica 257 (1969).
33. *See* Art. 2 of the Final Act of the Sixth International Conference of American States, 4 Hudson, *supra* note 6, at 2281.
34. Some of the rules of competency at they appear in the official English version seem obscure. The problem, as in other instances that have been referred to, stems in part from faulty translation. Thus, in Article 320, for instance, the translator used the English word "relief" for the Spanish *"recurso,"* confusing the meaning. *Recurso* is "relief" in a sense: relief from a ruling of some lower tribunal. Article 320 thus is a limitation on the power of parties to waive or circumvent local rules relating to *review* jurisdiction.
35. There is no "implied submission" if the defendant merely defaults, Art. 332. "Implied submission" is what we would call a "general appearance."
36. *See* Torres Gudiño, Derecho procesal civil 237–41 (1975), comparing provisions in the codes of Mexico, Chile, and Colombia.
37. Chap. 2, notes 145–49.
38. The text is: "Que las partes hayan sido citadas personalmente o por su representante legal, para el juicio." *"Juicio"* sometimes bears the meaning of "trial," but here it clearly means the "lawsuit" or "action."
39. In Panama, however, the rule that is applicable even to judgments of Bustamante Code countries is that the defendant or his personal repre-

sentative must have been served within the territory of the rendering state. *See* chap. 9 *infra* at note 27.

40. *But see* the Guatemala interpretation of Article 81; chap. 6 *infra* at note 12.
41. Accord, Salvadoran judgment, chap. 5 *infra* at note 21.
42. *See* Appendixes.
43. *But see* Carolina Power & Light Co. v. Uranex, 451 F.S. 1044 (D. Cal. N.D. 1977).
44. *See* chap. 7 *infra* at notes 12–14.
45. It is perhaps noteworthy that here the code refers to "country" (*país*), rather than "state" (*estado*) as in other places in the code. The reason for the different terminology, however, is not apparent.
46. BUSTAMANTE, TRES CONFERENCIAS SOBRE DERECHO INTERNACIONAL PRIVADO 64 (1929). (Apparently these lectures were not published

in an English version.)
47. *See* chap. 2 *supra* at notes 122–24.
48. *Quoted in* SOLANO VARGAS, LA AUSENCIA EN EL DERECHO PRIVADO 40 (1965, thesis, Universidad de Costa Rica).
49. *E.g.*, Argentina.
50. Procedures for letters requisitorial or letters rogatory appear in Articles 388–93 of the code.
51. Honduras and Panama.
52. Here, again, the official English translation of the code is deficient. The Spanish term *"Fiscal o Ministro Público"* was translated as "prosecuting attorney." In English, in the context of enforcement of a civil judgment, "prosecuting attorney," with lower-case initials, merely refers to the plaintiff's lawyer, and that is not what the code intended.
53. LAZCANO, . . . DERECHO INTERNACIONAL PRIVADO 662 (1965).

## CHAPTER 4

1. 4 HUDSON, INTERNATIONAL LEGISLATION 2348 (1932).
2. Anexo a LA GACETA no. 30 (6 February 1930).
3. Antillón, *El auxilio jurídico internacional en Costa Rica*, 15 REVISTA DE CIENCIAS JURÍDICAS 209, at 212 (1970).
4. Art. 423.3, Bustamante Code. *See supra*, pp. 53–54.
5. *See infra* section "Requirements for Recognition and Enforcement," subsection "Public Orders."
6. The Sala de Casación is a chamber of the Supreme Court, composed of five regular members, including the chief justice.
7. *See* discussion of the ambiguity of this term, chap. 3, section "Requirements for Recognition and Enforcement," subsection "Finality," *supra*.

8. There is one exception to this rule: No exequatur is required when the foreign judgment is introduced in a case as nonconclusive evidence. *See infra* pp. 70–71.
9. The exequatur procedure—which is sometimes called *pareatis*, or *pase de ley*—is common in Latin America (and the rest of the civil-law world). An extensive bibliography of the subject is provided in SENTÍS MELENDO, LA SENTENCIA EXTRANJERA (EXEQUATUR) 12–25 (1958). *See also* CAPPELLETTI, EL VALOR DE LAS SENTENCIAS Y DE LAS NORMAS EXTRANJERAS EN EL PROCESO CIVIL (1968; Spanish translations of several of Cappelletti's articles on this theme).
10. *See, e.g.*, folio 145, libro 1, 8:20 4 September 1944; folio 143, libro 1, 15:15 9 November 1943; folio

163, libro 1, 10:00 23 May 1950; and folio 170, libro 1, 16:00 15 June 1951. These cases appear in books kept in the archives of the Supreme Court of Costa Rica. Exequatur proceedings are registered in separate volumes. Before 1965, cases that were decided by the Supreme Court were regularly printed. After 1965, opinions or excerpts were distributed in mimeographed form till about 1972. For some reason, the exequatur proceedings were not reported in the regular reports, so the cases can only be found in San José, Costa Rica.

11. Code of Civil Procedure, Art. 98.
12. *Id.*, Art. 1026.
13. *See, e.g.*, folio 145, libro 1, 8:20 4 September 1944; and folio 148, libro 1, 16:00 15 May 1945.
14. Article 1021 declares that there can be no recourse against a judgment either granting or denying exequatur.
15. 3 ALSINA, TRATADO TEÓRICO PRÁCTICO DE DERECHO PROCESAL CIVIL Y COMERCIAL 127 (1943) (arguing that exequatur is not necessary where only *cosa juzgada*, not positive execution, is sought), and SENTÍS MELENDO, *supra* note 9, at 66 & 78 (arguing likewise, based on views of several Italian commentators).
16. *Sentencia* no. 101, 14:30 4 September 1968, pp. 48–49 (my translation). This case is not found among the exequatur cases but among the ordinary cases of casación.
17. Personal interview with Magistrado Coto, July 1976.
18. Folios 117–28, libro 1, 15:00 4 July 1941.
19. Bustamante Code, Art. 432.
20. *See* ANTILLÓN, *supra* note 3, at 244.
21. *See* 5 ALSINA, TRATADO TEÓRICO PRÁCTICO DE DERECHO PROCESAL

CIVIL Y COMERCIAL (2d ed.) 184–86 (1962); *see also* Costa Rica CCP, Art. 431.
22. Tribunal de Police du Liege v. Jean Moulaert, (exequatur) 1971.
23. *See, e.g.*, folio 143, libro 1, 15:15 9 November 1943.
24. Folios 198 & 199, libro 1, 16:30 6 August 1954.
25. *See* ORTIZ MARTIN, EL DERECHO INTERNACIONAL PRIVADO DE COSTA RICA 292 (1969).
26. Folio 143, libro 1, 15:15 9 November 1943.
27. "Costa Rican laws control immovable property situated in the Republic even though they may belong to foreigners, whether those properties are considered in isolation, or whether in relation to the rights of the owner as part of an inheritance or of other universality."
28. Folio 155, libro 1, 11:00 18 January 1947.
29. Art. 1024.
30. *Supra* note 29, chap. 3.
31. *See* ORTIZ MARTIN, *supra* note 25.
32. *See* Antillón, *supra* note 3, at 239–40.
33. Folio 282, libro 2, 10:30 27 December 1972 (exequatur was denied to a Florida divorce judgment which recited that defendant had been served but did not show the *form* or *manner* of service. The defendant denied having received notice, and the petitioner failed to bear the burden of proof).
34. *See* folio 9, libro 2, 15:15 18 May 1955.
35. Folio 203, libro 2, 15:30 14 June 1968.
36. Folio 250, libro 2, 15:15 28 May 1971.
37. *See infra* at notes 62–67.
38. Folio 199, libro 2, 14:30 8 May 1968. *See also* folio 270, libro 2, 15:45 9 August 1972 (denying exequatur to a Nicaraguan divorce judgment that was rendered

through such a procedure when the defendant's whereabouts in Costa Rica were in fact known).

39. Compare the application of Costa Rican standards relating to the grounds for divorce in actions that are seeking exequatur for foreign judgments divorcing nondomiciliaries of Costa Rica. *Infra* at note 63.

40. Folio 134, libro 1, April 1940.

41. Folio 165, libro 2, 9:00 29 July 1966. The defendant could not resist recognition of a Mexican divorce on this ground where he had married a second wife in Costa Rica, declaring publicly that he had been divorced from his first wife in Mexico.

42. *See* ORTIZ MARTIN, *supra* note 25.

43. With the exception referred to in note 8 *supra*.

44. Art. 423.4. *See supra* p. 60.

45. Art. 431.

46. *See* Antillón, *supra* note 3, at 238–39.

47. *See supra* at note 21.

48. Folio 276, libro 2, 8:00 6 October 1972.

49. Folios 87 & 88, libro 2, 15:00 10 October 1961; folio 141, libro 2, 15:00 21 July 1945.

50. Folios 18 & 19, libro 2, 16:10 21 May 1956; folios 22 & 23, libro 2, 16:00 12 April 1957; folio 132, libro 1, 15:00 13 November 1941.

51. *But see* Carolina Power & Light Co. v. Uranex, 451 F. Supp. 1044 (1977).

52. CCP, Art. 1023. The reference is to embargo generally. This can include embargoes issued as a feature of the execution procedure, as well as preliminary, provisional embargoes issued in the course of the main action on the merits.

53. Folio 154, libro 1, 13:00 17 January 1947; folio 162, libro 1, 10:00 2 December 1949.

54. Folio 142, libro 1, 9:20 3 November 1943.

55. Folios 35–51, libro 2, 15:45 9 September 1958.

56. *See* folio 285, libro 2, 8:00 25 January 1973. Two judges thought that exequatur should be granted subject to the condition that the appropriate guarantee be supplied.

57. Antillón, *supra* note 3, at 217–21. SOLANO VARGAS, LA AUSENCIA EN EL DERECHO PRIVADO 32–48 (1965, thesis, Universidad de Costa Rica).

58. Antillón, *supra* note 3, at 218.

59. *See supra* text at notes 39–46.

60. *See supra* note 27.

61. *See* ORTIZ MARTIN, *supra* note 25, at 234.

62. Art. 53. *See supra* chap. 3, p. 65.

63. *See* 4 HUDSON, *supra* note 1, at 2349.

64. Folio 137, libro 2, 15:00 28 January 1965.

65. Folio 140, libro 2, 10:00 21 July 1965. One party there was a Costa Rican citizen and domiciliary, but the court said that the rule applied "even to foreigners."

66. Folios 156–61, libro 2, 14:00 16 May 1966. The judge who wrote the opinion in the Honduran case discussed above dissented from this decision. The Nicaraguan judgment was based on invalid grounds. Under his view, Costa Rican "public order" cannot countenance that, even if there are now other valid grounds.

67. Folio 41, 1970.

68. *See* chap. 2 at notes 122–25.

69. *See* 1 AGUIRRE, DERECHO PROCESAL CIVIL DE GUATEMALA 790–825 (1973).

70. *See supra* chap. 3 at p. 54.

71. *See supra* note 16.

72. *See* chap. 2 *supra* at note 77. Civil Code of Costa Rica, Art. 723: "The authority of Cosa Juzgada is limited to the matter resolved in the

judgment, not to the grounds for the resolution."
73. See supra chap. 2 at note 169.
74. Civil Code, Art. 724.
75. See Antillón, supra note 3, at 241.
76. Id.

77. COUTURE, FUNDAMENTOS DEL DE-RECHO PROCESAL CIVIL (3d ed.) 487 (1958).
78. See supra chap. 2 at note 71.
79. See supra at notes 26 & 27.
80. See chap. 2 text at note 19.

## CHAPTER 5

1. See Ungo, El Salvador, in Kos-RABCEWICZ-ZUBKOWSKI, ED., INTER-NATIONAL COOPERATION IN CIVIL AND COMMERCIAL PROCEDURE, at 239 (1975).
2. Spanish Civil Judgment Law, Arts. 951–54.
3. Honduras, Nicaragua, and Panama.
4. CCP, Art. 261, pars. 3 & 4.
5. Cases are reported in the REVISTA JUDICIAL and are on file in the archives of the Supreme Court. However, there simply are not so many cases as were found in Costa Rica.
6. Case nos. 1–65 (pareatis), 13 August 1965.
7. Case no. 3 (pareatis), 136, 27 July 1973.
8. CCP, Art. 125.
9. Supra chap. 3 at note 8.
10. 72 REVISTA JUDICIAL 75 (1967).
11. Case nos. 1–69 (pareatis), 21 April 1969.
12. See CCP, Art. 64. Causes that cannot be subjects of arbitration include such matters as welfare claims, divorce, civil status of persons, and others. See also Bustamante Code, Art. 432.
13. Ungo, supra note 1, at 239–40.
14. "The prior permission that Article 453 C.C.P. prescribes is encountered only in cases in which there has been contention of the parties," case nos. 2–69, 25 August 1969.
15. Case nos. 1–69, 21 April 1969. See Civil Code, Art. 15: "Salvadorans remain subject to the national laws regulating civil rights and obliga-

tions, notwithstanding their residence or domicile in a foreign country: 1. In matters relating to the status of persons and their capacity to execute certain acts that are to have effect in El Salvador; 2. In the obligations and rights that arise from family relations; but only with respect to Salvadoran spouses or relatives." See also LINDO, EL DIVORCIO EN EL SALVA-DOR (2d ed.) 176–80 (1959), and FERNÁNDEZ FLORES, EL DIVORCIO EN DERECHO INTERNACIONAL PRI-VADO 114–19 (1967).
16. FERNÁNDEZ FLORES, id. at 119.
17. See LINDO, supra note 15, at 179.
18. Supra chap. 3 at note 8.
19. Bustamante Code, Art. 423.2.
20. 72 REVISTA JUDICIAL 76 (1967).
21. CCP, Art. 141; and see case holding this procedure valid against a non-Salvadoran, nondomiciliary (a Maryland corporation), whose address was known and who, accordingly, could have been notified more directly through rogatory process, 75 REVISTA JUDICIAL 465, at 474 (1970).
22. See Bustamante Code, Arts. 388–93.
23. See case no. 3, 3 February 1966, 74 REVISTA JUDICIAL 173 (1969), characterizing a Costa Rican order that directed the defendant to pay money as an embargo and ruling that pareatis was not permitted in such a case.
24. El Salvador extends its criminal laws outside its borders to reach

crimes committed by one Salvadoran citizen against another, Code of Criminal Procedure (Código de Instrucción Criminal), Art. 18.9. A prosecution cannot be undertaken, however, if there has been a final judgment based on the same acts in another country, Art. 21 of the

same code. *See* cases, 73 REVISTA JUDICIAL 111, 118, & 120 (1968).
25. *See supra* note 21.
26. Bustamante Code, Art. 431.
27. *Id.*, Art. 396.
28. 71 REVISTA JUDICIAL 117, at 124–26 (1966).
29. *Supra* text at note 14.

CHAPTER 6

1. ". . . [T]he Delegation of Guatemala is in perfect accord with the method which, with so much wisdom, caution, ingenuity, and scientific judgment, is set forth in the Project of Code of Private International Law, and it desires to leave express record of its absolute acceptance of the latter without reservations of any kind," 4 HUDSON, INTERNATIONAL LEGISLATION 2354 (1932).
2. *See infra* section "Basic Procedure for Recognition and Enforcement."
3. 1 AGUIRRE, DERECHO PROCESAL CIVIL DE GUATEMALA 354 (1973); MUÑOZ, CAMEY, & HALL, DERECHO INTERNACIONAL PRIVADO 225 (1953).
4. COLMENARES ARANDI, EJECUCIÓN DE SENTENCIAS EXTRANJERAS EN LA LEGISLACIÓN GUATEMALTECA VIGENTE 10 (1968, thesis, Universidad de San Carlos de Guatemala).
5. LJO (Law of the Judicial Organism), Art. 192.
6. LJO, Art. 191.
7. LJO, Art. 193.
8. Aguirre, *Guatemala, in* KOS-RABCEWICZ-ZUBOWSKI, ED., INTERNATIONAL COOPERATION IN CIVIL AND COMMERCIAL PROCEDURE, at p. 266 (1975).
9. CCMP, Art. 458.
10. *See* Civil Code, Arts. 924 & 926.
11. *See* COLMENARES, *supra* note 4, at 27.
12. Art. 81: "The local law shall be

applied for the purpose of deciding when the declaration of absence is made and takes effect and when and how the administration of the property of the absentee shall terminate as well as the obligation and manner of rendering accounts."
13. Civil Code, Art. 42.
14. COLMENARES, *supra* note 4, at 9–10.
15. CCMP, Art. 293.
16. Aguirre, *supra* note 8, at 262. *See also* Bustamante Code, Arts. 432 & 433.
17. Civil Code, Arts. 2158 & 2172.
18. Chap. 3 *supra* at notes 28–30.
19. CCMP, Art. 354.4.
20. MUÑOZ ET AL., *supra* note 3, at 228–29.
21. Art. 423.2.
22. *See supra* at notes 13 & 14.
23. COLMENARES ARANDI, *supra* note 4, at 19.
24. *Id.* at 11.
25. Aguirre, *supra* note 8, at 265.
26. 1 AGUIRRE, *supra* note 3, at 349–51.
27. Art. 423.3.
28. Aguirre, *supra* note 8.
29. José Antonio Copa López v. Juez Quinto de Primera Instancia de lo Civil., expediente no. 719, Sala Primera, Corte de Apelaciones (1969).
30. CONST., Art. 53.
31. CONST., Art. 245.
32. Sometimes slightly different terms are used.

33. *See generally,* 1 AGUIRRE, *supra* note 3, at 809–12.

34. *Id.* at 820.

## CHAPTER 7

1. *See* chap. 5 *supra* at p. 88.
2. *See, e.g., pareatis* no. 4320, 5 November 1968 (service of notice in connection with an Argentine divorce).
3. *Pareatis,* 31 January 1940.
4. *See pareatis* no. 2515, 13 November 1964 (recognition granted to Kentucky probate decree to determine rights in Honduran land). *Pareatis,* 17 February 1971 (recognition granted to Louisiana decree declaring petitioner the heir to stock in Honduran corporation). *See also pareatis* R 1411, 17 March 1972.
5. *See pareatis* no. 18, 1941 (denying recognition to a Salvadoran declaration of heirship of a Honduran who had died in El Salvador).
6. *Pareatis,* 29 December 1960; *pareatis,* 7 August 1953.
7. *Pareatis,* 10 June 1974 (effect given to a Florida default divorce on petition by defendant).

8. *Pareatis,* 16 October 1940 (recognition refused to a Salvadoran money judgment obtained against a Honduran, in accordance with Salvadoran law permitting the appointment by the court of a local representative without notice to defendant other than publication).
9. Civil Code, Arts. 2004 & 2005.
10. *See supra* note 8.
11. *Pareatis* no. 3121.
12. *See* chap. 5 *supra.*
13. *See* chap. 5, section "Kinds of Judgment Entitled to Recognition and Enforcement," subsection "Default Judgments."
14. *See pareatis,* 29 December 1960; *pareatis,* 7 August 1953; *pareatis,* 18 November 1941. A Costa Rican judgment declaring heirs was also denied recognition. *See pareatis,* 3 July 1942.
15. *See* chap. 3 text following note 36 *supra.*
16. Arts. 1251 & 1252.

## CHAPTER 8

1. "The Republic of Nicaragua will be unable to apply the provisions of the Code of Private International Law which may be in conflict with the Canon Law in matters which now or in the future Nicaragua may consider to be subject to such Canon Law.
   "The Nicaraguan Delegation declares, as it has previously done several times verbally throughout the discussions, that some of the provisions of the approved Code are in disagreement with express provisions of the legislation of Nicaragua or with principles which form the basis of such legislation; but, as deserved homage to the notable work of the illustrious author of this Code, it chooses, instead of formulating the corresponding reservations, to make these declarations and to leave to the public authorities of Nicaragua the formulation of such reservations or the modification, as far as possible, of the national legislation, in cases of conflict."
2. An official, similar to an auditor, who checks on municipal affairs to see that the laws are complied with.

3. In Nicaraguan cases, both the terms *"exequatur"* and *"pareatis"* are used, although in more recent years, *pareatis* seldom appears.

4. Art. 426.

5. 1964 BOLETÍN JUDICIAL (BJ) 319.

6. 1964 BJ 389.

7. 1959 BJ 19444.

8. 1959 BJ 19405.

9. *See* CCP, Art. 1119, *infra* at note 34.

10. 1964 BJ 378.

11. *See* CCP, Arts. 548 & 740.

12. *See* chap. 4 *supra* at pp. 72–73.

13. *See* 1950 BJ 15267.

14. *See* 1946 BJ 13507.

15. Unreported case, Trama v. Trama, 15 July 1975. Archives of Supreme Court of Nicaragua.

16. 1972 BJ 30.

17. *See* CCP, Art. 963.

18. *See* 1962 BJ 369.

19. *See* 1935 BJ 8967.

20. 1945 BJ 13038 (exequatur was denied to a Mississippi divorce of persons who were Nicaraguan nationals and domiciliaries according to Nicaraguan law. The court characterized its competency standards as of "international public order").

21. 1952 BJ 16000 (exequatur was granted to a Costa Rican divorce at petition of defendant even though it did not appear that he was domiciled in Costa Rica).

22. *See* 1959 BJ 19611; *see also* case cited *supra* note 19.

23. 1935 BJ 8967; 1946 BJ 13507; 1950 BJ 15267.

24. *See* 1959 BJ 19449; 1953 BJ 16449; 1962 BJ 369.

25. *See* 1945 BJ 13038.

26. *See supra* chap. 3, at p. 60.

27. *See supra* chap. 4, at p. 68.

28. *See* chap. 7 *supra,* at pp. 112–13.

29. *See* 1925 BJ 5323.

30. 1963 BJ 425. The court did note, however, that it had doubts about the French court's willingness to enforce Nicaraguan judgments without revision, based on the published writings of some French commentators. Perhaps a presumption was operating that would not apply to countries that were not well-known exponents of the power of *revision au fond.* The Nicaraguan decision antedated the reversal of the principle by the French Cour de Cassation in *Munzer v. Dame Munzer-Jacoby,* discussed in Nadelmann, *French Courts Recognize Foreign Money-Judgments: One Down and More to Go,* 13 AM. J. COMP. L. 72 (1964).

31. 1971 BJ 154.

32. Bustamante Code, Art. 423.3; CCP, Arts. 544.2 & 544.5; and CCP, Art. 16.4.

33. 1925 BJ 5323.

34. The basic rules of *cosa juzgada* are contained in Articles 1119–24 of the Code of Civil Procedure:

   Article 1119. Resolutions issued in proceedings of voluntary jurisdiction do not acquire the character of *cosa juzgada* to the extent that matters established in those resolutions cannot be impugned or refuted.

   Article 1120. One in whose favor a right has been declared in an action can have an action of *cosa juzgada* to secure compliance with the matter resolved, or to get execution of the judgment in the manner provided by this Code.

   Article 1121. The exception of *cosa juzgada* can be alleged by the litigant who obtained it in the [former] action and by all others who, under the law, can take advantage of the decision. "Cause of action" [*causa de pedir*] shall be understood to mean the immediate grounds [*fundamento immediato*] [ultimate facts?] of the right alleged in the action.

   Article 1122. Judgments rendered in a criminal process can be given effect in civil actions if the defendant was convicted.

Article 1123. Judgments of acquittal or which order a conclusive stay of proceedings will only produce *cosa juzgada* in civil matters if they rest on one or more of the following circumstances.

1. The nonexistence of the crime or tort that was the subject matter of the process. This does not include cases in which the acquittal or stay arose out of circumstances that provide an excuse from criminal responsibility;

2. No relation whatever exists between the [criminal] act and the accused person, not counting civil liability that may affect him by way of the acts of third parties or by way of damages resulting from accidents in accordance with the Civil Code;

3. No indication of anything against the accused appears in the record of the case. The exception of *cosa juzgada* in such a case can only be alleged with respect to persons who have intervened in the criminal process as direct or auxiliary parties. Judgments of acquittal or stay in criminal matters relating to guardians, administrators, auditors, receivers, treasurers and other persons who have received securities or objects of personal property through a title that creates an obligation to return them will in no way produce *cosa juzgada* in civil matters.

Article 1124. If the criminal judgment does produce *cosa juzgada* in a civil action, it will not be lawful in the latter to consider evidence or allegations incompatible with the result of that judgment or with the facts that necessarily serve as its basis.

(Those provisions are adopted from the Chilean Code of Civil Procedure.)

35. *See generally,* 1 AGUIRRE, DERECHO PROCESAL CIVIL DE GUATEMALA 789–825 (1973); and FÁBREGA P., COSA JUZGADA Y EJECUCIÓN DE SENTENCIA 1–38 (1975).

36. Art. 1121.

37. Art. 1124. *And see* 1972 BJ 190 (recognizing *cosa juzgada* effect of an earlier judgment declaring A not to be the father of B in a later action in which the children of A claimed to be brothers of B).

38. *See supra* chap. 4, section "Res Judicata (*Cosa Juzgada*) Effects."

39. *See, e.g.,* 1958 BJ 19162, at 19168. *See also* GUERRO, LA COSA JUZGADA (1957, thesis, Universidad Nacional Autonoma de Nicaragua).

40. 1949 BJ 14554.

41. *See supra* note 34.

CHAPTER 9

1. ODECA CHARTER, Transitional Provisions, Arts. 1 & 2 (1962).

2. For a discussion of the role of Panama in Central American integration generally, *see* 2 LINDO, LA INTEGRACIÓN CENTROAMERICANA ANTE EL DERECHO INTERNACIONAL (chap. 20, "Panama en el proceso de integración centroamericana") 51–63 (1970).

3. The term *auto* refers to judicial rulings that decide certain matters that are not mere questions of procedural form but which, at the same time, are not final, definitive resolutions of the whole case on the merits. *See* Judicial Code, Art. 546. Decisions on such matters as the judicial capacity of the parties, the jurisdiction (competency) of

the court, the rejection of or admission of a legal exception to the claim, etc., may be cast in the form of *autos*. See PRIETO-CASTRO, DERECHO PROCESAL CIVIL, primera parte, p. 473 (1964). Appeals of *autos*, as distinguished from *sentencias* (judgments), may have to be taken in a shorter time (Judicial Code, Art. 1044) and may not have the effect of divesting the inferior court of its jurisdiction pending the decision on appeal (Judicial Code, Art. 1047).

4. Ley de Enjuicimiento Civil, Arts. 951–54, based on Ley de Enjuicimiento of 1855, Arts. 922–25.

5. *See* Judicial Code, Art. 298. *And see* BERNAL GUARDIA, REGLAS COMUNES AL PROCEDIMIENTO CIVIL (2d ed.) 235 (1973).

6. *See* Judicial Code (Projected), Art. 1269, which uses the phrase "judgments rendered by foreign courts."

7. *Supra.*

8. *See* Barsallo J., *La ejecución de sentencia extranjera*, LEX, no. 2 (May 1973), 107, at 111.

9. *See* PALACIOS, RECONOCIMIENTO Y EJECUCIÓN DE SENTENCIAS EXTRANJERAS EN PANAMÁ 160–61 (1975, thesis, Universidad de Panamá).

10. *See* REPERTORIO JURÍDICO, no. 6 (June 1965), p. 29; REGISTRO JUDICIAL, no. 11 (1972), p. 825.

11. *See* chap. 3 *supra*, p. 54.

12. *Sentencia* 11 December 1972. *See* PALACIOS, *supra* note 9, at 170.

13. *See resolución*, Sala Cuarta (Fourth Chamber), 2 October 1974, cited in PALACIOS, *supra* note 9, at 175.

14. Judicial Code, Arts. 587 & 1105.

15. *Id.*, Art. 588.

16. *Id.*

17. Bustamante Code, Art. 425; Judicial Code, Art. 589.

18. *See* Ley 61 de 1946 and Ley 47 de 1956.

19. *See* BERNAL GUARDIA, *supra* note 5, at 233.

20. *See sentencias*, Sala Cuarta, Corte Suprema de Justicia, 29 July 1966. (REPERTORIO JURÍDICO, no. 7 [July 1966], p. 15), and 11 December 1972 (unpublished, but quoted in PALACIOS, *supra* note 9, at 185).

21. Bustamante Code, Arts. 429 & 430; Judicial Code, Art. 590.

22. *See* Civil Code, Art. 631.

23. Art. 423.2.

24. *See supra*, pp. 59–60.

25. Note 4 *supra*.

26. *See, e.g.*, BERNAL, *supra* note 5, at 167–89.

27. *See* PALACIOS, *supra* note 9, at 152.

28. *Id.*

29. *See* PALACIOS, *supra* note 9, at 112.

30. *See sentencias*, Sala Cuarta, Corte Suprema de Justicia, 25 August 1969 and 17 September 1971, 1969 REGISTRO JUDICIAL, no. 2 (July/August), p. 220, and 1971 REGISTRO JUDICIAL, no. 10 (August–December), p. 842.

31. *See* PALACIOS, *supra* note 9, at 117–18.

32. *See* Art. 432.

33. *See* PALACIOS, *supra* note 9, at 150.

34. *Supra* note 27.

35. The Bustamante Code does provide also for the extension of judicial assistance to foreign courts through letters requisitorial and rogatory (*exhortos* and *comisiones rogatorias*), Arts. 388–93.

36. 4 HERRERA LARA, JURISPRUDENCIA DE LA CORTE SUPREMA DE JUSTICIA 230 (1939).

37. Ley 47 de 1956. *See supra* at p. 129.

38. REGISTRO JUDICIAL, no. 2 (20 February 1961), p. 10.

39. *See, e.g., sentencia*, Sala Cuarta, Corte Suprema de Justicia, 4 December 1968 (REPERTORIO JURÍDICO, no. 12 [1968], p. 50), *quoted in* PALACIOS, *supra* note 9, at 111.

40. 2 Judicial Code (Projected), Art. 1269 (1971).

41. See chap. 4 supra, pp. 72–73; chap. 8 supra, p. 120.
42. See, e.g., BERNAL GUARDIA, supra note 5, at 231.
43. 2 Judicial Code (Projected), Art. 1269.
44. See PALACIOS, supra note 9, at 147.
45. Supra chap. 3, pp. 61–62.
46. Judicial Code, Arts. 768–70.

47. See FÁBREGA P., COSA JUZGADA Y EJECUCIÓN DE SENTENCIA 24 (1975).
48. Supra chap. 3, p. 64.
49. Private conversation, 21 July 1976, Panama.
50. See FÁBREGA P., supra note 47, at 24–26.

## CHAPTER 10

1. The details of the United States regime are discussed in chapter 2, at pages 24–35. Documentation is not repeated here.
2. The details of the EEC regime are discussed in chapter 2, at pages 35–43.
3. Convention, Art. 32. The Accession Convention of 9 October 1978 added provisions applying to Denmark, Ireland, and the United Kingdom.
4. Art. 34.
5. Jenard Report, p. 86.
6. Convention, Art. 27.
7. Id., Art. 28.
8. Id., Art. 37.
9. Id., Art. 40.
10. EEC Treaty, Art. 177.
11. De Wolf v. Harry Cox B.V. (Court of Justice of the European Communities, 1976) [1977], 2 C.M.L.R. 43.
12. Nicaragua requires notification of the state's representative as a step in the enforcement procedure in the case of Panamanian judgments and those of other non–Central American countries (CCP, Art. 546), but provides specially for enforcement of other Central American judgments. See supra chap. 8, pp. 115–17.
13. See chap. 4, note 75.
14. Bustamante Code, Art. 316.
15. See chap. 2, p. 30.
16. See, e.g., Magnolia Petroleum Co.

v. Hunt, 320 U.S. 430 (1943).
17. Convention, Art. 1.
18. See chap. 2, note 94.
19. See chap. 2, note 95.
20. See Jenard Report, p. 24.
21. Bustamante Code, Art. 437.
22. Id., Art. 432.
23. See chap. 4 at note 21; chap. 8 at note 12.
24. In the EEC Convention, the rendering court's competency is prescribed by the convention itself, and so there are not in fact two sets of standards. In the Bustamante Code, the requirement of competence under the rendering court's own rules is implicit in the requirement that the judgment be "executory" in the state of rendition, Art. 423.4.
25. See chap. 2 at note 40.
26. See chap. 2 at pp. 28–29.
27. See Gulf Oil Corp. v. Gilbert, 320 U.S. 501 (1947).
28. 20 U.S.C. 1332.
29. 28 U.S.C. 1404.a.
30. Convention, Art. 28.
31. Id., Art. 5.
32. Id., Art. 6.
33. Id., Art. 3.
34. Bustamante Code, Art. 318.
35. Id., Art. 323.
36. Id.
37. See chap. 4, note 31. The doctrine of collateral estoppel, which serves to prevent relitigation of jurisdictional facts in the United States

system, has no application in the Latin American concept of *cosa juzgada*.

38. *See* chap. 8, pp. 115–17.
39. United States: *see* chap. 2 at note 46; EEC: the right to resist enforcement on grounds of lack of notice is extended only to a "defaulting defendant," Convention, Art. 27.2; Bustamante Code: *see* chap. 3, p. 60.
40. *See* chap. 2 at note 42.
41. *See* Mullane v. Central Hanover Bank & Trust Co., 339 U.S. 306 (1950).
42. *Cf.* Baldwin v. Iowa State Travelling Men's Assn., 282 U.S. 522 (1931), where the jurisdictional defect concerned the basis element rather than the forum and adequacy of notice. The same principle applies in both situations, however.
43. Jenard Report, pp. 68–69.
44. *Id.*, p. 69.
45. Convention, Art. 27.2.
46. Jenard Report, pp. 76–77.
47. Bustamante Code, Art. 423.2.
48. *Cf.* note 39 *supra*.
49. *Compare* cases cited, chap. 4, notes 34–36. *See also* chap. 8, notes 23 & 24.
50. *See* chap. 3, p. 60.
51. *See* chap. 4, note 3; chap. 6, note 14; and chap. 7, note 10.
52. Nicaraguan Code of Civil Procedure, Art. 16.3.
53. *See* chap. 8, note 25.
54. *See* chap. 9, notes 26–28.
55. *See* Uniform Enforcement of Foreign Judgments Act § 6.
56. Convention, Art. 31.
57. Jenard Report, p. 82.
58. Bustamante Code, Art. 423.4.
59. *See* chap. 2, note 52.
60. *See* chap. 2, notes 53 & 54.
61. *See* Jenard Report, p. 23.
62. *Id.*, p. 19.
63. Bustamante Code, Art. 53.
64. 433 U.S. 186 at 210 (1977). *See*

Carolina Power & Light Co. v. Uranex, 451 F.Supp. 1044 (1977).
65. *See* Convention, Art. 24; Bustamante Code, Arts. 388–93.
66. *See* chap. 7, pp. 111–13.
67. *See* von Mehren & Trautman, *Recognition of Foreign Adjudications: A Survey and a Suggested Approach*, 81 HARV. L. REV. 1601, at 1670 (1968).
68. *See* chap. 2, note 63.
69. *See* Jenard Report, p. 75.
70. *Id.*, p. 76.
71. EEC Treaty, Art. 177.
72. *See* chap. 3, pp. 51–53.
73. *See* Bustamante Code, Art. 4.
74. *Id.*, Art. 53.
75. *See* chap. 6, p. 103.
76. *See* chap. 2, pp. 32–34.
77. Convention, Art. 26. If, however, recognition is sought, not as incidental to an action commenced for an independent purpose, but as an end in itself, the formalities prescribed for enforcement must be followed. Jenard Report, p. 74.
78. Jenard Report, *id.*
79. *See* HERZOG, CIVIL PROCEDURE IN FRANCE 554–55 (1967); CAPPELLETTI & PERILLO, CIVIL PROCEDURE IN ITALY 253–54 (1965); von Mehren & Trautman, *supra* note 67, at 1674–75.
80. *See supra* notes 45 & 46.
81. *See* 1 AGUIRRE, DERECHO PROCESAL CIVIL DE GUATEMALA 789–822 (1973).
82. *See* chap. 4, note 17, and chap. 9, note 49. *And see* SENTÍS MELENDO, LA SENTENCIA EXTRANJERA (EXEQUATUR) 66, 78 (1958).
83. *See* chap. 5, p. 94, and chap. 9, note 50. *And see* 3 ALSINA, TRATADO TEÓRICO PRÁCTICO DE DERECHO PROCESAL CIVIL Y COMERCIAL 127 (1973); 3 BUSTAMANTE, DERECHO INTERNACIONAL PRIVADO 285 (1931). *See* discussion in Lucas Sosa, *Eficacia de la sentencia extranjera, in* MORELLO, ED., PROBLE-

MÁTICA ACTUAL DEL DERECHO PRO-
CESAL 597–607 (1974).

84. If the official English translation of Article 396 is taken at face value, even compliance with all the prescribed formalities for notice to the defendant in the rendering state will not entitle the judgment to recognition if the defendant or his representative was not in fact "present." No recognition, in other words, could be extended to default judgments, even though such judgments may be enforceable. This is probably not the meaning intended, however. The Spanish term "comparecencia," translated as "presence," probably means, instead, "being made a party, by appearance or due citation." Cf. 3 BUSTAMANTE, supra note 83, at 285.

85. In his treatise discussing this article, Bustamante speaks, not of the lack of competence, but of doubt as to the competence of the rendering tribunal. 3 BUSTAMANTE, supra note 83, at 285.

86. See 3 BUSTAMANTE, supra note 83, at 281–82: "a dual interest—that of the administration of justice and that of the parties—demands that there be but one single litigation or process for each matter. This spares the individuals trouble and useless expenditures; the public administration, annoying duplications and perhaps sterile results; and the concept and application of law, the danger of divergent and contradictory resolutions."

87. See chap. 2, note 71.

88. Convention, Art. 21.

89. Id., Art. 22.

90. Id., Art. 27.3. The Accession Convention of 9 October 1978 also provided that recognition should be denied if there is a recognizable prior inconsistent judgment on the same cause of action in a noncontracting state, Art. 27.5.

91. See Jenard Report, p. 78.

92. Convention, Arts. 21–23.

93. Bustamante Code, Art. 395.

94. See chap. 4, note 75.

## CHAPTER 11

1. Brazil, Chile, Colombia, Costa Rica, the Dominican Republic, Ecuador, El Salvador, Guatemala, Haiti, Honduras, Panama, Paraguay, Peru, Uruguay, Venezuela.

2. Convention, Art. 1. Compare Bustamante Code, Art. 437.

3. Id. Compare Bustamante Code, Art. 432.

4. Convention, Art. 6.

5. The utility of the exequatur procedure was vigorously debated at the conference. See, e.g., vol. 2, Actas y Documentos, Segunda Conferencia Especializada Interamericana Sobre Derecho Internacional Privado (OEA/Ser. K/XX 1.2;

CIDIP-II/103), at pp. 51–95, 202–27.

6. Convention, Art. 2.d.

7. See Work Accomplished by the Interamerican Juridical Committee during Its Regular Meeting, 26 July to 27 August 1973 (CJI-17) (OEA/Ser. Q/IV.7), for the 1973 draft. The international competence provision is Article 4 (pp. 99–100).

8. 1977 Draft Convention Art. 2.d. The advisability of prescribing uniform competency standards in the convention was likewise vigorously debated. See note 5 supra.

9. Bustamante Code, Arts. 318–39.

10. Art. 2.e.

11. Convention, Art. 2.g. The language is very similar to that of the 1940 Montevideo Treaty on International Procedural Law, Art. 5.b.
12. Convention, Art. 4.
13. O.A.S. document, OEA/Ser. K/XXI.2, CIDIP-II/3 (English version), at p. 64.
14. Convention, Art. 10.
15. Bustamante Code, Art. 3.
16. Work Accomplished by the Interamerican Juridical Committee during Its Regular Meeting, 10 January to 18 February 1977 (CJI-31) (OEA/Ser. Q/IV.14), at 119.
17. Vienna Convention on the Law of Treaties, Art. 19, 8 INT. LEGAL MATERIALS 686 (1969).
18. 1973 Draft Convention, Art. 1.c.
19. 1977 Draft Convention, Art. 1.h.
20. Convention, Art. 2.h.
21. 1973 Draft Convention, Art. 5.
22. See chap. 2 supra at note 57.
23. See chap. 5 supra.
24. Bustamante Code, Art. 431.
25. Op. cit. supra note 16, at 116.

26. Convention, Art. 6.
27. 1973 Draft Convention, Art. 9; and see commentary, op. cit. supra note 7, at 131–33.
28. Op. cit. supra note 16, at 116.
29. See chap. 4 supra at note 15, and chap. 10 supra at notes 82 & 83.
30. Op. cit. supra note 5, at 51.
31. In the recently published third volume of his treatise, the rapporteur, Dr. Haroldo Valladão, describes his successful challenge to a Brazilian law that attempted to dispense with "homologation" (the Brazilian equivalent to exequatur) for judgments that were merely declaratory of the status of persons. 3 VALLADÃO, DIREITO INTERNACIONAL PRIVADO 190–91 (1978).
32. Op. cit. supra note 13, at 50.
33. See 3 BUSTAMANTE, DERECHO INTERNACIONAL PRIVADO 285 (1931).
34. Bustamante Code, Art. 394.
35. Op. cit. supra note 5, at 223–26.
36. Id. at 225.
37. Op. cit. supra note 16, at 117.

# Bibliography

## BOOKS

AGUIRRE GODOY, MARIO. DERECHO PROCESAL CIVIL DE GUATEMALA. Guatemala: Editorial Universitaria, 1973.

ALSINA, HUGO. TRATADO TEÓRICO PRÁCTICO DE DERECHO PROCESAL CIVIL Y COMERCIAL. Buenos Aires: Compañia Argentina de Editores, 1941–43.

——. TRATADO TEÓRICO PRÁCTICO DE DERECHO PROCESAL CIVIL Y COMERCIAL. 2d ed. Buenos Aires: EDIAR, 1956–57.

ARELLANO GARCIA, CARLOS. DERECHO INTERNACIONAL PRIVADO. Mexico: Porrua, 1974.

BEALE, JOSEPH HENRY. A TREATISE ON THE CONFLICT OF LAWS. Vol. 2. New York: Voorhis, 1935.

BERNAL GUARDIA, TARGIDIO A. REGLAS COMUNES AL PROCEDIMIENTO CIVIL. 2d ed. Panama: Universidad de Panamá, 1973.

BUSTAMANTE Y SIRVÉN, ANTONIO SANCHEZ DE. LA AUTARQUIA PERSONAL. Havana: Miranda, 1914.

——. DERECHO INTERNACIONAL PRIVADO. Havana: Carusa, 1931.

——. EL ORDEN PÚBLICO. Havana: Ruíz, 1893.

——. TRES CONFERENCIAS SOBRE DERECHO INTERNACIONAL PRIVADO. Havana: República de Cuba, 1929.

——. THE WORLD COURT. Translated by ELIZABETH F. READ. New York: Macmillan, 1925.

CAPPELLETTI, MAURO. EL VALOR DE LAS SENTENCIAS Y DE LAS NORMAS EXTRANJERAS EN EL PROCESO CIVIL. Translated by SANTIAGO SENTÍS MELENDO. Buenos Aires: Ed. Jurídicas Europa-América, 1968.

——, AND PERILLO, JOSEPH M. CIVIL PROCEDURE IN ITALY. The Hague: Martinus Nijhoff, 1965.

CLINE, WILLIAM R., AND DELGADO, ENRIQUE, EDS. ECONOMIC INTEGRATION IN CENTRAL AMERICA. Washington, D.C.: Brookings Institution, 1978.

COUTURE, EDUARDO J. FUNDAMENTOS DEL DERECHO PROCESAL CIVIL. 3d ed. Buenos Aires: R. Depalma, 1958.

EHRENZWEIG, ALBERT ARMIN. CONFLICT OF LAWS. St. Paul, Minn.: West, 1962.

ENCYCLOPEDIA OF EUROPEAN COMMU-
NITY LAW. New York: Matthew Ben-
der, 1973–.
FÁBREGA P., JORGE. COSA JUZGADA Y
EJECUCIÓN DE SENTENCIA. Panama:
privately printed, 1975. These are two
essays bound together.
FERNÁNDEZ FLORES, JOSÉ LUIS. EL DI-
VORCIO EN DERECHO INTERNACIONAL
PRIVADO. Buenos Aires: Ediciones De-
palma, 1967.
GALLARDO, RICARDO. LAS CONSTITU-
CIONES DE LA REPÚBLICA DE CENTRO-
AMÉRICA. Madrid: Instituto de Es-
tudios Políticos, 1958.
GOODRICH, HERBERT F., AND SCOLES, EU-
GENE F. HANDBOOK OF THE CONFLICT
OF LAWS. 4th ed. St. Paul, Minn.:
West, 1964.
GREEN, ANDREW WILSON. POLITICAL IN-
TEGRATION BY JURISPRUDENCE. Ley-
den: Sijthoff, 1970.
HERRARTE, ALBERTO. LA UNION DE CEN-
TROAMÉRICA: TRAGEDIA Y ESPERANZA.
Guatemala: Editorial del Ministerio de
Educación Pública, 1955.
HERRERA LARA, MANUEL ANTONIO,
COMP. JURISPRUDENCIA DE LA CORTE
SUPREMA DE JUSTICIA. Panama: Im-
prenta Nacional, 1921–.
HERZOG, PETER E. CIVIL PROCEDURE IN
FRANCE. The Hague: Martinus Nij-
hoff, 1967.
HUDSON, MANLEY OTTMER. INTERNA-
TIONAL LEGISLATION. Washington,
D.C.: Carnegie Endowment for Inter-
national Peace, 1931, 1932.
INTER-AMERICAN INSTITUTE OF INTERNA-
TIONAL LEGAL STUDIES. DERECHO CO-
MUNITARIO CENTROAMERICANO. San
José, Costa Rica: Trejos Hnos., 1968.
———. DERECHO DE LA INTEGRACIÓN
LATINAMERICANA. Buenos Aires: Edi-
ciones Depalma, 1969.
———. INSTRUMENTS RELATING TO THE
ECONOMIC INTEGRATION OF LATIN
AMERICA. Dobbs Ferry, N.Y.: Oceana
Publications, 1968.
KARNES, THOMAS L. THE FAILURE OF
UNION: CENTRAL AMERICA, 1824–

1960. Chapel Hill: University of North
Carolina Press, 1961.
KOS-RABCEWICZ-ZUBOWSKI, LUDWIK, ED.
INTERNATIONAL COOPERATION IN CIVIL
AND COMMERCIAL PROCEDURE. Ottawa,
Canada: University of Ottawa Press,
1975.
LAZCANO, CARLOS ALBERTO. . . . DE-
RECHO INTERNACIONAL PRIVADO. La
Plata: Editora Platense, 1965.
LINDO, HUGO. EL DIVORCIO EN EL SAL-
VADOR. 2d ed. San Salvador: Editorial
Universitaria, 1959.
———. LA INTEGRACIÓN CENTROAMER-
ICANA ANTE EL DERECHO INTERNA-
CIONAL. San Salvador: Ministerio de
Educación, 1970.
MANN, CLARENCE J. THE FUNCTION OF
JUDICIAL DECISION IN EUROPEAN ECO-
NOMIC INTEGRATION. The Hague: Mar-
tinus Nijhoff, 1972.
MATÁ GAVIDIA, JOSÉ. ANOTACIONES DE
HISTORIA PATRIA CENTROAMERICANA.
Guatemala: Cultural Centroamericana,
1953.
MONTÚFAR, LORENZO. RESEÑA HISTÓ-
RICA DE CENTRO-AMÉRICA. Guatemala:
"El Progreso," 1881.
MUÑOZ MEANY, ENRIQUE; CAMEY HER-
RERA, JULIO; AND HALL LLOREDA, CAR-
LOS. DERECHO INTERNACIONAL PRIVA-
DO. Guatemala: Editorial del Minis-
terio de Educación Pública, 1953.
ORTEZ COLINDRES, ENRIQUE. LA INTEGRA-
CIÓN POLÍTICA DE CENTROAMERICA.
Costa Rica: Editorial Universitaria
Centroamericana (EDUCA), 1975.
ORTIZ MARTIN, GONZALO. EL DERECHO
INTERNACIONAL PRIVADO DE COSTA
RICA. San José, Costa Rica: Colegio
de Abogados, 1969.
PRIETO-CASTRO, LEONARDO. DERECHO
PROCESAL CIVIL. Madrid: Editorial
Revista de Derecho Privado, 1964.
READ, HORACE EMERSON. RECOGNITION
AND ENFORCEMENT OF FOREIGN JUDG-
MENTS IN THE COMMON LAW UNITS
OF THE BRITISH COMMONWEALTH.
Cambridge, Mass.: Harvard University
Press, 1938.

Sentís Melendo, Santiago. La sentencia extranjera (exequatur). Buenos Aires: Ediciones Jurídica Europa-América, 1958.

Torres Gudiño, Secundino. Derecho procesal civil. Panama: Libreria Universitaria, 1975.

Treaties, Conventions, International Acts, Protocols and Other Agreements between the United States and Other Powers, 1776–1909. Compiled by William M. Malloy. Vol. 2. Washington, D.C.: United States Government Printing Office, 1910.

Uniform Laws Annotated. St. Paul, Minn.: West, 1968–.

Valladão, Haroldo. Direito internacional privado. Rio de Janeiro: Livraria Freitas Bastos, 1978.

Von Mehren, Arthur Taylor, and Trautman, Donald Theodore. The Law of Multistate Problems. Boston: Little, Brown, 1965.

Wright, Charles Alan. Handbook of the Law of Federal Courts. 3d ed. St. Paul, Minn.: West, 1976.

## ARTICLES

Aguirre Godoy, Mario. Guatemala. In International Cooperation in Civil and Commercial Procedure, edited by Ludwik Kos-Rabcewicz-Zubowski, pp. 245–72. Ottawa, Canada: University of Ottawa Press, 1975.

Antillón, Walter. El auxilio jurídico internacional en Costa Rica. Revista de Ciencias Jurídicas, vol. 15 (June 1970), pp. 209–50.

Barbante, Aldo. Estructura institucional del Mercado Común Centroamericano. Lecciones y Ensayos, no. 42 (1970). Universidad de Buenos Aires.

Barry, Herbert. Comity. Virginia Law Review, vol. 12, no. 5 (March 1926), pp. 353–75.

Barsallo J., Pedro A. La ejecución de sentencia extranjera. Lex, no. 2 (May 1973), pp. 107–16. Revista del Colegio Nacional de Abogados, Panamá.

Bartlett, Lee S. Full Faith and Credit Comes to the Common Market: An Analysis of the Provisions of the Convention on Jurisdiction and Enforcement of Judgments in Civil and Commercial Matters. International and Comparative Law Quarterly, vol. 24, pt. 1 (January 1975), pp. 44–60.

Carl, Beverly May. The Common Market Judgments Convention—Its Threat and Challenge to Americans. International Lawyer, vol. 8, no. 3 (July 1974), pp. 446–51.

Casad, Robert C. Shaffer v. Heitner: An End to Ambivalence in Jurisdiction Theory? University of Kansas Law Review, vol. 26, no. 1 (Fall 1977), pp. 61–83.

Ereli, Eliezer. The Central American Common Market: Integration in Practice. Tulane Law Review, vol. 43, no. 1 (December 1968), pp. 1–33.

Giardina, Andrea. The European Court and the Brussels Convention on Jurisdiction and Judgments. International and Comparative Law Quarterly, vol. 27, pt. 2 (April 1978), pp. 263–76.

Ginsburg, Ruth B. Judgments in Search of Full Faith and Credit: The Last-in-Time Rule for Conflicting Judgments. Harvard Law Review, vol. 82, no. 4 (February 1969), pp. 798–832.

Hay, Peter. The Common Market Preliminary Draft Convention of the Recognition and Enforcement of Judgments—Some Considerations of Policy and Interpretation. American Journal of Comparative Law, vol. 16, nos. 1 & 2 (1968), pp. 149–74.

———, and Walker, Robert J. The Proposed Recognition-of-Judgments Convention between the United States and the United Kingdom. Texas International Law Journal, vol. 11, no. 3 (Summer 1976), pp. 421–59.

Kurland, Philip B. The Supreme Court,

*the Due Process Clause and the In Personam Jurisdiction of State Courts: From Pennoyer to Denckla: A Review.* University of Chicago Law Review, vol. 25, no. 4 (Summer 1958), pp. 569–624.

Lorenzen, Ernest G. *The Pan-American Code of Private International Law.* Tulane Law Review, vol. 4, no. 4 (June 1930), pp. 499–528.

Lucas Sosa, Gualberto. *Eficacia de la sentencia extranjera.* In Problematica actual del derecho procesal, edited by Augusto M. Morello. La Plata: Ediar Platense, 1974.

Nadelmann, Kurt H. *The Common Market Judgments Convention and a Hague Conference Recommendation: What Steps Next?* Harvard Law Review, vol. 82, no. 6 (April 1969), pp. 1282–92.

———. *French Courts Recognize Foreign Money-Judgments: One Down and More to Go.* American Journal of Comparative Law, vol. 13 (1964), pp. 72–80.

———. *Jurisdictionally Improper Fora in Treaties on Recognition of Judgments: The Common Market Draft.* Columbia Law Review, vol. 67, no. 6 (June 1967), pp. 995–1023.

Simmonds, K. R. *The Central American Common Market: An Experiment in Regional Integration.* International And Comparative Law Quarterly, vol. 16, pt. 4 (October 1967), pp. 911–45.

———. *International Economic Organisations in Central and Latin America and the Caribbean: Regionalism and Sub-Regionalism in the Integration Process.* International and Comparative Law Quarterly, vol. 19, pt. 3 (July 1970), pp. 376–97.

Soto Jimenez, Rolando. *Sobre la justicia en la integración regional.* Revista de Ciencias Jurídicas, vols. 20 & 21 (October 1972), pp. 285–305. San José: Universidad de Costa Rica.

Ungo, Guillermo Manuel. *El Salvador.* In International Cooperation in Civil and Commercial Procedure, edited by Ludwik Kos-Rabcewicz-Zubowski, pp. 231–43. Ottawa, Canada: University of Ottawa Press, 1975.

Von Mehren, Arthur Taylor, and Trautman, Donald Theodore. *Recognition of Foreign Adjudications: A Survey and a Suggested Approach.* Harvard Law Review, vol. 81, no. 8 (June 1968), pp. 1601–96.

Weser, Martha. *Some Reflections on the Draft Treaty on Execution of Judgments in the E.E.C.* In International Trade, Investment, And Organization, edited by Wayne R. La Fave and Peter Hay, pp. 377–86. Urbana: University of Illinois Press, 1967.

## THESES

Colmenares Arandi, Roberto. Ejecución de sentencias extranjeras en la legislación guatemalteca vigente. Universidad de San Carlos de Guatemala, 1968.

Guerro, Alberto. La cosa juzgada. Universidad Nacional Autonoma de Nicaragua, 1957.

Palacios, Jesús. Reconocimiento y ejecución de sentencias extranjeras en Panamá. Universidad de Panamá, 1975.

Solano Vargas, Rodrigo. La ausencia en el derecho privado. Universidad de Costa Rica, 1965.

# Index